Disaster Management for Libraries and Archives

DISCLAIMER

No undertakings, express or implied, are given concerning the use of the contents of this book and neither the individual authors and editors nor publishers will accept liability for losses which might arise directly or indirectly from use of information herein.

DISASTER MANAGEMENT FOR LIBRARIES AND ARCHIVES

Edited by
Graham Matthews and John Feather

ASHGATE

Published by
Ashgate Publishing Limited
Gower House
Croft Road
Aldershot
Hampshire GU11 3HR
England

Ashgate Publishing Company
Suite 420
101 Cherry Street
Burlington, VT 05401–4405
USA

Ashgate website: http://www.ashgate.com

British Library Cataloguing in Publication Data
Disaster management for libraries and archives
1. Library administration 2. Emergency management 3. Archives
I. Matthews, Graham II. Feather, John
025.8'2

Library of Congress Cataloging-in-Publication Data
Disaster management for libraries and archives / edited by Graham Matthews and John Feather.
        p. cm.
    Includes bibliographical references and index.
    ISBN 0–7546–0917–0
        1. Libraries--Safety measures. 2. Archives--Safety measures. 3. Library materials--Conservation and restoration. 4. Archival materials--Conservation and restoration. 5. Emergency management. I. Matthews, Graham, 1953– II. Feather, John.

Z679.7.D565 2003
025.8'2–dc21

2003041915

ISBN 0 7546 0917 0

Printed and bound by MPG Books, Bodmin, Cornwall.

Contents

List of figures

List of tables

Notes on editors and contributors

EDITORS

GRAHAM MATTHEWS

Dr Graham Matthews is Professor of Information and Library Management and Director of Research, Faculty of Computing, Information and English, University of Central England in Birmingham. In 1995–96, he led a British Library Research and Development Department funded project that reviewed disaster management practice in British libraries (Matthews, G. and Eden, P. *Disaster management in British libraries. Project report with guidelines for library managers*, Library and Information Research Report 109, London: The British Library Board, 1996). He has written and presented widely on this topic and preservation management in general. He is co-author, with John Feather and Paul Eden of *Preservation management. Policies and practices in British libraries* (Gower, 1996). He has led research projects in the following areas: preservation of digital materials, preservation management training, preservation needs assessment, preservation research, and preservation surrogates.

JOHN FEATHER

John Feather has been Professor of Library and Information Studies at Loughborough University since 1988. He has been a member of the Arts and Humanities Research Board, and of the Library and Information Management Panel in the Research Assessment Exercise.

His academic interests include preservation management, a topic on which he has published extensively. His work in the field includes leading major investigations of preservation policies and practices in both libraries and archives in the UK, published as *Preservation management. Policies and practices in British libraries* (with Graham Matthews and Paul Eden, 1996) and *National preservation policy. Policy and practices in archives and record offices* (with Paul Eden, 1997). His other publications on the subject include *Preservation and the management of library collections* (2nd ed., 1996), and papers given at conferences of IFLA, LIBER, the American Library Association and the National Preservation Office. He is editor of the companion volume to this book, *Managing preservation in libraries and archives. Current practices and future developments* (2003).

CONTRIBUTORS

ALICE CANNON

Alice Cannon trained as a paper conservator at the University of Canberra and has worked in organizations in New Zealand, the USA and Australia. She is currently the Preventive Conservator at Artlab Australia (based in Adelaide, South Australia), where she is involved in risk management programmes, disaster preparedness, integrated pest management and environmental and storage issues for Artlab's government and private clients.

JOHN CREBER

John Creber was for many years Assistant Director of Libraries and Information for Norfolk Library and Information Service in the UK. He managed the recovery process following the fire of 1994 and his final project there was directing the client requirements during the building and fit-out of the Norfolk and Norwich Millennium Library, which replaced the one destroyed by the fire. He is now a library consultant, trading under the banner of Libraries Unlimited UK. John was for several years an active member of the national committee of the Information Services Group of the Library Association, and was national vice-chair from 1989–94.

SHERYL DAVIS

Sheryl J. Davis is Head, Preservation Services Department, Assistant Head, Special Collections, Tomás Rivera Library, University of California, Riverside. She has been Preservation Officer since 1986. She has served as a consultant to a number of institutions (including libraries and museums in Israel) for disaster recovery and preservation needs assessment. She is the author of several articles on disaster planning and regularly presents papers and training sessions on this topic. She teaches the *Preservation Management* course for the San Jose State

University School of Library and Information Science at the Fullerton, California campus. In 1987, Sheryl started the Inland Empire Libraries Disaster Response Network (IELDRN). The first of its kind, IELDRN libraries assist each other in times of disaster and conduct programmes to assist libraries and archives in the region to prepare for and respond to disasters. The IELDRN has been used as a model for similar groups now existing in California and other states.

BILL JACKSON

Bill Jackson joined the National Library of Scotland, Edinburgh, in 1988 as Buildings Manager and is now Estates Director responsible for all building maintenance, capital projects and support services. During the last 14 years there has been a capital investment of over £40 million in the Library's buildings. A considerable amount of this investment has been related to fire safety projects with the installation of fire suppression systems in the Library's collection storage buildings. Bill is a Chartered Building Surveyor who started his career in 1977 with the Property Services Agency. He has been Secretary of the Committee on the Protection of Cultural Resources of the National Fire Protection Association International since 1993.

KRISTEN KERN

Kristen Kern is Preservation/Catalog Librarian, Associate Professor, Branford Price Millar Library, Portland State University, Portland, Oregon, USA. She is Chair, Disaster Recovery Group (DIRG), PORTALS (Portland Area Library System); Chair, Preservation Committee, Orbis Consortium; member, ALA, Association for Library Collections and Technical Services, Preservation and Reformatting Section. She is a regular presenter at book repair workshops for state and local library organizations. In 2001, she achieved a Certificate from the Preservation Management Institute, Rutgers School of Communication, Information and Library Studies, Professional Development Studies.

MAJ KLASSON

Maj Klasson is Professor, Swedish School of Library and Information Studies, Göteborgs Universitet and Högskolan i Borås, Sweden. In addition to her recent research on the effects of a library fire on users, staff and society, other research interests include the development of adult education in Sweden, the Nordic countries and Europe; university libraries and change; educational aspects of user education, and information stratgies among emigrants. She has published widely in Sweden and abroad.

HEATHER MANSELL

Heather Mansell is Manager, Preservation, State Library of New South Wales, Sydney, Australia. She directs the Library's preservation policy function through the development and implementation of preservation policy strategies. She has a special interest in counter-disaster management and has been involved in a number of regional training activities including some in Brunei, Laos and India. Heather is a member of the Sydney Curatorial and Custodial Institutions Disaster Preparedness Group; a committee member of the Australian Institute for the Conservation of Cultural Material Inc, NSW division and Secretary of AusHeritage, Australia's export network for cultural heritage services.

KORNELIJA PETR

Kornelija Petr is Assistant Lecturer, Department of Library and Information Studies, Faculty of Education, University of J. J. Strossmayer, Osijek, Croatia. She teaches bibliographic control, reference services and information retrieval services. Her research interests include information networks and digital libraries. She is currently studying for a PhD in Information Sciences. She has presented papers about library services during war in Croatia, 1991–95, at international conferences.

CHRISTINE WISE

Christine Wise has been Head of Historic Collections, University of London Library, London, UK, since August 2001. From March 1994 to that date she was Librarian, The Fawcett Library, now The Women's Library, London Guildhall Library. Historic Collections in the University of London Library encompasses rare books and special collections of printed material; archives and manuscripts; the palaeography collection; and preservation and conservation. Christine has been a member of the M25 Consortium of Academic Libraries Disaster Management Group since 1997, becoming its Chair in July 2002.

Preface

This project grew out of a project to publish a collection of contemporary papers on preservation management (Feather, J. (ed.) (2003), *Preservation Management for Libraries and Archives: Current policies and Future Developments*, Ashgate). It seemed appropriate to produce a companion volume on disaster management, a key aspect of preservation management, with coverage that reflected current practice and issues, and with an international perspective. Drawing on experience from teaching, research and writing about this subject, we have drawn on worldwide contacts to solicit and edit a collection of chapters that offer advice and guidance on various aspects of disaster management based on first-hand experience, and reflection on this.

There has been considerable change and development in libraries and archives in recent years. Digital resources, services and networks have had considerable impact, the incidence of major disasters continues, and terrorism and war threaten cultural institutions on a global basis. New methods of tackling disaster management have been applied and the literature on the subject grows. It is timely to review practice and share experience as we move forward into an age where access to, and transfer and use of, documentation and other cultural heritage materials is dynamic. It is vital that we constantly review and consolidate good practice, and consider new issues and how to deal with them in order to safeguard the richness of resources in libraries and archives worldwide.

It is hoped that readers will benefit from contributors' considered views as they review, or address for the first time, disaster management practice. A disaster management text cannot be fully comprehensive, so references to other useful publications and sources are also included. Our purpose is to offer personal insights in specific contexts into key aspects of disaster management, which it is intended will prompt questions and solutions. It is hoped that it will be of broad interest and use to those involved in disaster management in libraries and archives.

Graham Matthews, Birmingham
John Feather, Loughborough

Acknowledgements

We are grateful to the contributors (and, where appropriate, to their employers) for their participation in the compilation of this book. Their prompt responses to deadlines and requests for information have been a source of encouragement to us. We are also grateful to organizations and individuals who have given permission for the reproduction of text, figures and tables. (Acknowledgement is made at appropriate points in the book.)

Likewise, our thanks are due to Suzie Duke, Commissioning Editor, Ashgate, for her patience and support.

1 Disaster management for libraries and archives – an introduction

Graham Matthews

GENERAL

By the mid 1990s, a significant amount of printed literature about, and guidance on, disaster planning in libraries and archives was available (see Matthews, 1994; Matthews, 1995; Feather, Eden and Matthews, 1996: 8–10). In 1995–96, a major review (funded by the then British Library Research and Development Department) of disaster management practice in the UK was undertaken and guidelines for library managers accompanied publication of its report (Matthews and Eden, 1996a). The now accepted use of the term disaster management rather than disaster planning in the UK acknowledges the fact that:

> Disaster management includes much more than the formulation of a written disaster control plan. It encompasses broader management issues such as finance, risk assessment and training. (Matthews and Eden, 1996a: 4)

In the years since the mid 1990s, while proponents of disaster management have continued to encourage its acceptance and implementation as an integral part of library and archival management, they have also had to incorporate within this the implications and impact of new developments within libraries and archives and the society in which they operate. These include the great changes brought about by the application of information and communication technologies with vast amounts of information now stored and disseminated electronically on a global basis. The digital environment at work (and at home) has developed at considerable pace over the last few years and this has brought about both benefits and concerns for those charged with disaster management in libraries and archives. The World Wide Web has made available an increasing amount of guidance and exchange of experience and expertise on disaster management via the internet. This, in keeping with professional developments, is not solely library or archive based, but has a broader perspective encompassing the whole cultural heritage sector including for example, museums and galleries as well.

Techniques from outside the field have been adapted, such as risk assessment and management from the business world. Experience in dealing with actual disasters, whether natural or man-made, continues to contribute to knowledge and practice in the field in an on-going, albeit unfortunate manner. This can range from advice on specific issues such as insurance requirements, or the salvage and treatment of particular media, to those of a broader nature such as training, assistance in setting up and maintaining a cooperative network or service continuity.

AIM OF THE BOOK

This book aims to bring together current professional and practical opinions and advice on key aspects of disaster management based on first-hand experience. It offers considered views on major activities and developments from a variety of authoritative backgrounds (the contributors include, for example, librarians, academics and conservators) and enriches existing information and knowledge on the subject. This is timely, as the basic principles of disaster management are well understood and widely disseminated, but still not applied as they ought to be. One recent review underlines this:

> It appears that the current reality is that many organizations, despite their good intentions, have yet to realize these intentions in the form of a disaster plan or integrated disaster planning. (Wellheiser and Scott, 2002: 4)

This is at a time of considerable change in libraries and archives, much of it driven by developments in information and communication technologies which are leading to a mixed digital and paper environment, and also at a time of increased threats to the cultural heritage from terrorism and armed conflict. The book offers evidence of the need for effective disaster management and examples of how it can be achieved, what it involves and how it can be facilitated, with examples in real contexts. It also demonstrates how disaster management is becoming more sophisticated where it is practised and supported and offers lessons from which others may learn. Simple and inexpensive measures and procedures can play just as important a role in effective disaster management and these are also included. The book is not a step-by-step how-to-do-it manual. It offers advice from individual views and experiences of particular activities set in the broader professional context. Sharing experience of these activities is at the heart of the book. The international nature of the contributions reflects the increasing amount of information and exchange of views now available on a global basis via the World Wide Web. While there are economic, geographical, political, technical and cultural aspects specific to particular regions and locations, much of the book's content is of wide application and interest. It is also hoped that it will give those involved in disaster management at local, national and international level an insight into the issues that still need to be addressed and developed, and thus play a part in professional debate and discussion.

To support this and the individual chapters, the book also provides bibliographic details of print and web-based sources, mainly English language and published from 1995 onwards, that will be of interest and help to those new to disaster management, or those reviewing procedures and/or documentation.

TOPICS ADDRESSED

The topics addressed have been selected because they are key activities within disaster management and they represent both those that have been practised for some time and now merit review in the light of experience and the current situation, and others which have come more to prominence in the last five years or so and about which less has yet been published.

DISASTER MANAGEMENT

The broad theme of the book, disaster management, is planning and being prepared for the unexpected in libraries and archives, and dealing with disasters effectively should they occur. *Disaster* is an emotive term. Disasters affecting libraries and archives can be man-made (for example, arson, poor maintenance or security) or natural (for example, earthquake, flood, hurricane) and vary in their scale and impact. In the UK overview (Matthews and Eden, 1996a), disaster in the context of library and information services is defined as:

> ... any incident which threatens human safety and/or damages, or threatens to damage, a library's buildings, collections, contents, facilities or services. (Matthews and Eden, 1996a: 4).

Perhaps, on reflection, and with more recent events in mind, the word 'destroy' could have been included in that definition. There are plenty of examples throughout history, including recent history, of the wanton destruction of libraries and archives and the cultural heritage they preserve (see, for example, van der Hoeven and van Albada, 1996, and Valencia, 2002). The events of 11 September 2001 have illustrated this in the most striking and poignant manner and have caused library and information services along with other public and commercial organizations to revisit emergency and security plans and procedures (see, for example, Di Mattia, 2001 and Kenney, 2001). The very wide range of the implications of the terrorist attacks on the World Trade Center and the Pentagon for library educators and future archive, library and information science professionals are identified and considered in a thought-provoking article, with numerous references, by a group of colleagues at the University of Pittsburgh School of Information Sciences (Cox, R.J., 2001).

THE DISASTER CONTROL PLAN

The book begins with a chapter on the disaster control plan, the framework around which good disaster management works, and a review of the effectiveness of disaster control plans in terms of their design and application, with practical advice based on experience. A disaster control plan is:

> … a clear, concise document which outlines preventive and preparatory measures intended to reduce potential risks, and which also provides details of reaction and recovery procedures to be undertaken in the event of a disaster to minimise its effect. (Matthews and Eden, 1996a: 4).

Many of the websites listed in Chapter 10, Guide to information sources on disaster management, provide links to examples of disaster control plans. While these may be helpful, it has to be stressed that disaster control plans should be organization specific, so generic templates and examples from elsewhere should be used carefully. (The author of this chapter has also been advised recently that some organizations in the USA have removed disaster plans from their websites in the aftermath of September 11 in order to remove the possibility of anyone exploiting weak points they might detect.) It is also important to recognize that just compiling a disaster control plan is not the end of the matter. For example, lines of authority must be clear, all who are to be involved in various parts of the plan need to be aware of their role, and receive appropriate training; aspects of the plan need to be tried and tested to check if they are feasible, and, importantly, the plan needs to be regularly reviewed to keep it up to date. It also needs to be reviewed following execution and amended if necessary.

The disaster control plan will normally address four phases of disaster management: prevention, preparedness, reaction and recovery. Increasingly, external funders of preservation and conservation initiatives or projects in libraries and archives will include a written disaster control plan as one of their basic criteria for consideration for an award and will thus insist on applicants having, *inter alia*, written disaster control plans as evidence of good preservation management practice and procedure.

The importance of the plan is underlined by a recent report of a survey of the impact of September 11 on the cultural heritage:

Although the events of September 11 were caused by an unprecedented act of terror, we found that standard, proven emergency management plans and responses turned out to be the most effective way of dealing with the disaster. (Heritage Preservation, 2002: 20)

RISK ASSESSMENT AND MANAGEMENT

Matthews and Eden (1996a) reported that:

All the disaster recovery experts interviewed stressed the fact that disasters – other than natural catastrophes – are seldom caused by a single incident. Rather, in the words of one such expert, 'they tend to be the result of a number of relatively minor events or situations occurring together or, more usually, over a period of time'. Assessments of the risks to people, buildings, collections, contents and facilities is accordingly the first and most important step in disaster prevention, and a necessary prerequisite to writing a disaster control plan. (Matthews and Eden, 1996a, 14)

Once hazards have been identified and the risk of their occurrence estimated, the reduction of the library or archive's vulnerability can be addressed (Wellheiser and Scott, 2002: 35). This is a continual process and risk assessment and management must be ongoing and effectively managed. From the author's experience in the UK, this topic seems to be of increasing interest and significance for librarians and archivists who are seeking advice as to how they might undertake risk assessments in developing their plans and/or managing potential actions (and their prioritization) which are under consideration following risk assessment. This may also signal an acknowledgement on the part of library and archival professionals that they need to understand more deeply the role and actions of the external experts and services that will need to be consulted and used (including those from other departments of the library's or archive's parent organization), and how they might work together better and forge mutual links. Chapter 3, which deals with this topic, is written from a broad cultural heritage sector perspective (for example, libraries, archives and museums), which is of considerable current relevance as these different domains are now working even more closely together and sharing expertise and experience.

FIRE AND WATER

Two of the major factors causing damage and destruction, whatever the cause of the disaster, are fire and water. Chapter 4 has its focus in prevention and preparedness as it deals with the planning and implementation of a major programme to prevent and deal with fire. Examples of the major impact of fire from around the world (see, for example, Watson, 1989 (Los Angeles Public Library), Sung, Leonov and Waters 1990 (Library of the Academy of Sciences of the USSR, Leningrad), Kennedy, 1995 (Norwich Central Library and Record Office) are, unfortunately many and well known. This chapter offers a case study of the planning and thinking behind the implementation of new fire prevention systems in a national library and offers straightforward advice of relevance to libraries and archives of different sizes.

Chapter 5 addresses water and its destructive powers, where, again there are recent incidents which testify to its impact, see, for example, Colorado State University (in July 1997, a massive flood hit Colorado State University where the Morgan Library and University bookstore were badly affected (Alive, 2000), and University of Sussex, 'Library salvage operation under way' (in October 2000, 70 000 volumes and documents in the University of Sussex Library book store were submerged in flood water). The chapter offers advice on prevention and preparedness, and, based on experience of a major incident of water ingress, on reaction and recovery as well.

COOPERATIVE ACTIVITY

One way in which some organizations have attempted to deal with disaster management has been to seek partners and work in a collaborative manner to achieve mutual support and assistance. In some instances, this may be informal, with personnel in libraries and archives in the same locale agreeing to provide help and expertise when requested. Increasingly, however, to facilitate effective disaster planning, this is formalized through written agreement of all parties involved. Alire (2000: 563) notes:

> It appears that very little has been written in the literature concerning disaster-recovery efforts involving partnerships, collaboration, and/or resource-sharing in libraries. And yet, there has probably not been a disaster of any magnitude that did not include most of these aspects. It is when a disaster occurs that there seems to be more cooperative sharing of resources, facilities, personnel, expertise, equipment, funds, etc.

She adds (2000: 571): ' ... learn from our disaster. Resource sharing external to your immediate library is not a given unless it is planned beforehand. Be prepared.' Chapter 6, based on practice and experience elsewhere in the USA, provides examples of how collaborative partnerships or networks can be established and maintained, with examples of cross-domain, cooperative activities that may be mutually beneficial. Reference to such networks elsewhere in the world is provided in Chapter 10.

HUMAN ASPECTS OF DISASTER MANAGEMENT

Training is vital to good disaster management (Matthews and Eden, 1996b). This is addressed in several chapters, as appropriate. Effective implementation of a disaster control plan depends on people: the people responsible for directing its application, the people carrying out the various tasks included in it. The plan is words on paper – people turn these words into action and action must be directed and managed. As well as training staff at all levels, attention should be paid to the well-being of all staff during and after a disaster. This will include ensuring health and safety regulations are adhered to and that staff are properly attired and equipped during salvage and recovery operations, that they are kept warm and well fed, and informed. They may do this in trying and difficult circumstances, perhaps in the midst of the palpable evidence of the destruction of a lifetime's work. This can have considerable impact on individuals and yet Matthews and Eden (1996a: 42) reported that:

> Interviewees with disaster experience invariably felt that the physical and mental stress which staff can suffer as the result of even a relatively minor disaster is generally underestimated ...

Furthermore,

> Librarians with disaster experience said they were surprised at how emotionally attached they and their staff had become to their library and its collections. They also pointed out how unsettling a disruption to normal working routines can be for some staff, especially if they are feeling insecure about their jobs. (Matthews and Eden, 1996a: 42)

In spite of such views, this is a topic which until recently has received little attention in libraries and archives. What is the impact of disasters on staff and what is the need for and the effectiveness of counselling? Based on a research project focusing on a major fire in Sweden, Chapter 7 considers these issues and one other aspect that has previously received little attention, the impact of such a disaster on library users.

WAR, ARMED CONFLICT, AND TERRORISM

When writing about disasters in libraries and archives, the use of the word disaster and other emotive words such as catastrophe, preceded evocatively by adjectives such as major, massive, overwhelming, can become commonplace and almost trite. One area where this is patently not the case is the damage to, and destruction of, libraries, archives and other storehouses of the cultural heritage through war and armed conflict (for accounts from around the world, see Sturges and Rosenberg (eds), 1999). Chapter 8 provides one example and one viewpoint of such damage and destruction through a personal account of events, and reflection upon them.

There is now an international movement seeking to work against such destruction and to offer a professional framework for support. In 1996, the International Committee of the Blue Shield (ICBS) was established. 'The Blue Shield is the cultural equivalent of the Red Cross. It is the symbol specified in the 1954 Hague Convention for marking cultural sites to give them protection from attack in the event of armed conflict' (International Committee of the Blue Shield, 2001). It covers museums, archives, historic sites and libraries. Its mission is 'to work for the protection of the world's cultural heritage by co-coordinating preparations to meet and respond to emergency situations'. Blue Shield Committees have been formed in a number of countries (Belgium, Italy, The Netherlands). The United Kingdom and Ireland Blue Shield Organisation (UKIRB) website <www.bl.uk/services/preservation/blueshield/content.html> provides links to these and offers basic disaster advice with links to web and other useful sources. The impact of terrorism, while not experienced before on the scale of September 11, has been felt before to a lesser degree, and lessons may still be applicable (see, for example, Saunders, 1993).

AFTERMATH AND RECOVERY

When undertaking research into disaster management in the mid 1990s, the author of this introductory chapter was extremely grateful for the assistance and cooperation of many individuals within Norfolk Library and Information Service, Norfolk County Record Office and their colleagues in departments of Norfolk County Council and Norfolk Fire Service. At a trying time, following the destruction by fire of Norwich Central Library, they willingly answered questions and offered advice and guidance. It is particularly satisfying that the penultimate chapter of the book offers a unique opportunity to look back from the time of the destruction by fire of a major central library (Norwich), through the immediate reaction to the disaster, to middle-term coping with the situation, and finally to long-term recovery, with the opening of a brand new state-of-the-art library and community resource. This considers not only the immediate and short-term issues such as the recovery, salvage and treatment of materials and the organization and operation of service continuity, but also the longer-term financial, political and technological issues which also had to be addressed. As this introduction is being written (July 2002), it is pleasing to note that Queen Elizabeth II has just officially opened the new Norfolk and Norwich Millennium Library.

GUIDE TO SOURCES OF INFORMATION

The chapters above include references to various sources, many of which are, naturally, topic-specific items. A more general guide to information sources on disaster management is provided in the final chapter. It concentrates on English-language sources, published from 1995 or so onwards (details of earlier publications can be found in some of these) and is arranged under the following headings: General, including books, journals, bibliographies, websites; Disaster Control Plans; Disasters – experiences; Computers and networks; Cooperative activity; Human aspects; Risk assessment; Security; War, civil unrest and terrorism. This guide should be consulted along with the references in appropriate chapters.

Sources for computers and networks, and security have been included to provide recent examples of useful sources in these areas which must be included in disaster planning, but which have often in the past been left to appropriate specialists within or without the parent organization, or service providers, who have been expected to implement back-up, security and recovery procedures. The dreaded 'crash' is a universal fear. Hardware and software can fail, files can inadvertently be erased, power supplies can be disrupted, security of networks and systems can be breached. Tried and tested steps, ranging from regular back-up of data and storage of critical data off-site to anti-virus and hacking activities, can be taken to prevent and minimize such occurrences, but cost may be high and risks need to be considered against this. An awareness now seems to be growing among librarians within the development of the digital library environment that they need to review disaster management procedures and practice relating to computers and networks, their use and security, and to communicate with all involved. Attention to this must be on-going with communication between all parties vital, as one library learned from experience:

> Regular *ongoing* communication must take place. The communication must involve all three points of the triangle: the library staff, the college systems staff, *and* the vendor. Had the vendor been in touch with the college's IT department more often, there might have been fewer questions on how to back up the data properly. Had we been in touch with the IT department more often, such discussions might have raised questions about how our data was being backed up. Had we communicated with the vendor more often, we would have known who our new customer service representative was, and we would have had an advocate during the emergency. Communication is particularly important during periods of staff changeover. (Brennan and O'Hara, 2002: 72)

The Joint Information Systems Committee's Committee for Awareness, Liaison and Training in the United Kingdom has recently investigated human and organizational issues relating to networked security (Cox et al., 2001). In the USA a group of educators, following the events of September 11, has underlined, along with the need for library and archival professional's to review their practices and procedures, the need for research into ways of effectively managing the mix of paper and electronic documents, which is still the situation in many organizations:

> Faculty in the School and their students need to research better techniques that ease the transition from paper to electronic systems, and they need to address whatever reasons are given for these enterprises' resistance. The importance of data replication and reliable network design was underscored by this disaster, and information science faculty and other experts must do more research in these areas. (Cox, A. et al., 2001: 6).

While no doubt some disasters are 'kept quiet' for reasons of security, or to avoid embarrassment perhaps, accounts of incidents and their aftermath continue to appear in the professional literature and on websites. While writing this chapter in July 2002, for example, the author noticed a brief report on the East Midlands Museums Service website of a fire which broke out in a local museum's roof space in April that year. The report focuses its advice to others on the importance of having an appropriate stockpile of emergency materials 'immediately to hand'. It ends with the reminder:

> Finally, are your Disaster Plans up to date and accessible? If housed in the building currently ablaze, there's little chance of you being allowed back in to fetch them! (Moyes and Lake, 2002)

Such articles offer help and advice based on the experience of others, and, along with details of major activities, often contain small but particularly useful, practical snippets of information. Even restating the obvious can be a timely reminder. A small selection of accounts is included in the Disasters – experiences section; others are indicated in publications and websites elsewhere in Chapter 10.

No matter how effective disaster management is, it can never totally remove the occurrence of disasters, but it can reduce the likelihood of them happening, and if they do, it can help to minimize their impact and facilitate service continuity. It is hoped that the contributions in this book will help others to prevent and be prepared for disasters and deal effectively and efficiently with them should they occur.

REFERENCES

Alire, C. (2000) 'Resource sharing: a requirement in library-disaster recovery', in, C. Alire (ed.) *Library Disaster Planning and Recovery Handbook*, New York: Neal–Schuman Publishers, pp. 561–73.

Alire, C. (ed.) (2000) *Library Disaster Planning and Recovery Handbook*, New York: Neal-Schuman Publishers. (Which is based on flood experience at Colorado.)

American Library Association (2002) *Loss and Recovery: Librarians Bearing Witness to September 11, 2001*, produced by American Libraries, the magazine of the American Library Association, in cooperation with Library Video Network, Chicago: American Library Association. (Distributed by Library Video Network, Towson, Maryland.) (This contains interviews with some of the librarians who were working in or near the World Trade Center when the terrorist attacks occurred. They recall the effects on information and library services and how they have recovered personally and professionally.)

Brennan, C. and O'Hara, E. (2002) 'Murphy was a librarian: a case study in how not to handle a systems crash', *Computers in Libraries*, 22 (3): 10–12, 72.

Cox, A., Currall, J. and Connolly, S. (2001) *The Human and Organizational Issues Associated with Network Security*, JISC Committee for Awareness, Liaison and Training (JCALT). Available at: <www.litc.sbu.ac.uk/jcalt/report.pdf>

Cox, R.J. (2001) 'The day the world changed: implications for archival, library, and information science education', *First Monday*, 6 (12). Available at: <www.firstmonday.org/issues/issues6_12/cox/index.html>

Di Mattia, S.S. (2001) 'Planning for continuity. Special libraries close to the events of September 11 can serve as a model for the importance of being prepared', *Library Journal*, 126 (19), 15 November 2001, 32–4.

Feather, J., Eden, P. and Matthews, G. (1996) *Preservation Management. Policies and Practices in British Libraries*, Aldershot: Gower.

Heritage Preservation (2002) *Cataclysm and Challenge. Impact of September 11, 2001, on Our Nation's Cultural Heritage. A Report from Heritage Preservation on behalf of the Heritage Emergency National Task Force*, Project Director Ruth Hargeaves, Heritage Preservation: Washington, DC. Available at: <www.heritagepreservation.org/news/cataclysm.htm> (Report of a survey of the impact of the events of September 11 on cultural and historic resources at the Pentagon and in Lower Manhattan, with recommendations.)

International Committee of the Blue Shield (ICBS) (2001) Available at: <www.ifla.org/VI/4/admin/protect.htm>

Kennedy, J. (1995) 'Norfolk Record Office fire: an initial report', *Journal of the Society of Archivists*, 16 (1): 3–6.

Kenney, B.J. (2001) 'Central libraries in uncertain times', *Library Journal*, 126 (19), 15 November 2001: 36–8.

Matthews, G. (1994) 'Disaster management: controlling the plan', *Managing Information*, 1 (7/8): 24–7.

Matthews, G. (1995) 'Disaster management: guidelines for library managers, in, A. Howell, H. Mansell and M. Roubos-Bennett (comps) *Redefining Disasters: A Decade of Counter-disaster Planning. Papers Submitted by Speakers Wednesday 20–Friday 22 September 1995, State Library of New South Wales, Sydney, Australia*, Sydney: Conservation Access, State Library of New South Wales, pp.137–51.

Matthews, G. and Eden, P. (1996a) *Disaster Management in British Libraries. Project Report with Guidelines for Library Managers*, Library and Information Research report 109, London: The British Library.

Matthews, G. and Eden, P. (1996b) 'Disaster management training in libraries', *Library Review*, 45 (1), 30–8.

Moyes, N. and Lake, S. (2002) 'REDS report. Fire at Derby Industrial Museum', *East Midlands Museum Service Hot News* (1). Available at: <www.emms.org.uk>

Saunders, M. (1993) 'How a library picked up the pieces after IRA blast', *Library Association Record*, 95 (2): 100–101.

Schmidt, F.C. (1999) 'Disasters: plans, clean-up, and recovery – the Colorado state experience', in MacGilvray, M.N. (ed.) *Proceedings of the 8th Annual Federal Depository Conference, April 12–15, 1999*, Holiday Inn – Bethesda, MD, Washington, DC: Library Programs Service, US Government Printing Office. Available at: <www.access.gpo.gov/su_docs/fdlp/pubs/proceedings/99pro31.html>

Sturges, P. and Rosenberg, D. (eds) (1999) *Disaster and After: the Practicalities of Information Service in Times of War and Other Catastrophes. Proceedings of an International Conference Sponsored by IGLA (The International Group of the Library Association), 4–6 September 1998, University of Bristol*, London: Taylor Graham.

Sung, C.H., Leonov, V.P. and Waters, P. (1990) 'Fire recovery at the Library of the Academy of Sciences of the USSR', *American Archivist*, 53 (2), 298–312.

University of Sussex, 'Library salvage operation under way' (2000) *Bulletin: The University of Sussex*

Newsletter, 1 December. Available at: <www.sussex.ac.uk/press_office/bulletin/01dec00/article15.html>

Valencia, M. (2002) 'Libraries, nationalism, and armed conflict in the 20th Century', *Libri*, 52 (1): 1–15.

van der Hoeven, H. and van Albada, J. (1996) *Lost Memory – Libraries and Archives Destroyed in the Twentieth Century*, prepared for UNESCO and IFLA, C-1196/WS/1, Paris; UNESCO available at: <www.unesco.org/webworld/mdn/administ/pdf/LOSTMEMO.pdf>

Watson, T. (1989) 'Out of the ashes: the Los Angeles Public Library', *Wilson Library Bulletin*, 64 (4): 34–8.

Wellheiser, J. and Scott, J. (2002) *An Ounce of Prevention: Integrated Disaster Planning for Archives, Libraries and Record Centers*, 2nd edn, Lanham, Maryland: Scarecrow Press and Canadian Archives Foundation.

2 The disaster control plan

Heather Mansell

INTRODUCTION AND OVERVIEW

There is a plethora of information dealing with how to write a disaster control plan (DCP); since the mid 1980s, in Australia certainly, there has been an enormous amount of activity related to writing and developing plans. This chapter takes an overview of that interest and looks at how such plans apply and how useful they really are. Considered mainly from personal experience and the preservation professional's point of view, it looks at what works and what doesn't in the process of developing, writing and reviewing DCPs.

For the purposes of this review I conducted a series of interviews with conservators and other related professionals working in both the public and private sectors in Australia. While this was not done in any quantitative or systematic manner it has provided some interesting insights into how DCPs are formulated and the way in which counter-disaster management is dealt with around the country. The information presented here comes from the perspective of preservation and conservation managers, conservators, trainers in counter-disaster management, consultants and salvage operators.

COUNTER-DISASTER PLANNING

This section discusses the development of counter-disaster planning in Australia, where it fits within organizational structures, and the implication for financial and managerial arrangements. The examples of incidents at the end of the section illustrate why we must continue making this time-consuming activity part of our organizational lives. Counter-disaster planning is an integral part of collection management and associated risk management for collections.

In Australia, the Heritage Collections Council (HCC) of the Cultural Ministers Council developed a *National Conservation and Preservation Policy and Strategy*

(Heritage Collections Council, 1998). As part of the activities outlined in the *National Strategy* document, a suite of publications was produced: *reCollections* (Heritage Collections Council, 1999b), *Assessment models* (Heritage Collections Council, 1999a), *Be prepared: guidelines for writing a disaster preparedness plan for small museums* (Heritage Collections Council, 2000) and *Significance: a guide to significance assessment in Australian museums* (Heritage Collections Council, 2001). Of these publications, *Be prepared*, a 'how to do it' manual, dealt specifically with counter-disaster management.

The term *counter-disaster management* to describe the total process of preparedness and planning, is gaining common usage in Australia, especially in the library and archive sector. By using the word 'management', disaster preparedness shifts from being solely the responsibility of conservators and is placed strategically with the corporate management of the organization.

A number of organizations report that DCPs form part of a bigger, corporate emergency plan which also covers risk management, staff, business resumption, information technology (IT), security and the media. Not surprisingly, IT plans became more prevalent as the year 2000 approached; the Y2K spectre encouraged activity not only for IT but also for those with responsibilities for building services and facilities.

Increasingly the responsibility for counter-disaster management is being spread throughout organizations and funded at a corporate level. The onus is no longer on conservation and preservation specialists, although they still need to play an active role in the process. Support at corporate level has added authority to the whole process.

COLLECTION MANAGEMENT AND ORGANIZATIONAL POLICY

There are good reasons for having DCPs in place, not the least of which are that they:

- provide a framework for people to work within
- require people to focus and think through potential problems and solutions in advance
- provide clear procedures; and clarify people's roles and responsibilities.

There is consensus that a good plan makes an incident much easier to manage and helps individuals to make decisions quickly and assess situations effectively and efficiently. Plans minimize risk, maximize the speed of recovery and help the organization to get back into business quickly. The development of a DCP is positive evidence of a duty of care for objects, collections and staff; it shows disaster control planning forms part of the risk management and overall operation of the entity.

For some organizations having a plan is a statutory requirement: government indemnity requires one and often insurance companies offer lower premiums where a plan has been developed and is shown to be in place. In New South Wales, the *State Records Act* stipulates that 'Each public office must ensure the safe custody and proper preservation of the State's records that it has control of' (1998, s.11).

Developing terms of reference or a policy document is a logical first step to producing a plan. The policy may not be a formal policy as such, but it is a high-level document which provides the rationale and outlines the scope of any plan. It also provides guidance on the approach to be followed and helps to ensure standard institutional practice. By necessity it is a short, straightforward document. An endorsed policy clearly shows that the organization supports the whole concept of counter-disaster management. Where one does not already exist, a formalized policy is recommended.

FINANCIAL AND MANAGERIAL IMPLICATIONS AND RESOURCES

In terms of organizational resources, staff time for disaster control planning is a significant factor. For example if the work is done in-house, one coordinator needs to be taken off-line to be given time to develop the plan. If a consultant is used, direct and indirect funds are required.

Undoubtedly, planning will need a significant financial contribution; the initial outlay for materials, equipment and supplies can be substantial. The implementation and maintenance of the DCP will be an on-going commitment. Often at least 25 per cent of a staff member's work programme will be required to maintain disaster bins, order supplies, organize stores and liaise with the building and facilities personnel. Allocating these tasks as a project and rotating them among staff on an annual basis works well.

Funds need to be accessible and available 24 hours a day, seven days a week (24/7). However, because of the prevailing 'it will never happen here' attitude, it is sometimes difficult to obtain a commitment of funds in this way. It can be challenging to persuade financial managers to consider the real costs to be incurred should a disaster occur.

Another factor often overlooked or misconstrued relates to the cost to restore versus the cost to replace items. The perception is that, where possible, it is easier and cheaper to replace items. However, a lot of resources can be involved in locating items that are likely to be rare or out of print. Even if found, the processing costs (cataloguing, labelling, and so on), need to be factored into the cost equation.

EXAMPLE INCIDENTS

Without the framework of a DCP, those affected tend to panic and confusion often reigns. Conservators generally find that their role is to calm people down, to get them to stop and think about their priorities. Faced with the unexpected, many people are galvanized into action, but when dealing with heritage and information records, it can easily be inappropriate action.

According to one conservator interviewed 'When there is no plan and things go awry, people tend to improvise and do something, but it's not always the right thing – they usually tell you after the event':

- For one large corporate's archives, the issues around the disaster were complicated by the fact that there was no DCP and consequently not enough information about the collection. Nobody knew what to do or whom to call immediately. Eventually when the right people were contacted it took several hours to calm everyone down. The response was very emotional. Before anything else, the conservator called to the site had to '… talk calmly but firmly and appear to be in control – basically, provide some strong leadership'.

Storage areas for records and heritage collections should not be below water level. We know from experience that sumps overflow, pumps break down and basements flood, but the reality is that buildings continue to be constructed in this way.

- A major herbarium experienced the problem of the specimens germinating when the sump overflowed in the collection storage area.

'Below water level' of course can also mean under the roof. Very often water tanks and caretaker's accommodation are situated on the rooftops of buildings:

- In one instance a small, grant-supported, organization faced problems when the washing machine in the caretaker's flat overflowed. As the water seeped through the floor to the storage area below it took with it dirt and debris. There was no DCP in place, but fortunately the staff member who discovered the problem knew whom to call, so the damage was minimized. That organization is now lobbying for more funds to undertake a thorough risk assessment and possible reorganization of the caretaker accommodation.
- An intriguing case involves an office building containing vital Human Resource (HR) records, where increasing numbers of staff were becoming ill. Air-quality tests revealed high levels of bacteria, fungi and yeasts. A disused well, discovered under the floor was thought to be the cause. The salvage operator called in to decontaminate the records is in the process of working out what to do with the documents. Apart from a strange odour everything appears normal. The records themselves look perfectly sound, with no evidence of mould growth or other activity.

- A distressing example relates to the use of volunteers in a disaster recovery situation. There was no plan in place and no formal procedure for recording the movement of the collection in this small organization. The records of what the collection contained were incomplete. As operations returned to normal it was discovered that a large proportion of the collection had disappeared. Unfortunately there was no tracking mechanism in place. A number of conservators reported that using volunteers can be problematic, not only from the perspective of security but because of the very nature of the arrangement, organizations have no authority over them unless specific agreements are in place.

- In another organization the plan is under review. It regularly experiences small and medium-scale incidents, usually related to water. These incidents are dealt with on a routine basis because the general staff have been trained in immediate response procedures. In some instances the person discovering the incident deals with it and reports back later; in other cases the appropriate parties are alerted and introduce a more complex series of procedures. Whatever the incident, the benefit is that panic is removed and the issues are dealt with efficiently and effectively.

- Events did not proceed so well for that same institution, when blocked gutters caused water damage to a number of items in an off-site storage area. The off-site storage personnel had not yet received any disaster awareness training or any instruction on how to use the emergency supplies in the disaster bins located in the storage areas. Because they did not know what to do or understand the consequences of inaction, some of the items grew mould and all items were very misshapen by the time they were found.

PURPOSE OF THE DCP

This section brings together views on the purpose behind the DCP. Answers to the question about why we bother having such plans reveal that it is the discipline of writing and the putting together of the plan that are important. The essential elements required to deal with the emergency event include conducting a risk analysis and establishing staff roles. It is about achieving higher levels of organizational control through staff familiarization with the issues.

ROLES AND RESPONSIBILITIES

When a disaster occurs the plan may not be consulted, but the knowledge of the collection and what to do will be familiar to organizational staff. A number of the conservators interviewed stated that they do not refer to the plan when disaster

Table 2.1 Roles and responsibilities of a typical disaster response committee for a large organization

Role	Comment	Responsibility
Disaster Leader/Controller	Person in charge of the recovery operation, but who is not actively involved in the recovery	• Liaises with the CEO • Approves major funding • Approves salvage plan and related strategies
Disaster Response Coordinator	Acts as a response and recovery team leader	• Liaises with the Disaster Controller • Ensures priorities for salvage comply with agreed priority list • Estimates the amount of financial funding required for the salvage operation • Compiles information for an insurance claim
Communications Manager	Commands the communications networks throughout the entire recovery operation	• Notifies relevant personnel • Ensures that the communication infrastructure is operational
Media Specialist	Media spokesperson	• Liaises with the CEO re media releases and interviews • Presents organizational message to the media
Recovery Specialist	Specialist in the recovery techniques required for cultural heritage collections	• Liaises with the Disaster Leader/ Controller • Assesses the extent of the damage to the collection • Determines the methods and procedures required for the salvage operation • Liaises with Recovery Team Leaders, re working procedures and use of supplies
Recovery Team leaders	Manage the salvage operation of the collection	• Train and instruct the recovery team in the required salvage methods • Liaise with Recovery Specialist • Liaise with HR Manager re Occupational Health Safety and Welfare (OHS&W) issues
Team Recorder	Maintains and oversees all of the records generated during and after the recovery procedure	• Organizes photography of the damage prior to and during the salvage operation • Organizes and files records of damaged materials and insurance records
Building Manager	Specialist in the building(s) fabric, structure, operations and security	• Assesses damage to the building(s) • Liaises with external contractors and authorities

18

		• Provides important information about the building, for example, building plans, utility locations, and alternative power sources
		• Ensures security measures in place
HR Manager	Specialist in obtaining and managing human resources	• Coordinates available staff resources
		• Administers volunteer labour
		• Employs additional staff as required
		• Coordinates OHS&W strategies
Messenger	Must hold a current driver's licence	• Delivers and exchanges messages for the Disaster Response Committee members
		• Maintains a current list of outside service organizations, equipment and suppliers
		• Assembles supplies and equipment
		• Organizes transportation
		• Ensures availability of food and water during the work breaks
		• Runs other errands as required

strikes, other than to obtain contact numbers and addresses. Most organizations rely on a telephone 'tree' arrangement for contacting appropriate staff. Some organizations have a 'mobile phone holder' who is on call 24 hours a day: that person assesses the situation and then contacts others as necessary.

Roles and responsibilities during an emergency situation are determined in the preparedness phase of the plan. A Disaster Response Committee is normally established with each person having a specific role to play, although organizations report different approaches. In small organizations members of such committees take on multiple roles. Because of the diversity of membership, there is often difficulty in getting this team of people together on a regular basis. Interestingly, one organization reported that the idea of the disaster response team had become redundant for them as most of the incidents experienced were of a small scale and dealt with easily. However, the recent threat of large-scale, local bushfires had highlighted the need to have a mechanism in place to mount a major response; they have therefore come full circle in their approach to response teams.

While the terminology differs between one organization and the next, the composition of the disaster response committee or team is very similar. The number of people in the disaster response team depends on the size of the organization. Table 2.1 outlines a typical disaster response committee for a large organization. There are two key positions: the Disaster Controller and the Disaster Response Coordinator. The Disaster Controller is usually the most senior person with the highest financial delegation; the Disaster Response Coordinator is usually a person who has had some experience dealing with disasters – this might be a management or conservation representative. What is generally agreed though, is that the Director or Chief Executive will take on neither of these roles. When dealing with a large-scale incident the Director will be fully committed to quelling fears and rumours, briefing politicians, responding to the media and possibly calling for public or private support.

RISK MANAGEMENT

Developing a risk management profile for a building and its collection can be an exigent undertaking for an organization. Some conservators believe that understanding a risk management study of buildings and collections is often the most crucial part of the planning process.

For many institutions, accounting for risk management is a statutory requirement. Risk assessment or analysis provides a focus, as it helps to formulate strategies to limit and minimize damage to people or objects, collections or the building(s). Only by assessing risks can we reduce risks. We need to know our buildings and our collections; to understand how they behave historically in their environment.

A number of training providers and institutions use a simple grid system for risk analysis, where probability is measured against effect (1 being high risk or high effect and 4 being low risk or low effect). This is illustrated in Figure 2.1.

For many organizations, off-site storage facilities compound the degree of difficulty in defining risks. A positive aspect of off-site storage facilities, of course, is that they distribute the risk. On-site storage space is increasingly at a premium for organizations located in the central business district (CBD) of large cities. Consequently there is a growth in the need for extra storage facilities located some distance away. Some organizations are fortunate enough to occupy purpose-built off-site storage; others rely on warehouse space which may or may not have been modified to suit. It is usually impossible to be aware of or control the activities of other tenants. For example, in one shared building, after a fire on the second level was extinguished, nobody thought to check the level beneath. Inevitably the water had penetrated the expansion joints in the floor and wet the material in store underneath. This was only discovered by chance some weeks later.

Risk analyses produce different prognoses for different institutions and it is important to remember that not all risks are known. It must also be remembered that documents produced through such exercises are not static and that the risks change depending on what is happening to the collection or the building at any one time. For example, many organizations rely on raising revenue through hiring out rooms and gallery type spaces for weddings, parties, book launches and the like. Many conservators and collection managers have problems with

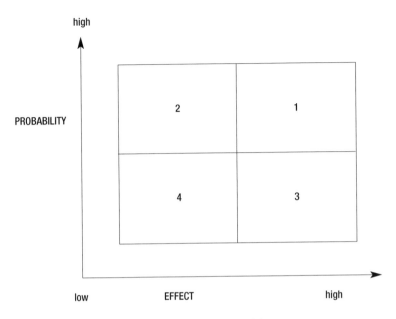

Figure 2.1   Risk analysis model

such activities, but the reality is that it happens. There have been reports where inappropriate parties have damaged historic objects: paintings (portraits) have been kissed and dignitaries and VIPs have been seen to smoke cigarettes at such functions.

The risks presented by hiring out such spaces for social functions have to be measured and managed accordingly. It is critical to have a good relationship with the organization's venue hire facility and be on the circulation list for the calendar of events. At least then any necessary precautions can be taken.

Buildings and collections are more at risk during building work, renovations and collection moves. There are many tales of problems during building renovations, especially where the old building meets new work. Having conservators on building project committees tends to work well. Building a rapport with the architect and project manager often helps; taking them on a tour of the building to point out areas of concern and previous damage, is an approach that has worked well for some. This can result in being notified of work schedules and provides the opportunity to take protective action (or not, depending upon the risk).

Another strategy which has proved useful is the development of a 'code of conduct' document for contractors, such as a 'hot works permit'. This document, though simple in structure, clearly defines what is expected of the contractor(s) and what is acceptable when on-site. It needs to be remembered that the majority

21

of contractors used by heritage organizations are normally employed on unoccupied building sites. Much of the unacceptable behaviour in occupied heritage buildings (smoking, eating, being careless about dirt and dust transfer and so on) is acceptable in other places. Contractors need to be made aware of any special requirements.

It is necessary to be ever vigilant. In one instance, the hot works permit had been issued and signed by the contractors, who were replacing wooden shingles on a roof. Arriving to work one morning, a staff member noticed that the contractors were smoking on the roof. The contractors were duly briefed and the situation resolved – no further evidence of smoking. However, arriving later to work some days following, the staff member noticed the contractors smoking again. Evidently monitoring needs to be not only constant, but also designed to obtain an adequate picture of activities and behaviours.

Another risk management strategy suggests producing the DCP in phases. The first phase involves undertaking the preliminary exercises such as risk assessment, prioritising the collection. The second phase might include awareness raising exercises and purchasing basic supplies for disaster kits and stores. As funding or resources permit, other phases and plan components are added. Continuous improvement is a more realistic approach for organizations where plans do not exist and resources are limited.

ELEMENTS OF A DISASTER CONTROL PLAN

This section focuses on the essential components of a DCP itself. Discussions indicate similarity between organizations in the basic elements of a DCP and include preparedness, prevention, reaction and recovery. It is in the approach and application where differences are clearly evident. Most organizations consider preparedness and prevention as complementary components.

Over the last 10 years or so there has been a definite move away from large plans weighing many kilos towards discrete documents which form parts of a suite of related products (for example, the institution's total emergency plan, produced at the corporate level).

Appendices are useful and normally contain salvage priorities, supplier lists, contacts, floor plans and proposed relocation sites. They are especially useful where they can be used as standalone documents.

Some conservators believe that lists of priority collection items should not be included in the plan at all, as they not only add to the size of the document but also represent a concise shopping list for the unscrupulous. The crux here is that such documents exist and that the appropriate people have access to them when necessary.

FITTING THE ELEMENTS TOGETHER

At the simplest level a good plan will contain details sufficient for any member of staff to initiate the vital steps in disaster management: prevention, containment of problems during the emergency, and recovery.

The shorter and simpler the plan, the more accessible, easily understood and readily introduced into an organization it will be. During times of stress it is necessary to be able to access information quickly and easily. The current trend is for DCPs to form a set of documents comprising:

- easy to follow, immediate response sheets
- a ratified policy document
- a detailed resource list
- a recovery document which is really only relevant to conservators or those undertaking the recovery process.

One organization has its plan divided into seven separate sections, arranged such that individual parts can be selected and removed as required.

Although the information may not be presented in the same fashion, four common headings have been used to formulate the information:

- Prevention
- Preparedness
- Reaction/response
- Recovery and post recovery.

Prevention

The most obvious prevention strategies are the regular maintenance checks on all building systems (for example, electrical, roof, gutter, HVAC (heating, ventilation and air-conditioning), and water). Even when these regular checks occur there are always times when an extraordinary event happens. For example, only days prior to a heavy rainstorm, one organization had carried out a routine gutter inspection. Unpredictably during the storm, a dead bat became trapped in the down pipe and caused extensive damage to the ceiling and floor as a result of the built-up rainwater seeping under the eaves.

Maintaining an 'incident log' of disaster events is a practical way of keeping track of vulnerable sites in the building. When reviewing incident logs, it becomes apparent what faults have been attended to and what remains to be done. Such logs have been used effectively to support insurance claims and bids for funding for building maintenance and alterations.

Interestingly, a provider of disaster management services to a number of organizations is about to introduce an e-mail reminder service for its clients (see

Chapter 3 p. 66). The messages will be based on a log of previous events and alert clients to take appropriate action (for example, 'the rainy season is coming: it is time to check the gutters', and so on).

Preparedness

Being prepared for a disaster or emergency event is considered by many to be the most important section of the disaster control plan as it will reduce the level of response and recovery. It is closely linked with disaster prevention and the two are often dealt with together.

Basic elements under preparedness include:

- the formation of the disaster control committee
- the creation of telephone trees
- the production of suppliers and contact lists
- the assembly and distribution of disaster kits (see Table 2.2, p. 31)
- the production, distribution and training for staff in the use of disaster response procedures.

It is vital to ensure that any contractors and suppliers listed have the capacity to deal with situations for which they may be required, such as knowing that the designated cold store only takes pallets of material which have been wrapped in a specific way or that unclean material is not acceptable.

Simple, accurate floor plans are invaluable. It is essential to keep these up to date by recording any changes and building modifications.

Reaction

Response or reaction to incidents is normally categorized as:

- immediate actions relating to who needs to be informed, actions taken by whoever discovers the incident
- short-term actions taken by the conservators and building facilities personnel
- long-term actions relating to decisions about priorities, treatments, drying out, freezing; collaborative approaches involving collection managers, conservators and building facilities personnel.

Recovery and post-recovery

This section of the plan, which provides information on recovery techniques for various media is regarded as being primarily for conservators or those responsible for carrying out the actual salvage work. This information certainly needs to be readily available, but including it as part of a single plan document is considered to cause bulk and confusion.

Of necessity the recovery plan can only be produced after the incident. What it contains will be directly related to the event. It provides a structure for recovery and post-recovery. The exercise of producing it has been found to be useful even for relatively small incidents.

ARE THERE DIFFERENCES BETWEEN TYPES OF ORGANIZATION?

The philosophy of why a plan is necessary and the mechanics of developing the plan (for example, Occupational Health Safety and Welfare (OHS&W) and financial aspects, and so on) are the same or similar for all types of collecting organizations, large and small. It is in the response and recovery phases, where individual organizations use distinct approaches to suit the materials in the collection, that differences will become obvious.

One area of difference is evident between government and private organizations. Australia has three tiers of government: federal government, state government and local government. It seems that all government organizations are concerned with maintaining and providing public access to collections and records in their custody. Private sector organizations, by necessity, are concerned with keeping business records and collections.

Some Australian organisations have a national role with agency offices in each state (for example, the National Archives of Australia). These state agencies rely on a state business recovery plan. The crisis management team for the agency then produces a specific, immediate response document.

Some of the larger heritage institutions, which mount exhibitions, have a specific plan for the display space, taking into account any borrowed works and lender requirements. In these instances it is normal to prepare specific documentation for each major exhibition. For other organizations, the display space and its contents are considered in the general procedures of the disaster control plan.

DEVELOPMENT OF A DISASTER CONTROL PLAN

The processes involved in developing a plan are examined in this section. Critical to these processes are understanding the culture of an organization; the collection and how it is used; and the availability of resources.

Issues discussed include prioritizing the collection, occupational health and safety, salvage, insurance, dealing with the media and the length of time required for producing a plan. Some of these issues appear to be relatively straightforward, others are complex and very often take a long time to resolve.

WHAT WILL BE SAVED FIRST?

Ostensibly, prioritizing collections is one of the most difficult issues on which to reach agreement; it is also one of the most crucial components to be completed when developing the plan. It is somewhat easier where organizations have undergone the rigours of collection valuation, as this at least provides a starting point for discussion. A number of organizations have found the strategies outlined in *Significance* useful in this process (Heritage Collections Council, 2001: 20).

Identifying and documenting the location of high-priority collections are both fundamental to the preparedness process. Where priority items are stored over several locations (a good risk management strategy), there is a need to have a finding aid or listing to help with locating these items quickly.

An interesting situation and potential dilemma exists for one commercial conservation service provider which deals with items ranging from documents to large, three-dimensional objects. Because of the nature of the business, the items in the building change frequently and all belong to other institutions or individuals. In the event of a disaster, staff will need to make judgements about what to save first. This is a good example of where early retrieval of vital records is important. Access to the records of what is actually in the building at any one time is crucial. This organization is in the process of developing a set of salvage priorities based on significance, physical susceptibility and physical restraint.

OCCUPATIONAL HEALTH SAFETY & WELFARE

Many organizations have an OHS&W Committee and in some, the Chief Warden or Chief Security Officer has oversight of this activity. Usually Wardens and Security Officers deal with bomb threats and with the evacuation of personnel during an emergency. The role of the OHS&W Committee is wider and involves ensuring that staff are familiar with manual handling procedures, ergonomic work practices, the correct handling of dangerous materials and perhaps the use of fire extinguishers.

An important role for the OHS&W person on the disaster response committee is to manage the process of ensuring that workers take regular breaks and have access to refreshments.

Stress management is normally covered in counter-disaster awareness and training sessions. It is not until the disaster strikes that people realize the impact of stress on performance and behaviour. The effects of stress are unpredictable. When dealing with large-scale incidents it is recommended that meetings with staff and contractors are held off-site where at all possible. This provides both physical and mental distance from the problem.

Engaging the Human Resources or Personnel unit ensures that an appropriate stress management environment exists and that counselling is available during or directly after an incident. Post traumatic stress disorder is a recognized phenomenon.

SALVAGE PLANS

The salvage operation cannot take effect until a recovery plan has been developed. Personnel responding to even small incidents need to follow some logical strategy. When facing medium to large-scale incidents, the preparation of the recovery plan is normally a consultative process. Usually conservators drive the process, liaising with collection managers, registrars and curators. A course of action is recommended to senior management.

Possibly because water problems are more frequent, conservators consider attending to the effects of water to be more urgent than those from dust. Problems associated with dust are typically not seen as dangerous. However potential impacts can be severe and a similar set of strategies has to be put in place. It can be an expensive problem from which to recover.

INSURANCE

While insurance is considered to be the responsibility of finance or administration departments, the organization's insurance arrangements should be noted in the disaster planning policy document. This simplifies procedures for those dealing with emergency situations if the person with delegated responsibility is unavailable at the time of the incident.

Before processing any claims, insurance companies normally require an account or summary of actions taken and costs involved (staff hours, resources, cost of damage and the like). It has been found that maintaining disaster incident logs is useful.

For smaller organizations without a plan, the insurance company may play a commanding role. In one reported instance, where 10 000 financial records were affected by water, the insurance company directed the recovery operation. Overwhelmed and untrained, volunteers did what they thought best and placed wet items in lidded buckets. Eventually, expert advice was sought, but only after mould had started to grow. This particular incident was expensive, not only in monetary terms but also in terms of the psychological impact on personnel.

How do you know when it's time to get help? This is a pertinent question, even where a disaster control plan exists. For organizations with experienced conservators on staff this does not present such a difficult decision; experience allows these professionals to make educated assessments about what can be dealt with in-house and what requires external assistance. The difficulty comes, however, where there are inexperienced or no conservation staff. Dealing with 2000 wet items requires a different response from the reality of dealing with 200 000 wet items.

MEDIA

During a major disaster or emergency event, media management is likely to be critical for the organization. Responses and interactions must be handled strategically.

Anyone dealing with the media on behalf of the organization needs to be well versed in doing so. It is a task best handled by the Public Relations (PR) officer. If such a position does not exist within the organizational structure then the Chief Executive Officer (CEO) would be the obvious choice. Presenting well-considered, consistent information is of the utmost importance. It is interesting to note that the media often listen to emergency radio and arrive at the scene of the incident before the fire or other emergency services!

Many incidents are not reported to the media for a variety of reasons, such as the wish to avoid bad publicity or because the incident is small and can be dealt with quickly and easily. There generally appears to be a reluctance to report incidents relating to building failure, especially in new buildings. Conversely, incidents related to and damage caused by 'acts of God' often make the headlines.

What to tell the media can be a complex issue. In one example a major part of a collection was affected by a toxic mould. Consequently, access to that part of the collection was withdrawn. Not surprisingly library users were upset at this inconvenience. Initially the organization was wary of announcing the full extent of the problem as it was likely that accusations would be made about the 'mismanagement of public collections'. However once the public were fully informed they were very supportive of the organization and its problem; they recognized that they were being protected rather than inconvenienced.

HOW LONG WILL IT TAKE TO PRODUCE A PLAN?

From discussions with colleagues and actual experience there is neither consensus nor benchmark for how long it takes to develop and produce a DCP. However, there is agreement that it will use considerable resources and take anywhere from two to twelve months. It will depend upon whether it is done on a full-time basis and whether or not it is undertaken in-house or by a consultant. Even when an in-house person has been dedicated to this task there is a tendency to call on that person to be involved in other organizational activities. Using a consultant will consume internal resources too: that person will need to talk to staff in order to understand how the organization operates and then work with them to obtain ownership and commitment.

Some parts of a plan take longer than others to develop. For example, most agree that obtaining information on collection priorities is a protracted process and one organization found that agreeing on the contents of the disaster kits was lengthy because they decided against using one of the standard 'off the shelf' versions. It is important to remember that time is required for editing, reviewing and obtaining approval for the plan; approval often takes a long time.

PARTICIPATION

This section discusses the various partners and stakeholders who need to be involved in producing a DCP. It is recognized that the processes cannot take place in isolation and that seeking advice widely and gaining input facilitates the process. Well-managed communication strategies are vital.

COMMITTEE VERSUS SINGLE PERSON

Because the ethos behind a disaster control plan relies on every stakeholder having some ownership, good communication strategies are essential. For this reason it is advisable to have a committee comprising representatives of any organization involved. It would be naive, though, to imagine that a committee is going to produce a tangible document; committees have been notoriously unsuccessful at completing plans. The production of an actual plan can probably only be achieved by one person, well supported by a committee. The role of the committee of stakeholders is to provide input from across the organization and channel information in both directions; the role of the individual is to coordinate and drive the process, not to be responsible for the whole project.

Once a plan has been developed and put in place, an individual can be responsible for updating information. Some organizations prefer to rotate this task among a small group of staff as it intensifies the learning and awareness process.

There will always be pressure to look at specifics, but it is critical that the committee does not become enmeshed in too much detail. Tight management of committee deliberations is imperative in order to achieve effective outcomes.

INTERNAL

Stakeholders within the organization are many and varied. Establishing the disaster response committee is a powerful communication tool and an excellent mechanism for representing stakeholder interests.

EXTERNAL

Partners, external stakeholders and suppliers need to be kept informed of expectations and activities. It is useful to investigate the likely response times for businesses supplying emergency materials and equipment. This also applies to plumbing, electricity, air-conditioning and any other contractor services.

It is beneficial to have informal reciprocal arrangements in place with like institutions. This can be as simple as a first point of contact number or as detailed as sharing lists of available equipment, supplies and staff expertise.

A number of relatively formal support groups have been established in Australia. For example: the risk management group of the Cooperative Action Between Victorian Academic Libraries (CAVAL); the DISACT (Disaster Australian Capital Territory) group; the Sydney Curatorial and Custodial Institutions Disaster Preparedness Group; and the Arts SA (South Australia) Collecting Institutions Disaster Management Group.

SUPPORTING INFRASTRUCTURE

This section looks at the physical elements considered as essential to support the DCP.

DISASTER RESPONSE SUPPLIES, STOREROOMS AND BINS

Opinion varies on what is essential in terms of equipment and supplies, even among similar collecting institutions. The major determining criteria are the types of collections and the resources available (that is, financial and physical). Most agree that there are layers or levels of preparedness. This can range from disaster trolleys to disaster rooms filled with supplies and equipment. Some organizations have space to assess, isolate and air-dry items and cope with small incidents.

Table 2.2 lists a typical range of disaster supplies necessary to cope with an immediate response. Such supplies are housed in a variety of containers, such as mobile storage bins, trolleys, cupboards and trunks.

Table 2.2   Disaster kits: basic contents

Perforated paper towelling	Clear polythene storage bags for collection items)
Pre-cut plastic sheeting	Blue garbage bags (for rubbish)
Gloves: cotton and rubber	Twist ties
Pencils, paper, clipboards	Chalk
Masking tape	String
Plastic buckets	Foam sponges
Scissors	Tie labels

Where organizations are in a position to have storerooms for equipment and supplies, having both internal and external access to the store is seen as a benefit. A list of typical stores and equipment is included in Table 2.3.

Large-scale, major incidents need to be dealt with using external resources and normally require assistance from community and state emergency services.

INFORMATION MANAGEMENT

Once plans have been produced it is necessary to make them available to stakeholders and keep track of updated versions. Whether or not to make them available to the wider community is a contentious issue.

STORAGE OF AND ACCESS TO THE PLAN

Opinions differ on this issue, but basically it is believed that the plan in total should only be available to those identified as key players on the disaster committee. It is considered that general staff should have simple handouts appropriate to their needs and responsibilities. Many organizations require key personnel to keep copies of the plan in their cars or at home for ready access.

HARD COPY VERSUS ELECTRONIC COPY

Hard-copy disaster control plans are preferred. An electronic version may not be accessible during the disaster and it may not be easy to use even if it is available. Nevertheless electronic format is ideal for updating and distributing plans

Table 2.3 Typical store contents

Protection	Removal	Recovery	Monitoring equipment	Communications
Plastic sheeting	Cardboard boxes	Clothes lines	Dehumidifiers	Radio
Adhesive waterproof tape	Trolleys	Spray bottles/misters	Temperature and RH monitoring equipment	Whistles
Ties (gardening twine)	Blotting paper	Clean newsprint, blotter	Fans	Loud hailers
Stanley knife	Plastic bags (2 colours)	Distilled water		Walkie-talkies
Pins	Plastic crates	Clean work space, trestle tables		Telephones
Scissors	Bins			Chalk
Sandbags	Plastic sheeting, Mylar™			Large sheet of paper
				Thick waterproof pens

Plant/safety equipment	Clothing	Clean-up	Documentation
Torches, batteries, globes	Rubber boots	Mops (sponge type)	Paper, pens, chalk
Emergency lighting	Raincoats	Buckets	Tags
Generators	Masks	Paper towelling – perforated, dimpled, non-coloured	Camera, flash, batteries, film
First aid kits	Aprons	Brooms	Disaster lists
Pumps	Overalls	Sponges	Clipboards
	Gloves		Disposable cameras
	Hard hats		
	Respirators		
	Sleeve protectors		

through the organization's intranet. A number of organizations use both formats. Whatever the choice, it is important to ensure staff know where the plan is located and how it can be accessed.

When placing disaster control plans on the internet it must be remembered that not only are there staff privacy issues to be considered but also organizational security issues. Sensitive information (such as collection priorities and key locations) must be excluded, so a generic form of plan is recommended.

One major organization, referred to by a number of conservators as having a useful DCP to follow, recently removed its disaster plan from its website. The organization's risk management officer believed that 'terrorists' could work out any weaknesses in the plan and use those to their advantage.

CD-ROM

Consultants providing counter-disaster management services have used CD-ROM for supplying and storing DCPs. It is a compact way of sending the finished product to the client who can then print and distribute the documents as required.

TRAINING

This section reviews the various categories of training identified as necessary to help personnel deal with emergency events and cope with the aftermath. Not everyone requires the same level or type of training. Probably the most difficult to convince that training is relevant are the heads of organizations, so it is encouraging to see that an attempt has been made to target this group.

TARGETED TRAINING

There is a need for different types and levels of training to be available. There has been a limited attempt to raise awareness among senior executives by providing them with an overview of the whole process of counter-disaster management. It was successful in the Australian Capital Territory (ACT), where senior executives from organizations with DCPs demonstrated a better understanding of the costs and commitment involved in counter-disaster management activities. It is testing to persuade senior executives to take time out from their, often punishing, schedules to focus on something which might never happen.

Preservation and conservation managers are keen to receive training at a more strategic level. In the emergency situation these people are likely to be responsible for coordinating or managing the recovery process. Much of the training currently available is irrelevant for this group.

Regular training sessions for the disaster response committee to practise specific roles is obviously necessary, but team building for this group is also recommended. This group must be able to communicate with each other effectively. In large organizations it is probable that the team members do not work together on a regular basis, if at all. Team building could conceivably assist communication during the stress of an emergency event or situation.

In recognition of the fact that disasters rarely occur between 9.00am and 5.00pm, it is important to train security and other staff who occupy the building after normal business hours. This group should possibly be among the first to be instructed in any counter-disaster awareness, training programme.

General staff require broad counter-disaster awareness training. To be useful, this training needs to be held regularly, allowing staff to attend refresher sessions. Conservators reported that this type of training has helped spread responsibility for counter-disaster management and enhances the feeling of ownership.

IMPORTANCE OF SIMULATION EXERCISES

There is general agreement that it is at the simulation stage of any training exercise or programme that people gain vital experience of what to do in a disaster situation. For most people it is difficult to conceptualize what this might entail. Interestingly, record keeping seems to be the hardest aspect for many during these exercises.

Short courses are provided regularly in the Australian Capital Territory (ACT), New South Wales (NSW), South Australia (SA) and Victoria (VIC). These courses are similar in their approach: training is generally presented over two days and ends with a simulated disaster, followed by a debrief. These courses are aimed at people who need to write disaster plans and who will be involved in, or responsible for recovery processes.

Indisputably, training is forgotten unless it is put to use. In one organization, disaster simulation exercises have been dismissed in favour of *in situ* scenarios. This is seen to work especially well, as there is a number of collection sites with specific problems and issues. The training methodology relies on the staff completing damage checklists by following written or physical prompts.

One method of training provided by CAVAL uses disaster simulation during the first session, the object being to test responses and reactions to the emergency situation. Feedback is provided to the participants through a 'how it could have been done better' exercise. Not surprisingly, this can be difficult for some people.

APPLICATION

This section looks at the difficulties in moving from preparation, preparedness and disaster simulation to reality. Examples illustrate unexpected occurrences.

REALITY AND THE MOMENT OF TRUTH

- A major difficulty occurred with dual occupancy of a building. One part of the building housed a municipal heritage collection where a DCP was in existence. The other part housed the municipal offices where there was no DCP. When water penetrated both buildings there were problems for both parties. The plan for the heritage materials swung into action, but because there had been no communication between the two parties there were two separate approaches to the resolution of the problem. The lack of communication caused particular difficulties for the drying contractors, as disputes erupted over access to power supplies and equipment. Valuable time was lost and more money than perhaps necessary was spent.
- For one organization the disaster incident log reads like a double entry for two consecutive months. The ingress of water, caused by what appeared to be a blocked drainage system, resulted in major inconvenience (closure of the reading room) and the expenditure of a relatively large sum of money (drying concrete floors, replacing carpets and checking electrical fittings in floors and ceilings). Unbelievably, almost to the day a month later, the scenario was repeated. Apparently the cause was not only the immediate drainage system but also involved a related sump problem.
- In the same organization, trained staff were observed paddling about in water with bare feet, reportedly because they did not want to get their shoes wet. Rubber boots were available. All training and awareness sessions in that organization discuss the potential for water to be contaminated and to have electricity running through it. Such incidents illustrate too well the fact that stress can cause irrational behaviour.

CONTINUOUS IMPROVEMENT (REVIEWING)

DCPs are dynamic documents. To be effective they need to be updated regularly to reflect changes to personnel, suppliers, contractors and building structures.

HELPFUL TIPS ON WHAT MAKES A PLAN EFFECTIVE

The effectiveness of a plan is compromised through not paying attention to certain factors and by not completing certain tasks.

- Ask for advice; ownership by stakeholders is crucial: consult them. All active players need to understand and agree to their role(s).
- The physical appearance and design of the DCP document(s) have a strong bearing on how people interact with the plan and how easy it is to use. Does it have the right 'feel' about it?
- There is a set of tasks which need to be carried out on a regular basis:
  - updating contact numbers for staff, suppliers and contractors
  - updating and review of floor plans
  - restocking and reviewing disaster response supplies.
- Never become complacent. Remember that the plan is not 'set in concrete'. If there has been a disaster incident, review the plan very soon afterwards. What could have been done better or differently?
- Ensure that appropriate counter-disaster management training programmes are available and that these programmes are current and relevant.
- Perhaps most important tasks of all, review risks and update analyses documents.

LESSONS TO BE LEARNED

Some comments from experienced disaster response professionals are significant: 'It [the plan] will never be perfect'; 'Get the insurance assessor in very quickly'; 'It's impossible to be prepared for everything'; and 'Every event is a learning process.'

INPUT INTO NEW BUILDING DESIGN AND REFURBISHMENT

In theory a DCP should have an impact on refurbishment, extension work and the construction of new buildings. Through first hand experience, conservators have acquired a good knowledge of what does not work in buildings in terms of potential hazards for disaster incidents. It should therefore be possible for them to brief architects, designers and builders about 'things to look out for'. Indications are, though, that this interaction is not welcome and really seen as interfering or causing problems. Conservators and other preservation specialists need to position themselves such that they are consulted early in the building process, during the consultation and design phases.

COOPERATIVE NETWORKS AND PARTNERSHIPS

Cooperative, regional activities in terms of support and sharing resources seem like a good idea and are popular in Australia, with both formal and informal groups established in a number of states. Some of these groups have been in existence for a number of years.

Pivotal to the formation of DISACT was the 1998 report of the Australian National Audit Office (ANAO), which examined collection management issues at four of the national collecting institutions in Canberra. Deficiencies in counter-disaster preparedness were found although the limits on staff and funding were noted as significant factors. Through meetings of the DISACT group, a Memorandum of Understanding (MoU) was developed (Hughes, 2000).

Seven Federal Government institutions[1] are about to be signatories to the MoU, which among other things agrees to:

- aim to have a common standard and format of disaster plan to increase efficiency of mutual assistance
- hold one annual training exercise on Disaster Recovery Techniques to be arranged by member institutions on a rotational basis to improve communication between staff and institutions
- hold an annual seminar on issues relevant to Disaster Planning to raise disaster awareness
- provide specialist staff in emergencies and an agreed method will be used to request emergency assistance including providing staff from member institutions to assist for up to two days without undue formality that could delay recovery
- each institution will provide indemnity cover for their staff assisting disaster recovery at other member institutions with the agreement of their own institution.

A less formal arrangement applies in New South Wales. Formed in 1985, the Sydney Curatorial and Custodial Institutions Disaster Preparedness Group includes various state and federal government organizations. The group's sphere of activity focuses on sharing of information and resources across the organizations. A central register of supplies, equipment and expertise is maintained and distributed among members. The group meets around twice a year. Although established to encourage heads of organizations to embrace disaster preparedness, in reality it is collection managers and heads of conservation who attend. There are plans to promote the group to building facilities managers, registrars, curators and librarians.

In South Australia, ArtLab Australia (the state's central conservation facility for government heritage collections), maintains the relationship among the cultural institutions. The close proximity of the institutions to each other facilitates this network for sharing of supplies, equipment, facilities and expertise. As a service provider, ArtLab Australia assists these organizations in formulating their plans and is also available to provide advice and assist with any recovery or salvage operations as required.

The Victorian group, CAVAL, is a consortium of Victorian university and Institute of Technology libraries. It was established in 1978 to enhance the effectiveness of educational and research activities of the consortium members. Its structure and focus has changed over the years, but this group continues to be active in the provision of disaster preparedness training and advice. CAVAL has a risk management group which meets quarterly.

CONCLUSION

Over the last ten years counter-disaster management has shifted from being solely the responsibility of conservators and preservation managers to being a corporate concern; this is a positive outcome.

It is interesting to note that while there is a multiplicity of approaches to counter-disaster management, there is also a high level of consistency across organizations as to how disasters are prepared for and actually dealt with.

The example incidents in this chapter, both major and minor, illustrate that they are neither rigid nor totally predictable in their effects; very often things are not what they seem. In our eagerness to find a quick and simple resolution to a problem it is easy to focus on the effect and not the cause. We need to be aware that dealing with disasters is a creative process, that there is no 'right' way. By creating a framework (a DCP) we become familiar with the concepts and principles which enable us to deal with the unexpected.

ACKNOWLEDGEMENTS

My thanks to colleagues in a range of Australia-wide institutions and organizations, who have broad experience in dealing with disasters and emergency events and who were happy to answer questions and provide comment:

State Library of New South Wales: Anna Higgs, Tegan Henderson (assistance with conducting interviews), Nichola Parshall
Conservation Access, State Library of New South Wales: Catherine Thomson
National Museum of Australia: Eric Archer
National Gallery of Australia: Fiona Kemp, Janet Hughes
National Archives of Australia (Canberra): Ellie McFadyen
National Archives of Australia (Victoria): Elizabeth Donovan

State Library of Victoria: Mary Cox
State Library of Queensland: Grant Collins
Library & Information Services, Western Australia (LISWA): Stephanie Baily
ArtLab Australia (Adelaide): Ian Cook, Alice Cannon, Vicki Humphrey
Art & Archival (Canberra): Kim Morris,
Historic Houses Trust of New South Wales: Tamara Lavrencic
Munters Pty Ltd: Tim Butler

NOTE

1. Australian Institute for Aboriginal and Torres Strait Islanders; Australian War Memorial; National Archives of Australia; National Gallery of Australia; National Herbarium; National Library of Australia; National Museum of Australia; Screen Sound Australia (formerly National Film and Sound Archive).

REFERENCES AND SELECT BIBLIOGRAPHY

BOOKS AND PAPERS

Alire, C. (ed.) (2000) *Library Planning and Recovery Handbook*, New York: Neal-Schuman.
Doig, J. (1997) *Disaster Recovery for Archives, Libraries and Records Management Systems in Australia and New Zealand*, Wagga Wagga: Centre for Information Studies, Charles Sturt University.
Dorge, V. and Jones, S. (1999) *Building an Emergency Plan: A Guide for Museums and Other Cultural Institutions*, Los Angeles: Getty Conservation Institute.
Fox, L. (1998) *Disaster Preparedness Workbook for US Navy Libraries and Archives*, Newport, RI: US Naval War College Library.
Heritage Collections Council (1998) *National Conservation and Preservation Policy and Strategy: Australia's Heritage Collections*, Canberra: Commonwealth Department of Communications and the Arts.
Heritage Collections Council (1999a) *Assessment Models*, Canberra: Commonwealth Department of Communications and the Arts.
Heritage Collections Council (1999b) *reCollections: Caring for Collections Across Australia*, Canberra: Department of Communications, Information Technology and the Arts.
Heritage Collections Council (2000) *Be Prepared: Guidelines for Small Museums for Writing a Disaster Preparedness Plan*, Söderlund Consulting Pty Ltd., Canberra: Commonwealth Department of Communications, Information Technology and the Arts.
Heritage Collections Council (2001) *Significance*, Canberra: Commonwealth Department of Communications, Information Technology and the Arts.
Hughes, J. (2000) 'A strategy to increase cooperation for disaster preparedness: some Australian examples for saving resources and raising awareness', paper presented at the Prevention 2000 conference, Draguignan, France 7–10 November 2000 (in press).
Lavrencic, T. (2000) *The Evolution of Disaster Plans at the Historic Houses Trust of New South Wales*, ICOMOS.
State Records Act of New South Wales (1998) Sydney: State Records New South Wales.
Toigo, J. (2000) *Disaster Recovery Planning: Strategies for Protecting Critical Information*, 2nd edition, Upper Saddler River, NJ: Prentice Hall PTR.

WEBSITES

American Institute for Conservation (USA), available at: <www.aic.stanford.edu/disaster>

Australian Museums On-Line (Australia), available at: <www.amol.org.au>

Conservation OnLine (USA), available at: <www.palimpsest.stanford.edu>

Federal Emergency Management Agency (USA), available at: <www.fema.gov>

Inland Empire Libraries Disaster Response Network (USA), available at: <www.palimpsest.stanford.edu/bytopic/disasters/misc/inland.html>

Northeast Documentation Centre (USA), available at: <www.nedcc.org>

SOLINET (USA), available at: <www.solinet.net>

Office of Information Technology (Australia), available at: <www.oit.nsw.gov.au/Guidelines/Security>

3 Risk management

Alice Cannon

INTRODUCTION

Many people working within the cultural heritage industry already practise risk management, although they may not be conscious of doing so. For example, when developing a treatment proposal for an object, a conservator will consider both the expected benefits to the object and the risks posed by the treatment itself before choosing the most appropriate method. Similarly, developing a disaster plan or reviewing the storage arrangements for collections will contain elements of risk management – the current situation will be assessed to determine what risks threaten the collection, so that new strategies can be developed to address these risks.

Risk management is essentially, therefore, a framework for making better decisions. It is a formal method for collecting information about something – in our case, collections – and identifying current or potential risks, prioritizing these risks according to their predicted occurrence and severity, and then using that information to decide what activities will best contribute to the longevity of the collection. This allows an organization to manage risks, rather than merely reacting to any situations that occur. Preventive conservation is all about risk management, but is not always discussed in these terms.

At Artlab Australia we have started to use risk management as a tool within our Preventive Conservation programme. We find it useful for a number of reasons:

- It is a useful way to organize information about collections.
- It is a useful way to standardize information about collections – Artlab carries out work for a number of government arts organizations, and this system allows us to compare risks between organizations, if necessary.
- It helps us to justify our position on collection issues to other stakeholders. Risk management is a more transparent way of making decisions and therefore we find it is easier to argue our case, as it is not just presented as an

intuitive response or position. For example, instead of saying, 'these items mustn't travel', we can say, 'if these items travel, this is the probable outcome, and this is the probable cost', which is more likely to carry weight with those making the final decision.

- It is a recognized methodology used in many organizations and by many professions and thus assists us in communicating with other disciplines.
- Staff involved in the process learn a great deal about their environment, collection and management structure. This helps to build a more cohesive organization and a more integrated approach to decision making at all levels.

This chapter examines why risk management is important for cultural heritage organizations and outlines the risk management process itself, step-by-step. While our focus is on risk management for collections, it is important to remember that this process is used extensively outside of the cultural heritage industry – for example, in the insurance industry, the construction industry, the agricultural industry, and by governments, hospitals and schools. Although each of these industry sectors use risk management to regulate different activities, such as project management, occupational health and safety initiatives or investment strategies, the process of risk management is the same throughout. This means that we can learn much from other industries, as it is from these industries that the formal processes of risk management originally developed. Artlab's approach to risk management is based on the Australian and New Zealand Standard for Risk Management (AS/NZS 4360:1999), and therefore much of the discussion in this chapter will be based on this model. However, discussions and examples of other models used within the heritage industry will also be included.

ABOUT ARTLAB AUSTRALIA

Artlab Australia is the State Conservation Centre for South Australia and is based in Adelaide. Artlab provides preservation and conservation assistance for eight government-owned collecting organizations in the Adelaide metropolitan and country regions, as well as for a number of private individuals and organizations both within Australia and internationally.

Artlab and the government collecting organizations are part of Arts SA (South Australia), a portfolio within the Government's Department of Premier and Cabinet. The collecting organizations within Arts SA receive government funding to spend on conservation treatments and on preservation programmes, which are provided by Artlab. Artlab is expected to provide direction and guidelines for risk management activities related to collections. Being a separate organization in itself, Artlab also requires its own risk management programme to protect items and collections under its temporary care.

Artlab's risk management programmes

Artlab has started to use the risk management approach extensively in recent years. As part of our Preventive Conservation programme, Artlab is undertaking risk assessments internally and for all State Government collecting organizations, in order to establish a broader risk management structure. The information gathered from this process is being used to aid other preventive projects – for example, disaster preparedness, environmental monitoring upgrades and storage reviews – and to develop conservation management plans. Recommendations arising from these risk assessments can also be used by the organizations in developing appropriate risk treatment programmes. We hope to link this programme to other risk management activities within the State Government – for example, to the State Disaster Committee, which exists to respond to statewide emergency situations.

We have also used the risk management approach on a project level in order to develop Integrated Pest Management (IPM) plans for government clients. As these clients share both infrastructure and buildings, a coordinated approach to IPM has seemed the most sensible option. In a less formal way, risk management has also been applied to various building and exhibition redevelopment programmes. Throughout this chapter, these programmes are used to illustrate the application of risk management to the cultural heritage industry.

ABOUT RISK MANAGEMENT

THE ORIGINS OF RISK MANAGEMENT

As a formal concept, risk management only became prominent during the 1970s. This was largely in response to the stock market crash of 1974, after which risk management became 'the biggest game in town' for investment managers and their clients (Bernstein, 1998: 301). A great deal of the existing risk management literature has come from the insurance and stock market industry.

Prior to the 1970s, the main strategy in dealing with risks was to purchase an appropriate insurance policy, thereby 'transferring' the risk to another party. However, some companies began to see prevention of risk as just as important as financing risk, as insurance could not cover all the potential costs that may arise from a loss – for example, lost time, goodwill or reputation (Drennan, 2001: 1–2). Rising levels of litigation and insurance premiums and changes to government legislation have also affected the global approach to risk management (Drennan, 2001: 6).

The risk management standard developed by Australia and New Zealand was the first major milestone in the worldwide movement towards risk management,

43

and was followed by similar work from organizations in Canada, the USA, Germany and the UK (Kloman, 2000: 4). The last few years have seen the appointment of risk managers in many industries, in recognition of the need for companies to take an holistic approach to risk management, rather than individual departments each being responsible for their own risk management programmes – an approach that often leads to the repetition of some tasks, and the omission of others (Drennan, 2001: 6).

RISK – IS IT ALL BAD?

People have a tendency to view all risk as 'bad' (Kloman, 2000: 1). In the cultural heritage industry, a risk is generally seen as something that endangers the safety of collections, that is, if the hazard in question occurs, some level of damage will also occur. However, risk does not necessarily have to have a negative outcome. Risk represents uncertainty and change, which is why people find it disturbing, but risk can result in positive outcomes that may not have occurred if the prevailing order had been maintained (Kloman, 2000: 2–3). For example, a higher risk investment strategy can result in higher returns, a risky or unproven medical treatment can cure an illness. Possible examples in the cultural heritage industry include the following:

- An invasive, high-risk or unproven treatment may stabilize an object that would otherwise have been lost.
- Shipping an exhibition overseas involves risk to the items travelling, but may also raise the profile of an organization, create political favour, and/or result in increased funding for collections.
- Loosening the environmental set points for the organization's air conditioning system may save money for the organization, without compromising collection safety.

On the whole, conservators tend to have a very low risk tolerance when it comes to collections, and are therefore generally unwilling to take risks unless there is sufficient evidence that the outcome will be favourable. This is a valid approach – the idea of risk management is, after all, that you can quantify the risk to a certain extent, in order to be more certain of the outcome. However, it is beneficial to remember that risks may have some outcomes that are positive, as well as those that are negative. Risk management can be used to provide a framework for managing these outcomes.

VIRTUAL RISK

When making decisions, people tend to choose a course of action that bears a level of risk they feel comfortable with – for example, when choosing investment strategies, a cautious person will tend to choose a low-risk option, whereas a less cautious person may choose options with a higher degree of risk.

But is the risk in any given situation real, or perceived? For example, abseiling is often seen as a risky activity. However, as a person abseiling is attached to a great deal of supportive equipment, the actual risk of bodily harm is quite low. Adams talks of this notion as 'virtual risk' (Adams, 1999: 25–38) – what people perceive as a threat, regardless of the actual level of risk present. He uses as examples various diseases that the public may regard as a serious threat but are in fact unlikely to threaten public health. A parallel from the cultural heritage industry may be the effect of environmental fluctuations on the deterioration of collection items. Recent research suggests that most materials may be more resilient over a greater range of relative humidity and temperature than was previously thought. Previously our recommended set points and allowable fluctuations were set very tightly; these may now relax (see Erhardt and Mecklenburg, 1994, Michalski, 1994 and Padfield, 1994: 196).

THE RISKS OF RISK MANAGEMENT

Although risk management is a useful tool for collection preservation, it is well to remember that every system has its flaws.

- Risk management is still a developing field. Improvements or changes in the process over time are likely. It is necessary to stay abreast of current thinking.
- Risk management relies on human judgement – which is not known for its accuracy. Some estimates will be wrong and some risks may be overlooked entirely. This is one reason why risk management must be an on-going process, allowing mistakes to be corrected.
- Sometimes it is not possible to predict accurately either the likelihood or consequences of a risk due to lack of information. For instance, some deterioration reactions are not understood well enough for a conservator to be able to estimate the expected lifespan of an object before or after treatment. Conservators are often asked to quantify the lifespan of a treated object to that of an untreated object. Invariably the answer is 'it all depends'.
- Once a risk management system is in place, people can become complacent – the system is not infallible and will require frequent evaluation and revision if it is to remain useful.
- Once a system or workplace is seen to be 'safer' due to various risk management programmes, it is possible for people to introduce new risks into the system. One study suggested that the introduction of seatbelts caused people to drive more aggressively, as they felt safer in their cars (Adams, 1999:

6–10). As a parallel within cultural heritage organizations, better risk management of loans may see an increase in loans, due to a perception of the process being less risky.

RISK MANAGEMENT FOR CULTURAL HERITAGE ORGANIZATIONS

Although conservators and other cultural heritage workers frequently discuss risks to collections in a general sense, it has only been within the last ten years that a more strategic approach to risk management has begun to take hold in the cultural heritage industry.

One of the most influential papers published so far regarding risk management as a management tool is Robert Waller's 1994 paper 'Conservation risk assessment: a strategy for managing resources for preventive conservation'. This paper (Waller, 1994) describes the detailed risk assessment carried out at the Canadian Museum of Nature, where the process was used to quantify risks and to determine the most cost-effective ways of reducing overall risks to their natural history collections. This article has influenced work carried out by a number of organizations, including the Australian Museum in Sydney (see Valis, 2001 AICCM Bulletin, 25, 41–46) and our own programmes at Artlab Australia. Other articles relating to risk management have been written within the conservation field – Stephen Michalski of the Canadian Conservation Institute (CCI) has written extensively about the perceived and actual risks associated with various environmental factors (see Michalski, 1993 and 1994), and Jonathan Ashley-Smith of the Victoria and Albert Museum, London, has discussed the use of risk analysis for making decisions about object treatments (Ashley-Smith, 1999). While many other authors have used the word 'risk' when describing various situations, what the authors above have in common is that they have attempted to quantify the risks in question, have analysed the potential costs and benefits, and used this information to temper their recommendations for caution. In other words, there is recognition that all risks are not equal – some risks may be so small as to be ignored, and in other cases it is necessary to balance the cost of preventive strategies with the expected benefits to the collection.

RISK, DISASTER AND PRESERVATION MANAGEMENT

The majority of cultural organizations these days recognize the need for disaster preparedness. A good disaster preparedness programme involves the identification of risks to collections and the development of strategies to reduce both the likelihood of a disaster occurring and the resulting consequences for the collections. Similarly, most cultural organizations have some kind of large-scale preservation management or preventive conservation programme in place, which also identifies risks to collections from various agents of deterioration, such as light, pests or adverse storage conditions. These programmes then aim to minimize the deterioration of collections as much as possible, through such things as IPM programmes, display guidelines and environmental monitoring. A disaster preparedness plan is often a component of an organization's preventive conservation programme – as it is at Artlab Australia.

Fewer organizations have a formal risk management programme for collections, although this process is often included as a step in the development of a disaster plan, as explained in Chapter 2. The Australian disaster preparedness publication *Be Prepared* (Commonwealth of Australia, 2000) lists four stages to disaster preparedness: *prevention, preparation, response* and *recovery*; it is in the *prevention* stage where risks to the collections are assessed and reduced.

This is an entirely valid approach; however, at Artlab we have preferred to see disaster planning as a component of risk management for collections, rather than the other way around, as a means of reducing the consequences of risk. Risk management thus becomes the primary information-gathering tool that helps to direct and prioritize other activities within our general preventive management programme. We feel this system is the most effective means of managing the large and varied collections for which we are responsible, and enables us to connect various programmes within the Arts portfolio more easily. For example, it can be easier to obtain support for an IPM programme if it is seen as part of a larger 'risk management programme' – a concept that is more familiar to administrators and other staff. As the government organizations share infrastructure and buildings, centralizing various risk management programmes also allows us to better manage resources.

DEVELOPING A RISK MANAGEMENT PROGRAMME

WHAT IS INVOLVED?

Developing a risk management programme involves working through a series of steps in order to collect, organize and analyse information about risks. Collecting, organizing and analysing the information is the step generally called *risk assessment*. Developing strategies to counter these risks is where this information is turned into a *risk management plan*.

HOW LONG WILL IT TAKE?

The length of time taken to establish a risk management programme will vary according to a number of factors:

- What resources are available? The largest 'investment' of time and/or money will be in the initial start-up stages; however, once the programme is up and running, staff time or funds will still be required on a regular basis in order to maintain the programme adequately.
- How urgent is the need for change? For example, the threat of the Y2K bug brought about some rapid changes within organizations, even in the last few months of 1999.
- What end result is required? More detailed information will require the investment of more time in the process.

Generally, however, the process will take at least a few years to become properly established. Although the assessment itself may be carried out relatively quickly – say, within a month – analysing the information gathered and turning this into a strategy for risk management will take much longer. Longer still is the time required to change the work culture within an organization, which is often necessary. Changing work or management practices generally requires an evolutionary approach, rather than a revolutionary one.

WHAT ARE THE POTENTIAL COSTS?

The main resource required will be staff time, unless a consultant is paid to carry out the assessment. Even when an external consultant is engaged to carry out the bulk of the work, staff will still need to contribute time to the project in order for the best results to be obtained and for the organization to 'own' the process properly.

A risk assessment will invariably identify areas that require 'fixing' and therefore will incur further costs. The prioritization of risks that occurs during the risk assessment allows these costs to be worked gradually into an organization's budget, as appropriate.

THE MAIN ELEMENTS

The process of risk management is described differently according to different standards and guidelines. In the Australian/New Zealand Standard (AS/NZS 4360:1999: 7–8) there are six steps identified:

1. Establishing the context
2. Identifying risks
3. Analysing risks

4. Assessing risks
5. Treating risks
6. Monitoring and reviewing risks.

The six stages form a cyclical process in which the review stage leads back to the beginning, for re-evaluation and refinement (AS/NZS 4360:1999: 8). Risk management is not just done once – ideally the process will be carried out annually, biennially, or however often is appropriate. This ensures the project stays active, useful and up-to-date.

Documentation is another critical factor – with so much information gathering taking place, it is important to keep good records, so that with each cycle of risk management the outcomes can be strengthened and improved.

ESTABLISHING THE CONTEXT – THE PLANNING STAGE

As mentioned previously, risk management can be applied on a large scale, to the functioning of the organization as a whole, or to a particular project or process – for example, in order to manage a redevelopment project. The process is the same, but the focus is different. This is why it is important to establish the context of the project before any other work takes place. This step can make or break the success of the programme, and therefore deserves significant attention. Without clear direction, the process will become confused and it is likely that much time will be wasted.

The Australian and New Zealand Standard (AS/NZS 4360:1999: 9–12) identifies five major components of this first step of the risk assessment:

1. Establish the strategic context.
2. Establish the organizational context.
3. Establish the risk management context.
4. Develop risk evaluation criteria.
5. Define the structure.

THE STRATEGIC CONTEXT

The strategic goals and working environment of the organization must be considered if the results of the project are to be useful.

What are the aims of the organization?

In general, our government clients all aim to preserve their respective collections and to make them available to the people of South Australia. However, the

49

mechanism by which they make their collections accessible varies considerably from organization to organization – most through exhibitions of some kind, some through research, scientific analysis or search facilities and some through the provision of services and advice. This means that each organization can have quite a different relationship with the general public and very different operational contexts and working environments. Identifying the way in which the organization operates to fulfil its aims helps to identify potential risks to collections later on in the process.

Who are the primary stakeholders?

All those with an interest in the collections – and those who have an impact on the risks affecting the collections – need to be included in the risk assessment programme. In our case, the entire population of South Australia could be said to be stakeholders, as our government clients preserve their respective collections for the benefit of the state. However, for the purposes of communication and consultation, we have developed a list of primary stakeholders who act on behalf of the broader population. This list includes appropriate representatives from the client organizations, key staff from Artlab and the Arts SA head office, the building landlords and the contractors who provide our maintenance, security and cleaning services. Developing this list took more time than expected and it is still evolving. The South Australian government network is large and we are always discovering more people that need to be included in our communications.

What elements support or impair your ability to manage risks?

The level of commitment an organization has to the risk management programme will affect the success of any future risk management strategies. For example, many of our government clients do not yet have a formal policy relating to risk management for collections, nor do they have an identified staff member who is responsible for overseeing the programme. Without this formal recognition and allocation of responsibilities, it is difficult for a risk management programme to be successful. In general, it is advisable to have the support and involvement of senior management (to an appropriate degree) before beginning the project. The first step should be to develop a formal policy for risk management, which will need to be discussed, approved and supported by senior management if the project is to succeed (AS/NZS 4360:1999: 5 and 25). This will enable the programme to be included in programme planning and resource allocation.

The level of control an organization has over its immediate environment will also affect the success of any risk management programme. For our government clients, maintenance work is administered outside of the organizations themselves and is carried out by contractors. This limits the control we have over these processes and necessitates close collaboration with another large group of stakeholders to ensure the success of our programme.

What related strategies are already in place?

The organization may already have various health and safety or financial risk management strategies in place. Some of these existing programmes may be required by law, or for insurance purposes. If the risk management programme for collections can be linked to these existing programmes, they will all be easier to manage. It is also useful to identify anything similar already being carried out within the organization, such as an existing disaster plan or conservation management plan, to avoid repetition and to prevent resources from being wasted.

THE ORGANIZATIONAL CONTEXT

The resources available and the working conditions of the organization will have a large impact on the project. There may only be a certain amount of staff time available to dedicate to the project. Alternatively, the timeframe of the project may have to be tailored to take staff rosters into account. Accommodating the realities and capabilities of the working environment will make the project more workable.

THE RISK MANAGEMENT CONTEXT

The first step in this process is to define the extent and comprehensiveness of the risk management activities to be carried out.

What kind of information is needed, and how will it be used?

The risk assessments carried out by Artlab are generally broad in nature and are needed in order to help plan a variety of other preventive programmes, such as disaster preparedness, pest management and storage plans. The information gathered will also be used to form conservation management plans and to set budget priorities and project timeframes. We want to be able to monitor the change in identified risks as our treatment programmes are implemented. This engenders a different sort of project and a different level of analysis from, for example, the risk assessment carried out to determine if a discrete collection should be moved and/or placed in storage during a building redevelopment.

What parts of the collection or organization will be included?

It is worth defining the scope of the risk assessment at the start. For example, will it focus only on collection issues or will it include other functions, such as financial security or the maintenance of critical services? Risks in all areas of the organization and its activities will, of course, impact on each other; however, even if there is some overlap, the focus of the assessment should be clear. As many people use risk management techniques in their work for other purposes, such as managing financial security, this definition will avoid confusion as to the expected results.

Is the risk assessment for internal use only, or will the results be used to argue for resources in a wider government or management context?

This will also affect how information will be gathered and presented. For example, are word descriptions of risk ratings sufficient (qualitative analysis), or are more precise figures required (quantitative analysis)? (See p. 56). This will also have a major impact on the time required to complete the project – in general, quantitative analysis is more complex and time consuming.

How frequently will risk assessments occur?

It is also worth considering at the start how often risk assessments are to be carried out and therefore how long the results of the current review are to be of use. This must be balanced with the complexity of the project – for example, if a risk assessment takes three years to complete because of the degree of detail desired, there is no use in scheduling a review annually.

What resources are required?

It is useful for planning purposes to estimate the staff numbers and the amount of time to be devoted to the project and to set approximate timeframes and milestones to the process. Our risk management programmes began more as 'trial and error', and we have found the lack of a concrete plan and timetable makes the project more difficult to manage; having no formal structure, the project often seemed overwhelmingly large, and the lack of identified milestones made it difficult to monitor progress.

How long will the project take, and when will it begin and end?

This will be affected by how detailed the risk assessment process needs to be and by resource availability. Setting milestones – whether through goals achieved or by reviews at particular dates – helps the programme to maintain momentum, and gives staff a goal to work towards.

Is specialist knowledge required to complete the programme?

It is often useful to consult external professionals and experts for advice – for example, meteorologists, seismologists, architects, fire prevention and security experts may be useful contacts. Specialists such as these are consulted in order to obtain a more accurate assessment of risks from various sources that are outside the average conservator's area of expertise.

Who will carry out the review?

While there may be one or two people running the risk management programme – for example, the Preventive Conservator or the Head of Collections – it is best to consult with as many people involved with the collections as possible. It is also useful to have someone from outside the organization present when carrying out a risk assessment. When Artlab carried out its own risk assessment, we asked a colleague from the State Library to assist us with our review. This person noticed issues that had become invisible to our staff.

What records need to be kept?

As a great deal of information will be collected during the programme, some thought as to how and what records will be kept is beneficial – for example, survey forms, interview transcripts, and so on. One problem that regularly arises during risk assessments – particularly qualitative assessments – is that people have different ideas of what constitutes a 'high' risk and what constitutes a 'low' risk. They may also use different terminology to describe various events or activities. Ensuring that there is some standardization of the way in which data is defined and collected helps to streamline the process.

DEVELOPING RISK EVALUATION CRITERIA

Risks to the collections are the primary criteria to be considered within the type of projects discussed here. Criteria other than risks to collections, such as risks to income, building structure, public safety/liability, as well as other intangibles, like reputation and staff morale, may be included (AS/NZS 4360:1999: 10). However, this will require the involvement of a wider group of people and will make the project more complex. This step also involves thinking about what level of risk is considered acceptable; that is, once the risk assessment has been completed and risk ratings assigned, how will these ratings be divided into those deserving immediate action to those deserving no action at all? For example, when developing our IPM plan for government organizations, we assigned each building a risk rating, according to the types of collection material contained within them and the existing controls to minimize pest infestations. Those buildings that received a high or serious rating for pest infestation are to be given more immediate attention to reduce the risk of pest infestation – more frequent inspections, review of quarantine procedures and so on – whereas no extra activities are to be carried out in buildings with a moderate or low rating for the meantime. In other words, we have decided that the level of risk presented by pests in these buildings is acceptable. This notion is discussed further in the section, Evaluating risks – which should be treated? (p. 56).

DEFINING THE STRUCTURE

This involves breaking down the project into steps – for example, writing the proposal, seeking approval and support for the programme, gathering preliminary information, conducting interviews and so on.

It is also useful to define the assessable units of the project. For example, it is common for cultural heritage organizations to consist of a number of buildings and collections. Depending on the complexity of the organization and the nature of the assessment, it may be more practical to assess each building separately, or to consider each floor, room or collection. Alternatively, if the risk assessment is being applied to a process, such as loan and travel arrangements, or to a treatment proposal, the project will need to be divided into steps – for example, by location, action or end results.

Whatever the approach, some generalization will inevitably occur – for example, the risk from water to collections may vary throughout the building and a decision will need to be made whether to include the 'average' figure or the most extreme risk, or whether to present both results separately.

The greater number of assessable units included, the more detailed and specific the resulting information will be. It can be more difficult to obtain an overall, general picture of the risks to collections if this approach is taken. At Artlab we have tended to assess risks by buildings, giving one 'score' for the entire building, and in some cases by collection. Sometimes also we have combined these approaches – for example, in assessing the risks to the South Australian Museum collections, we gave overall risk ratings for each building, but with some additional notes for each major collection category, after discussions with scientists and curators.

IDENTIFYING RISKS – WHAT CAN HAPPEN, AND HOW?

This step is reasonably self-explanatory. The Australian and New Zealand Standard outlines the steps involved as follows (AS/NZS 4360:1999: 12):

- Generate a list of events that could occur that pose a risk to the elements identified in the previous step (that is, the collections).
- Identify how and why these events could occur.

The more information available at this stage, the more comprehensive the list of events and causes will be.

Obviously there are thousands of possibilities to be considered. For this reason, we have found it useful to group individual events into categories and have adopted the risk categories developed by Waller (1994: 2) at the Canadian Museum of Nature. Waller developed a list of risk categories for collections, according to the principal causative agent – for example, physical forces, water, fire, criminals, pests, contaminants, light and ultra-violet, inappropriate relative humidity, inappropriate temperature and custodial factors. These principal causes were also separated into more specific categories – for example, the category *Physical Forces Type 1* included risks from earthquakes, building collapse and large-scale events, *Physical Forces Type 2* included risks from handling, use and transportation and *Physical Forces Type 3* included risks from long-term vibration or distortion.

This approach allows individual events such as a leaking water pipe, overflowing gutters during a rainstorm or a plumbing disaster to be grouped together under one risk category – in this case, *Water Type 2*. A specific event such as 'the building next door burns down' can be put under the heading *Fire*. This makes it easier to organize information and to carry out the subsequent analysis.

COLLECTING INFORMATION – HOW TO THINK OF EVERYTHING

Risks can be identified via many different techniques. To start off, the old-fashioned 'brainstorm' between colleagues is a very useful way to identify a range of hazards. Past records of disasters and staff experiences during these times will also be invaluable. The conservation literature can provide further examples of possible hazards (see AS/NZS 4360:1999: 13).

Other techniques for collecting information include on-site inspections, interviews, surveys and questionnaires. These activities aim to provide details about the processes and procedures carried out by the organization that may have an effect on various risk factors (Drennan, 2001: 3). For cultural organizations, in particular, inspection of the building is vital. Include maintenance, security and cleaning staff in surveys, as they often know much about the building that other staff do not. It is best to gather information from as many different sources as possible in order to reduce any subjective bias.

ANALYSING RISKS – HOW SERIOUS ARE THEY?

This can be a complicated step. The aim of analysing the identified risks is to predict their likelihood and impact and thus obtain an overall risk rating for each risk category to allow them to be prioritized in order of severity (AS/NZS 4360:1999: 12).

EXAMINING EXISTING CONTROLS

When examining each category of risk, look at what measures are already in place to prevent or minimize their occurrence (AS/NZS 4360:1999: 13). For example, disaster plans, regular preventive maintenance programmes and regular back-ups of computer networks all help to prevent loss from occurring.

It is then necessary to examine how well these existing measures are carried out: for example, the disaster plan may not have been updated for five years; the preventive maintenance programme may have been cut back as a cost saving measure; or the back-up tapes for the network may be stored on-site.

TYPES OF ANALYSIS: QUALITATIVE VERSUS QUANTITATIVE ASSESSMENTS

There are two major types of analysis that can be used in risk management. *Qualitative* assessments use words to describe the likelihood and consequences of the risks identified – for example, the likelihood of an event may be described as high, moderate or low. *Quantitative* assessments use numbers to describe the same – for example, probabilities of event occurrence, or the percentage of loss to be expected (see AS/NZS 4360:1999: 14–15).

Recent advances in information technology have made quantitative analysis a more viable option in other professions – for example, in predicting the likelihood and effect of epidemics or disease in the agricultural industry (New Zealand Ministry of Agriculture, 1996: 7). For us, statistics of natural events such as rainfall, flood patterns, bushfires, and high tides can help with predictions, as can records of past disasters and building weaknesses. However, at this stage, there is generally too much uncertainty about deterioration reactions, event frequency and expected losses in value to affected collections for meaningful quantitative figures to be obtained (Waller, 1994: 15). The disadvantage of qualitative analysis is that it is more likely to be inaccurate, as ratings are generally estimated and dependent on individual value systems. However, we have still found it accurate enough to provide suitable direction for prioritization and programme planning, while allowing the project to be completed more quickly.

Another class of risk assessment is carried out via *semi-quantitative* analysis. The Canadian Museum of Nature study has been described as a semi-quantitative method (Ashley-Smith, 2001: 59). In this project they estimated the *probability* of an event (P), the *fraction* of the collection *susceptible* to the event (FS) and the *loss in value* (LV) of the collection expected if an event occurred. This enabled the authors to calculate the magnitude of risk as a numerical figure, allowing them to easily identify which risks were most serious. The method is semi-quantitative in that there is still a degree of estimation in the figures assigned – that is, some of the figures were obtained in a qualitative manner and may have been 'little better than guesses' (Waller, 1994: 15).

DETERMINING THE CONSEQUENCES

Once risks have been identified, it is necessary to estimate how serious the damage would be if an event occurred, taking into account any existing controls. For qualitative assessments a descriptive level is assigned to the risk in question. At Artlab, we have based our qualitative measures of consequence on the Australian and New Zealand Standard, which has five levels of impact that can be assigned, from *1: insignificant* to *5: catastrophic*. The standard gives a descriptive example of each level, which we have modified to suit our circumstances. For example, in the standard, *insignificant* is described as 'no injuries, low financial loss' (AS/NZS 4360:1999: 34). We have modified this to 'loss of some work hours in recovery operation, no damage to collection'. Any individual or organization can modify these descriptions as appropriate to their situation.

DETERMINING THE LIKELIHOOD OF OCCURRENCE

Again, the way in which this is expressed will depend on whether a qualitative or quantitative method has been chosen. For qualitative analysis, descriptive levels again are used. The Australian and New Zealand Standard has five levels of likelihood that can be assigned, ranging from *A: almost certain* to *E: rare* (AS/NZS 4360:1999: 34).

Thus, in metropolitan Adelaide, a flood may occur only in exceptional circumstances, as the city is not situated on a flood plain and rainfall levels are low. This risk would be assigned an E (*rare*). However, the building of one of our government clients located outside the city is next to a river that has flooded before. In this situation, the same risk would be allocated a C (*should occur at some time*). A pest infestation, for certain collections, should occur at some time, thus also earning itself a C. From our experience, the likelihood of a water leak during redevelopment projects would be an A (*almost certain*) or B (*likely*).

ASSIGNING RISK RATINGS

The values determined for *consequence* and *likelihood* are then combined to assign a level of risk to each risk category. For qualitative assessments, the standard provides a matrix where the values previously assigned to consequence and likelihood are combined to give a risk rating of *high, significant, moderate* or *low*. As an example, a risk that is *likely* to occur (B), with *critical* consequences expected (4), will earn a risk rating of *high*. A risk that is *unlikely* to occur (D) and with *minor* consequences expected (2), will earn a risk rating of *low* (AS/NZS 4360:1999: 35).

During this step, a quantitative or semi-quantitative method, such as that employed by Waller, will generally produce a risk rating expressed as a decimal figure between zero and one, as the figures assigned to consequence and likelihood are multiplied together. The closer the value is to 1, the more serious the risk. Some kind of qualitative description may also be necessary in order to divide the resultant figures into categories such as *high, significant, moderate* and *low*.

SUBJECTIVITY

When assigning values for consequences and likelihood, subjective bias or other inaccuracies are, of course, possible. The standard recommends including a figure indicating your confidence in the risk rating estimated (AS/NZS 4360:1999: 15). There is particular value in taking this uncertainty into account in the cultural heritage industry, as so many of our predictions are based on human judgment. However, at Artlab we have yet to build this factor into our risk assessments, mainly because calculating these figures is in itself a large and difficult task.

If such a figure were to be calculated, it may take into account the variety of sources on which estimates were based – for example, if only one person was consulted to obtain an estimate, this would create greater uncertainty than if five people were consulted. Alternatively, it may reflect a lack of knowledge – for example, it is known that artificial ageing, on which many of our expectations of deterioration are based, does not always proceed in the same manner or at the same rate as natural ageing (see Erhardt, et al., 2000).

There will obviously be a difference in the level of risk assigned to an action (or non-action), depending on who is carrying out the assessment and what the context of their assessment may be. For example, the management of state government assets in South Australia relies on the decisions of two different departments: one administers the buildings owned by the government, while another administers the collections housed within these buildings. Ideally the two departments would have similar priorities; however, this is not necessarily the case – what may be perceived as a 'bad' risk by one department could be perceived as a 'good' risk by the other. The risk management framework allows us to establish a common language for communicating the potential costs that could result from decisions made by either department.

There is another way in which bias can creep into estimations. While the standard gives relatively equal ratings to consequences and likelihood when assigning priorities to risks, there is often a tendency to give more weight to one of these factors than the other. For example, it has been said that governments tend to put more weight on consequences, particularly those that their public fear, whereas corporations tend to give greater weight to likelihood, dismissing less likely events as being too remote to consider. The first approach lessens the chance of serious loss but probably involves more expenditure; the second is more cost effective but does not necessarily prevent loss or damage from occurring (Kloman, 2001b: 1–2). Again, the bias reflects the context of the risk assessment carried out.

However, as Kloman states (2001b: 1): 'None of us will ever be privy to the complete information, so we must make decisions with the best information to hand.' Risk ratings will always need to be revised; uncertainty should not prevent us from attempting the process at all.

ASSESSING RISKS – WHICH SHOULD BE TREATED?

In the previous step, risks were assigned a risk rating of *high, significant, moderate* and *low*, according to the qualitative method outlined in the Australian and New Zealand Standard. These ratings allow various risks to be separated into those that are minor and acceptable and those that are more serious and require further action (see AS/NZS 4360: 1999: 12 and 35). In other words, not all risks will be treated equally. High or significant risks will receive the more immediate and detailed attention. Moderate and low risks may be accepted at their current level and only monitored for change. The level of risk deemed acceptable to the organization would have been decided when establishing the context of the project.

Conservators can find it difficult to come to terms with the concept of 'acceptable risk'. Nobody likes to think that any damage to collections is acceptable. This idea is becoming more widespread, however, particularly when it comes to loans and exhibitions. For example, most people recognize that displaying a textile or watercolour will cause some degree of damage to that item, yet these items are still displayed. In other words, we have decided that the risk to the item is acceptable, and is balanced by the benefits that the exhibition of the work can bring to the organization. The emphasis now is on quantifying that risk more exactly, by considering how long we want the item to be 'useful' and by using concepts such as the time taken to achieve one 'just noticeable fade' to determine what total light exposure an item can receive over a given timeframe (see Derbyshire and Ashley-Smith, 1999 and Tait, et al., 2000).

RISK TREATMENT – DEVELOPING YOUR STRATEGY

The next step involves identifying and assessing the options available for treating the identified risks, and preparing and implementing risk treatment plans. Treatment options include those listed in Table 3.1 (see AS/NZS 4360:1999: 16).

The most appropriate option in any given circumstance will be that which achieves a balance between the costs of implementation and the benefits that it will provide (AS/NZS 4360:1999: 18). In the cultural heritage industry, the costs of loss are not only financial – loss of unique heritage has an intangible as well as a financial cost. However, excessive or inappropriate treatment of risk can be expensive and can also damage the reputation of the organization if the expense is seen as wasteful. The cost of managing risks should generally be balanced with the benefits obtained.

Table 3.1   Risk treatment options

Risk treatment option	Example
Avoiding the risk by not proceeding with the activity.	Deciding not to loan or display fragile or sensitive objects.
Reducing the likelihood of occurrence.	Increasing the amount of preventive maintenance for the building, or relocating sensitive items stored in areas with inappropriate environmental conditions.
Reducing the consequences of the risk.	Ensuring the organization has an up-to-date disaster preparedness programme and carrying out disaster training for staff.
Accepting the risk and monitoring the situation for change.	Maintaining existing arrangements in a low-risk storage area and instead monitoring climate and pest levels in case of change.
Accepting the risk and organizing finance to deal with the consequences.	Insuring items going on loan.
Transferring or sharing the risk, for example, by insurance or partnerships.	Hiring a company to store records or to undertake risk management activities, such as pest control or the development of a disaster plan. **Note**: Transferring or 'sharing' the risk does not necessarily eliminate or even reduce the risk in question; it only spreads the responsibility (Kloman, 2000: 7).

As an example, the maintenance of the air-conditioning plant for many of our buildings has not been documented over the last 10 years, in order to save costs. This means we are unable to determine which areas have humidity control, what plant is still working and which air-handling units service various areas. This reduces our ability to use collection spaces in the most effective manner. To document this information would now cost thousands of dollars, as contractors will have to go on site to physically inspect the existing plant. We have to decide whether the cost of such a process is worth the equivalent reduction in risks – perhaps these funds would be better spent on more advanced monitoring equipment, or some other project altogether.

Rare but severe risks can be the most difficult to make decisions about, as the risk reduction measures may be very expensive. For example, a decision was made to 'earthquake-proof' a number of buildings in the Adelaide region, based on an expert assessment of the situation. This is an expensive process and Australia is (relatively) not subject to a great deal of seismic activity. Although an earthquake of medium magnitude is expected in Adelaide within the next 50–100 years, it would be easy to dismiss this risk as unjustifiable purely on economic grounds. However, the earthquake could happen tomorrow. If an earthquake did occur and steps had not been taken to make buildings safe, lives could be lost in the subsequent building damage. So, the decision was made to carry out the building works. This was primarily a public liability issue rather than one of collection safety. However, it does illustrate the need to take public perception into account when choosing risk treatment options. Generally a combination of risk treatment options will prove to be the best solution for any particular problem. For example, to reduce the risk from water leakage requires reduction in the likelihood of this event occurring – through preventive maintenance programmes and good storage methods – and a reduction of the consequences if this event should occur – by ensuring the disaster plan is up to date and the disaster team well trained. It may also be necessary to prioritize risk treatment strategies, as there may not be sufficient funds or human resources to implement them all at once (AS/NZS 4360:1999: 19).

It has also been noted that overly harsh risk treatment measures may not always be fully effective – people tend to rebel against them. In general, it is preferable to have a more workable solution that does not tempt people to take short cuts or to ignore rules (New Zealand Ministry of Agriculture, 1996: 3–4).

ACTING ON RESULTS – PUTTING WORDS INTO ACTION

The risk treatment plan that is developed from all this analysis will need to identify responsibilities, timeframes and schedules, the expected outcomes of treatments, allocated resources and performance measures. The plan should also include a mechanism for assessing the progress of the programme. Defining these elements will help to keep the programme moving (AS/NZS 4360:1999: 19–20).

However, it is not enough that a policy has been written down and approved. To be successful, staff must be familiar with the policy and committed to its implementation (Drennan, 2001: 3). Planning the change is relatively easy – making it happen is the hard part. Risk management invariably involves cultural change within a workplace, and this is something that can take a great deal of time to achieve. We have yet to fully realize this part of the risk management programme and are expecting it to be a gradual process that will occur over many years.

Communication, through updates, meetings and/or staff training, is the key to keeping the project active. This enables staff to understand the part they have to play in the programme and to see how the programme is progressing. Studies across industries reveal that failures in communication, management responsibility, supervision and training are the most common causes of incidents resulting in loss (Drennan, 2001: 9).

RISK MANAGEMENT IN DIFFERENT TYPES OF ORGANIZATIONS

Risk management is a process that can be applied equally to all types of heritage organizations – large city galleries or museums, regional archives or libraries, even private collections.

While the process is the same, the context will be different, as well as the types of risks faced and the risk ratings assigned to them. Geographical location will have a critical impact on the level of risk from natural events such as earthquakes, volcano, windstorms or fire. The differences between city and country locations will also affect the type of risks affecting an organization – for example, in Adelaide, buildings located near bushland or in regional areas are at greater risk from bushfire compared to those in the central business district. Consequently the risk treatment plans arising from an assessment of each will be quite different.

The nature of the collections will also have an impact on the results. Clearly, different formats are subject to different risks – for example, electronic media and farm machinery are subject to quite different risks and so a library will have a different risk treatment plan from an agricultural museum. However, their respective risk treatment plans are still likely to have much in common – preventive maintenance programmes, disaster plans, IPM plans and so on.

MONITORING AND REVIEW – KEEPING THE PROGRAMME ACTIVE

Deterioration continues; change always occurs. Review is essential to maintain the effectiveness of the risk management process – after all, the risks themselves may change, as could many factors affecting the suitability or cost of various treatment options (AS/NZS 4360:1999: 20).

Risk management information must remain current and relevant. The frequency of review will depend, among other things, on the severity of the identified risks and the resources allocated to maintaining the risk management programme. The rate of change within an organization may also affect how often reviews are carried out – for example, during a redevelopment change is occurring more rapidly than normal, however for this reason it is possible that staff will have less time to devote to normal operational practices. It is useful to prepare a timetable of risk assessment reviews, allowing time for consultation and comments from all interested parties.

DEVELOPING A RISK MANAGEMENT SCHEDULE

The initial assessment and implementation of the risk management programme is what takes the longest time. The review process can be quicker, as it can refer to the original assessment and note any changes.

At Artlab, we are looking at carrying out three types of risk assessment for our government clients: the initial assessment, a review assessment and a reassessment. As we need to carry out assessments for nine organizations, including ourselves, we are currently looking at carrying out a briefer 'review' of each organization every three years. Every third review – that is, every nine years – a 'reassessment' will be carried out, which will be more detailed in nature than a review. After each review, changes that need to be made to the risk management plan will be identified and implemented.

Management

Keeping the programme active involves good management. Stewart describes the five critical attributes for a risk manager as follows (see Tilghman, 2001: 1):

1. Daydreams
2. Is flexible
3. Communicates both successes and failures
4. Takes responsibility
5. Works with and as part of a team.

It is the first point that Stewart thought was the most important – the ability to think creatively, to ask 'what if ...?' and to look at situations elsewhere and wonder how they might occur in your own organization. Asking this question can also help to decide what is the most appropriate risk treatment method – that is, by asking 'if we do A, what is the expected result?' and comparing this to the expected results of implementing B, C or any combination of these, helps to identify the most appropriate option.

Being a 'risk manager' also involves taking on several roles. For example, we have identified that the person steering the project will need to act in the following capacities (see Robbins et al., 2000: 12):

- As a *liaison officer*, by maintaining networks and contacts.
- As an *information monitor*, by keeping track of relevant information internally and externally.
- As a *disseminator of information*, by transmitting information to others in the network.
- As a *negotiator*, by representing organizations at tender selection meetings and other relevant occasions.
- As a *disturbance handler*, by taking corrective actions when processes did not work effectively.
- As an *entrepreneur*, by searching for 'improvement projects' and other activities that could make the programme more workable.

DOCUMENTATION

Each stage of the risk management process should be documented in order to provide a record of risk-related activities (AS/NZS 4360:1999: 21). A lack of adequate documentation causes three major negative effects:

- A loss of information and/or corporate knowledge – for example, a historical record of disasters that have occurred is invaluable in developing a risk profile for an organization. Such a record allows the risk manager to identify what risks are the most likely and what effect they have had on collections. However, it is often difficult to obtain information on events such as these, as organizations may be reluctant to disclose details of their problems, fearing censure. The loss of experienced staff through retirement is another way corporate knowledge can be lost if their knowledge has not been adequately documented.
- Repetition of work – for example information may already have been collected or activities may be duplicated. This is a waste of time and resources.
- An inability to accurately assess existing controls and hence levels of risk – the example given previously of the lack of documentation of our air-

conditioning plant is an example of this situation (see Risk Treatment, p. 60).

One of our recent documentation projects is our 'Disasters Database', which we use to record what disaster situations have occurred, small and large, and pertinent details about their cause and effect. For example, of the events recorded so far, 78 per cent have involved damage due to water and 22 per cent were due to dust. Of these, 51 per cent occurred during minor or major building works, and 33 per cent were preventive maintenance issues. This historical perspective is invaluable in determining where our major problems lie and providing statistics for arguing our case for change.

COMMUNICATION AND CONSULTATION

If risk management is to serve all stakeholders in a cultural heritage organization, the most important function of the risk management process is to communicate with stakeholder groups. Communication will build and maintain trust within these groups, and their confidence in both the future of the organization and the safety of the collection. This involves delivering risk information in a way that is easy to understand and to utilize, as well as ensuring that those making the decisions have the time, tools and incentive to act on this information (Kloman, 2000: 5). Effective communication pathways will need to be constructed so that there is a consultative process occurring, rather than just a one-way flow of information (AS/NZS 4360:1999: 20).

Perceptions of risk can vary greatly from actual levels of risk. As stakeholders can have a large impact on decision making, it is important that the perceptions of those involved accurately reflect the actual state of affairs. Stakeholders also need to understand the reasoning behind the treatment plan. Kloman (2000: 6) calls this creating a culture of 'risk understanding', which is a large and important step towards developing an effective risk management programme.

The fear of bad publicity or censure when making disasters known to the public can also be managed by good communication. For example, a recent mould outbreak at the State Library of Victoria (SLV) restricted public access to newspaper collections. SLV staff found that the lack of access to material was more readily accepted when the public knew the facts of the situation. The SLV internet site was used to relay information about the situation and expected delays, augmented by in-house signage, handouts and staff briefings (Cox, 2002: 153).

DEVELOPING EFFECTIVE SYSTEMS

We have found effective communication to be one of the most difficult parts of our risk management process. We have found it difficult even to determine who we need to include in our information loop. This is partly to do with the structure of the South Australian government. For example, all our maintenance work, IT support, security and building pest management is contracted out to three different Facilities Management companies, who then subcontract the work out to others. A number of our buildings are owned by another government department, and, of those buildings, many are shared by more than one organization. We share an air-conditioning plant, access points and grounds. We are not all on the same e-mail network. All of this makes it difficult to discover just who the correct contact person is, let alone keeping all the right people informed. People change or leave jobs constantly, or even just change their telephone number.

We are finding that e-mail is a very effective way to keep a large number of people informed, and makes it easy for staff to respond to this information. One project we are just beginning is an e-mail-based 'Disasters Update', a monthly newsletter e-mail to be distributed to relevant people within Arts SA. This will provide information on the latest risk management initiatives, as well as reminding staff of review dates and likely risks during the coming month – for example, in April/May the first heavy rains of the year coincide with autumn leaf drops and hence overflowing gutters are common. September is when the weather begins to warm, and when the carpet beetles and clothes moths are more active. November/December is the start of our bushfire season, and so we can use the update to remind people to ensure appropriate preventive measures have been taken. Prolonged hot, dry spells are likely during January and February (up to 40°C and as low as 10 per cent relative humidity (RH), making air-conditioning failures or power shortages more likely. In the future, we are hoping to make use of a service provided by the Department of Meteorology, so that we can use the update to provide people with storm warnings and weather advice.

E-mail is a useful system for Artlab and its clients, as every government employee has a personal e-mail address. It may not suit everyone, as people may not have regular, or any, access to computers. The communication strategy within an organization must be tailored according to the resources available and the way in which information is generally communicated.

RISK MANAGEMENT FOR SPECIAL CIRCUMSTANCES

NEW BUILDINGS AND REFURBISHMENTS/EXTENSIONS

Building works create a whole new set of risk for collections – anything from increased risk of damage due to dust, vibration, water and fire, to inappropriate selection of building materials or the design of exhibition galleries. Increasingly, conservators and collection safety are being included in these projects to minimize the chance of unsatisfactory outcomes for the collections – although there is still room for improvement.

In Adelaide, curators and conservators have been included in the Project Control Group meetings for a recent redevelopment of one wing of the South Australian Museum since the start of the project. This has given us the opportunity to raise concerns early on in the project, at the design stage, and to include potential risks to the collections within the larger risk management plan for the project. This risk management plan aims to ensure the project is completed on time, within budget and with a satisfactory outcome for the museum. This is an example of how risk management can be used in a different context, while still impacting on collection issues – the risk manager in charge of this project has to consider risks to health and safety, possible budget blowouts and incidents that could cause delays or affect the quality of the end result. Collection safety is one component of this larger programme.

Approaching redevelopment projects from a risk management perspective helps to ensure that collection issues are considered from the beginning, rather than as an afterthought, as they can be more easily accommodated within existing risk management programmes.

MOVING COLLECTIONS OR LOANS/TRAVEL

Travel is a fact of life for many organizations – while movement of collections continues, risk will always be present. Risk management can be applied to the process of a planned move or loan, to identify possible hazards to the collection.

In Adelaide, we have had instances where collections have been moved between buildings without such a process taking place. Subsequently, loss and damage has occurred. It is not reasonable to expect 'zero risk' for such a large undertaking (or for any process at all – see New Zealand Ministry of Agriculture, 1996: 3), but in retrospect some of this loss could have been prevented had a risk management approach been adopted from the beginning. Identifying the stages at which the collections could be damaged (for example, during packing, handling, transport and unpacking) and identifying processes that could minimize this damage (for example, better tender selection criteria, training for

67

contractors, itemization of packed boxes and so on) would have helped to reduce loss. One very clear risk is that the commercial removal company may not have any experience in handling cultural collections and therefore may use inappropriate packing, handling and transport methods.

Loans are commonly approached from a risk management perspective, even though it is not put in those terms. Loan agreements, packing methods, condition reports, quarantine, couriers and light and environmental control are all ways in which risks to the collection are reduced and controlled. Large shipments of collections are frequently split into groups and sent on different trucks or flights, so that the entire collection will not be affected should a disaster occur.

DISPLAY

The exhibition of collections is also considered in terms of risk – most commonly, the risk created by prolonged exposure to light. It is generally accepted that display causes damage to susceptible materials, such as paper and textiles, and that the acceptable *rate* of change is the critical factor that must be decided. This involves deciding what the useful life of the object is expected to be, and therefore how much time can pass before one 'just noticeable fade' is considered appropriate (see Derbyshire and Ashley-Smith, 1999 and Tait et al., 2000). In this manner, risk management can be useful in determining display guidelines for collection items – this form of deterioration is better understood and more accurately predictable than many others.

There are other risks from display: inappropriate environmental conditions, exposure to dust and pollutants, risks of pest infestation and physical damage. Often, it is the design of the exhibition area that can have the greatest bearing on these factors. For example, in a recent gallery renovation in South Australia, fragile bark paintings were placed on open display, putting them at greater risk of physical damage and dust exposure. This indicates the need for risk management to be applied to the *process* of exhibition preparation, so that areas where damage could occur can be identified prior to the completion of the project.

Large galleries often apply this kind of thinking to their exhibitions, particularly when the subject of the exhibition is controversial. An illustration of the need for this type of thinking is a 1997 exhibition at the National Gallery of Victoria that included the controversial work *Piss Christ*, a photograph depicting a plastic crucifix immersed in urine. Offended members of the public demonstrated outside the gallery and two acts of vandalism were attempted, one successfully. This led to the early closure of the exhibition, as the gallery felt it could no longer guarantee the safety of staff, visitors and other works in the gallery (see Arts Law, n.d., 97: 4). The gallery was strongly criticized, by some for displaying the work in the first place and by others for succumbing to pressure to close.

TREATMENT

The risk management approach can also be used in determining the most suitable treatment methodology for collection items. Conservation treatment can pose risks to objects, and some treatment methods are more risky than others – for example, there is a greater potential for damage associated with washing a watercolour than, say, for a simple paper repair, as the treatment is more invasive. A treatment must balance the potential benefits to the object with the potential for damage or change from the treatment. This idea has been explored thoroughly by Jonathan Ashley-Smith in *Risk Assessment for Object Conservation* (1999).

CONCLUSIONS

THE FUTURE

Risk management is a useful way to organize information, prioritize actions and make better decisions regarding the future of collections. It is currently used in an informal manner among cultural organizations. Artlab Australia believes that greater formalization of the process will be beneficial, especially in creating effective links with other activities within the organization and better communication with other professional sectors.

It seems likely that organizations around the world will adopt risk management techniques with greater frequency in coming years. The profile of risk management is growing, hence the marked increase in training courses for risk management, and it is being actively promoted as a management tool by various professional bodies worldwide. Risk management is also often a means of reducing insurance premiums (Drennan, 2001: 7–8). For these reasons, the risk management trend is also likely to be adopted by the cultural heritage sector, particularly those organizations affiliated with the government. Risk management applied to collections is likely to become more integrated with other risk management activities within an organization. Those working in risk management usually find that the separation of risk management functions is inefficient. Greater integration means that collection needs can be put on the same table as other needs, and can be more easily included in the allocation of resources; adopting common risk languages and frameworks for all functions of an organization will streamline management (Kloman, 2000: 5–6).

Some industries are working towards the development of common international standards to help reduce risk worldwide – for example, common standards for animal and plant health and food hygiene issues are being developed in the agricultural sector, where trade agreements are increasingly based on risk analysis (New Zealand Ministry of Agriculture, 2001: 9). Such arrangements are still far away in the cultural heritage industry, but are likely to be beneficial – particularly with loans, where the risks present in different locations need to be compared in a more systematic and realistic manner (see Ashley-Smith, et al., 1994).

There is a degree of uncertainty inherent in the measurement of risk – perhaps more so in the cultural heritage industry than in others. Increasingly, software and computer programs are being offered to aid organizations with risk management and disaster planning, and as diagnostic tools for calculating the magnitude of risks more accurately. As yet, they cannot undertake the whole task and are not designed specifically with cultural heritage organizations in mind, but may still be useful tools (Drennan, 2001: 5–6). Some examples of conservation resources that can be used to help predict the measurement of risk include the Image Permanence Institute's (IDI) *Storage Guide for Acetate Film* (Reilly, 1993) and the Canadian Conservation Institute's *A Slide Rule to Determine Light Damage* (1987). While not necessarily in digital form, both of these tools help to predict the lifespan of collection items subject to various conditions. With further research, more accurate predictions will be possible.

At Artlab, we still have some way to go before our risk management programmes are running smoothly and are integrated with other government processes. Our greatest challenges are to ensure that communication is effective and in motivating people to actually make the changes that will reduce risks to the collections. We envisage that this process will take some years to achieve. Despite the clear need for patience as organizational cultures evolve and embrace the risk management approach, the benefits of risk management as a tool for collection management are already becoming apparent.

ACKNOWLEDGEMENTS

The author would like to thank the following people (very much!) for their advice and assistance in the preparation of this chapter: Graham Matthews, Vicki Humphrey, Ian Cook and Heather Mansell.

REFERENCES

Adams, J. (1999) *Cars, Cholera, and Cows: The Management of Risk and Uncertainty*, Policy Analysis, Washington DC: Cato Institute.
Arts Law, n.d., *Piss Christ Exhibition 97.4*. The Arts Law Centre of Australia. See <www.artslaw.com.au/reference/piss974/>
Ashley-Smith, J. (1999) *Risk Assessment for Object Conservation*, Oxford: Butterworth Heinemann.
Ashley-Smith, J. (2001) 'Practical uses of risk analysis', *The Paper Conservator*, 25: 59–63.
Ashley-Smith, J., Umney, N. and Ford, D. (1994) 'Let's be honest – realistic environmental parameters for loaned objects', in *Preventive Conservation Practice, Theory and Research: Preprints of the*

Contributions to the Ottawa Congress, 12–16 September 1994, London: The International Institute for Conservation of Historic and Artistic Works (IIC).

Australian/New Zealand Standard AS/NZS 4360:1999 (1999) *Risk Management*, Homebush, NSW and Wellington, NZ: Standards Australia and Standards New Zealand.

Bernstein, P.L. (1998) *Against the Gods: The Remarkable Story of Risk*, New York: John Wiley & Sons, Inc.

Canadian Conservation Institute (1987) *A Slide Rule to Determine Light Damage*, Ottawa: National Museums of Canada & Canadian Conservation Institute.

Commonwealth of Australia on behalf of the Heritage Collections Council (2000) *Be Prepared: Guidelines for Small Museums for writing a Disaster Preparedness Plan*, Canberra, ACT: Commonwealth of Australia.

Cox, M. (2002) 'Managing mould outbreaks in a newspaper archive', in *AICCM Symposium 2002 – Conservation of Paper, Books and Photographic Materials* (Preprints), AICCM: Canberra.

Derbyshire, A. and Ashley-Smith, J. (1999) 'A proposed practical lighting policy for works of art on paper at the V&A', in *ICOM Lyon 1999 Conference Proceedings Vol. 1*, ICOM Committee for Conservation, pp. 38–41.

Drennan, L. T. (2001) *Risk Management: A Holistic Approach*, Lyme, Connecticut: Seawrack Press. See <www.riskmanagement.com.au/ARTICLES/> (accessed 30 November 2001).

Erhardt, D. and Mecklenburg, M. (1994) 'Relative humidity re-examined', in *Preventive Conservation Practice, Theory and Research: Preprints of the Contributions to the Ottawa Congress, 12–16 September 1994*, London: The International Institute for Conservation of Historic and Artistic Works (IIC).

Erhardt, D., Tumosa, C.S. and Mecklenburg M.F. (2000) 'Can artists' oil paints be accelerated aged?', *Polymer Preprints*, 41 (2), 1790–91.

Kloman, H. F., (2000) *An Iconoclastic View of Risk*, Lyme, Connecticut: Seawrack Press. See <www.riskmanagement.com.au/ARTICLES/> (accessed 5 December 2000).

Kloman, H. F. (2001a) *Risk Odyssey*, Lyme, Connecticut: Seawrack Press. See <www.riskmanagement.com.au/ARTICLES/> (accessed 9 January 2001).

Kloman, H. F. (2001b) *Consequences*, Lyme, Connecticut: Seawrack Press. See <www.riskmanagement.com.au/ARTICLES/> (accessed 10 December 2001).

Michalski, S. (1993) 'Relative humidity: a discussion of correct/incorrect values', in *ICOM-CC 10th Meeting, Washington, D.C.*, Paris: ICOM-CC, pp. 624–9.

Michalski, S. (1994), 'Relative humidity and temperature guidelines: What's happening?', *CCI Newsletter*, **14**, September 1994, Ottawa: Canadian Conservation Institute.

New Zealand Ministry of Agriculture (1996) *Risk Analysis – Opening the way for Agricultural Trade*, Lyme, Connecticut: Seawrack Press. See <www.riskmanagement.com.au/ARTICLES/> (accessed 25 July 2001).

Padfield, T., (1994) 'The role of standards and guidelines: are they a substitute for understanding a problem or a protection against the consequences of ignorance?, in *Durability and Change: The Science, Responsibility, and Cost of Sustaining Cultural Heritage*, New York: John Wiley & Sons Ltd, Inc.

Reilly, J.M. (1993) *IPI Storage Guide for Acetate Film*, available from the IPI website: <www.rit.edum661www1/>.

Reilly, J.M. (1998) *The IPI Storage Guide for Acetate Film*, Rochester, NY: Image Permanence Institute.

Robbins, S.P., Bergman, R., Staff, I and Coulter, M. (2000) *Management*, 2nd edn, Frenchs Forest, NSW: Prentice Hall Australia Pty Ltd.

Tait, R., Hughes, J. and Hallam, D. (2000) 'Light level guidelines at the National Museum of Australia', *AICCM National Newsletter*, 74.

Tilghman, S. M. (2001) *Nonprofit Risk Management Centre*, Lyme, Connecticut: Seawrack Press. See <www.riskmanagement.com.au/ARTICLES/> (accessed 9 November 2001).

Valis, S. (2001) 'Conservation strategy for the Natural Science Collections at the Australian Museum: a technical note', *AICCM Bulletin*, March: 40–42.

Waller, R. (1994), 'Conservation risk assessment: a strategy for managing resources for preventive conservation', paper presented at *Preventive Conservation Practice, Theory and Research: Preprints of the Contributions to the Ottawa Congress, 12–16 September 1994*. London: The International Institute for Conservation of Historic and Artistic Works (IIC).

4   In case of fire

■ Bill Jackson

INTRODUCTION

This chapter is based on my experience as Buildings Manager in the National Library of Scotland (NLS) since 1988. My understanding of how fire affects libraries is based on the refurbishment and fire safety project carried out at the NLS George IV Bridge Building between 1990 and 1999, and the research and investigation I had to undertake to direct the project itself.

It is perhaps a surprising thought that when I began the process of research it was necessary to look outside the UK for expertise in this specialist area. My first approach was to the Library of Congress in Washington DC. From that point I was introduced to a new way of thinking, first by FIREPRO (FIREPRO, 2002) and second through the National Fire Protection Association International.

FIREPRO, a fire safety consulting firm based in Andover, MA, produced a fire safety report for the Library of Congress during the 1970s. This type of analysis and research was applied to the NLS situation, and the resultant report that FIREPRO produced for the NLS (FIREPRO Incorporated, 1990) was key to changing the library's perception of various problems and assumptions. More significantly, perhaps, it was an essential tool for the eventual work of advocacy that had to be undertaken to obtain funding to address the severe problems that had been identified. Much of this work is explained in the second part of this chapter.

The issues relating to disasters in libraries are not constrained by national boundaries. Currently a great deal of experience in this area has been developed and codified in North America. Various elements of this work are incorporated in this chapter and further consultation of *NFPA 909 Code for the Protection of Cultural Resources* (NFPA, 2001a) is recommended.

The process of facing up to the actual and specific risks which relate to libraries as warehouses full of paper was as difficult for me as a buildings manager as it was for my curatorial colleagues. This chapter tries to describe some of those changes in thought processes which are essential if a proper understanding of both risks and solutions is to be reached. It must be stressed strongly that the processes are much more about *people* and their convictions, opinions and beliefs, than they are about the selection and installation of expensive *equipment.*

BACKGROUND

The Library's George IV Bridge Building was designed by Reginald Fairlie in the early 1930s specifically to contain the library's collections. It was constructed between 1934 and 1939 and completed in 1950 to 1954, and is now a category B listed building. (Category B buildings are those ' ... of regional or more than local importance, or major examples of some particular period, style or building type which may have been altered' (Historic Scotland, 2002). The catalyst for fire prevention work carried out in the building came in 1988 when the ownership (and therefore the legal responsibility for management) was transferred from the Crown to the Library's Board of Trustees.

The trustees appointed a Buildings Manager to carry out the work previously undertaken by the Property Services Agency (PSA). When the new manager

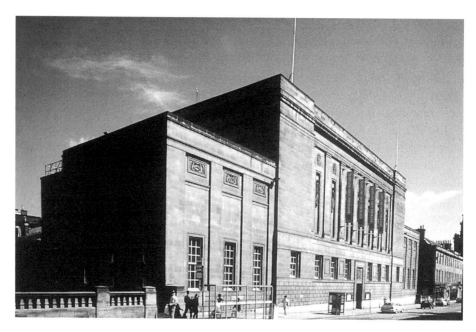

Figure 4.1   The National Library of Scotland George IV Bridge Building (Crown copyright. Reproduced by kind permission of the National Library of Scotland)

examined the legal and physical status of the property, the George IV Bridge Building did not have a fire certificate; while it was Crown property none was needed under the provision of 'Crown Immunity'. Fire safety improvements up to that date had been targeted to ensure that the buildings complied with relevant fire safety legislation. However, UK fire safety law is primarily concerned with ensuring that provision is made for the safety of life rather than the contents of buildings, which are the responsibility of the owners and occupiers. The consequence of the new manager's investigations was that the contents were found to be at serious risk should a fire occur in the building.

This was important because the contents have a unique importance. The library is a repository of Scotland's culture, ideals, experience and ethos as preserved in printed and written records. The conventional approaches to risk management are inappropriate. For example, insurance or other forms of financial risk transfer are irrelevant: how can money replace the irreplaceable?

Given the irrelevance of insurance in these circumstances therefore, and the need to maintain the collection in a form that is accessible to readers, it became clear that the only acceptable solution was to carry out a thorough examination of how the building and contents could be protected from the effects of fire, and how the structure could be upgraded to allow it to qualify for a fire certificate.

THE PROBLEM

An initial risk assessment of the George IV Bridge Building was undertaken by Edinburgh University Consultants in 1989. The study made a number of recommendations including the need to provide structural improvements and fire compartmentation. A full structural survey and the FIREPRO report were, therefore, commissioned and these highlighted serious flaws in the design and construction of the building which can be summarized as follows:

- Book stackage upright supports in the core of the building were found to be supporting the intermediate book stack floors.
- The intermediate floors of concrete, which were supported by the book stack uprights below, were only 65mm thick.
- A fire in such a book stack could reach 1000°C in under three minutes and would result in deformation of the steel stack elements.
- Any fire would be likely to deform the stacks to the extent that within eight minutes they would collapse, leading to progressive collapse of the whole building and the loss of the national collections.

These very serious risks made it clear to the library's management that they had to confront not only a range of newly discovered fire safety problems, but also the

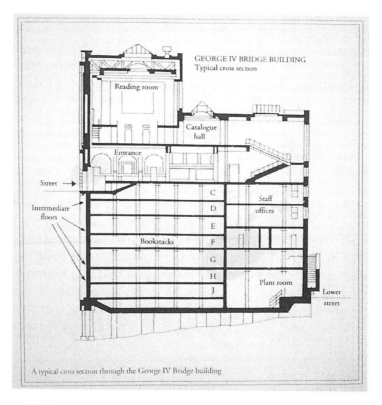

Figure 4.2   A cross section of George IV Bridge Building (Crown copyright. Reproduced by kind permission of the National Library of Scotland)

fundamental fact that even a relatively small fire could result in the loss of a major part of the library's collections and very significant damage to the building itself.

FIRST STEPS

The studies of the fire and structural risk contained a number of recommendations which could be acted on rapidly:

- The outdated fire alarm system, which relied on bi-metal strip detectors, was replaced by a modern smoke detector system so that detection of fire was immediately much more effective.
- Intrusive and dangerous use of stack areas for non-storage purposes (offices and the computer room, for example) were eliminated to reduce the level of ignition risk.

- 'First-aid' fire suppression devices (fire extinguishers and so on) were increased in number and upgraded.
- A programme of staff training in procedures for fire prevention was implemented.

However, the situation became more complicated when the way in which the fire brigade would be expected to fight a fire was examined. The absence of windows to give access to the stack floors which form the heart of the building; the presence of staff offices running across the back of the building creating a barrier to the inner core of the building; and the peculiar geography of the George IV Bridge site presented serious difficulties because it would be extremely difficult to ensure access by fire-fighters to tackle a fire at, or near, its source. The inevitable delay in doing so would allow a fire to grow to the point at which serious structural damage would occur.

After consultation with the fire authority it became clear that the nature of the building design, with the book stackage supporting much of the structure, could only lead to the library being listed as a dangerous structure. In turn, this meant that great caution would be exercised before committing fire-fighters to working in the building during an incident. The worst case scenario was that fire-fighters would only prevent the spread of fire to adjacent properties while the interior and its contents were ravaged by fire.

DIFFICULT DECISIONS

At this point the library was faced with the realization that:

- The physical structure, layout and use of the George IV Bridge Building was fundamentally unsafe and unsatisfactory for its purpose.
- These problems, combined with the fuel load which the mainly paper-based collections constituted, made it inevitable that anything other than a minor fire would be utterly disastrous.
- The building design no longer matched the requirements of fire safety regulations and could not be given a fire certificate (which the loss of Crown Immunity had made necessary), so that occupation by staff and users would become highly problematic.

The discussions which then took place looked at the two possible alternatives:

- **Vacate the building** – that is, relocate the archival and storage functions to another site. This was unrealistic and incompatible with the library's mission and objectives.
- **Protect the building** – by installing an active fire-fighting system (probably

based on automatic water sprinklers) into the building to provide immediate response to any fire in the library and ensure that the steelwork was kept below its deformation temperature, thus offering the protection needed to prevent structural collapse.

There was, theoretically, a third alternative and that was **to do nothing** – in the hope that the building, which had avoided a serious fire for some 50 years, would continue to be lucky.

In the event, the decision to retain the George IV Bridge Building was perhaps the easiest part of the process. The site was too steeped in its history and the central city location was too firmly established for a move to another location to be a realistic option.

THE MASTER PLAN

From the various studies undertaken, the library defined the fire safety objectives for the project to be:

1. Put in place the maximum practical measures for the safety of the public users, visitors and staff.
2. Put in place the maximum practical measures for the safety of the collections.
3. Put in place the maximum practical measures for the additional safety of highly valued items, or 'national treasures', within the collections.

The decision to install a fire suppression system was only part of the overall fire protection work needed. Improvements in the provision of means of escape to bring the library's fire safety regime up to an acceptable contemporary standard were also part of the work, together with a range of other related work including renewal of electrical wiring and the air-conditioning plant and its associated ductwork.

A Master Plan for all the required work – not just the sprinkler system – had to be prepared and a bid made to the Scottish Office for the necessary finance. Approval for a project with a total budget of £12.7 million (covering fees, VAT and forecast inflation) was obtained in June 1991. The Design Team was appointed in 1992 to undertake the development of the Master Plan and to oversee the programme of works. The Design Team was given additional responsibilities including:

- carrying out a risk assessment of the new designs to ensure that problems associated with the designs would be avoided in the future
- management of the risks implicit in the construction and engineering works.

Although the fire safety problems had been identified, it was clear to the library staff that it was essential that everyone involved with the library (the trustees, Scottish Office, staff, readers) understood what was to happen. To this end a detailed series of briefings took place. It was felt that if all parties were to 'sign-up' to the project, everyone needed to understand what was to happen during a period of very intense disruption to normal work.

The idea was to avoid the usual problems that can happen when, for example, a fire protection project is imposed on a building regardless of the needs or sensibilities of those who have to use that building. Given that the intention was to maintain a normal range of library services for the duration of the project it was clear that staff cooperation and the understanding of the readers was even more important. It was also helpful to be able to point out to staff the other benefits (additional space, better air conditioning, new accommodation) which would result from the project. In the last analysis, it had to be accepted by everyone that the risk of losing the national collection was so great that almost any amount of disruption would need to be tolerated.

THE PROGRESS OF THE WORKS

Work began in 1992 and was phased to minimize the impact of the work on the provision of public services.

- The Contract 1 phase involved the construction of a new 'north staircase' which was literally driven through all of the floors in the building in order to provide (for the first time) a direct fire exit route from the Reading Room. This staircase significantly enhances the personal safety of those who work in or visit the library, and greatly simplifies the way in which fire-fighters can access this part of the building, with consequential benefits for the protection of the collections and for salvage and damage control.

  Other benefits from this phase of the contract included the creation of additional space at the same level as the Reading Room – now used as the Catalogue Hall, and this, in turn, has allowed a complete reorganisation of the layout of services in the Issue Hall which is the main focal point for contact with readers.
- The Contract 2 phase involved:
  - the installation of a second external fire evacuation staircase running the full height of the building
  - the installation of a sprinkler system on all stack floors and public spaces
  - the renewal of electrical, heating and ventilation plant and lifts.

  Additional benefits provided under Contract 2 included the creation of a new rooftop space (made possible by the relocation of the ventilation plant on the roof itself), which was subsequently fitted out for staff accommodation.

One of the problems of the very complex nature of the site and the library's intention to remain open while work was in progress was the decision to retain the collections in the book stacks, meaning that the contractors needed to work around collections *in situ*. Given the relatively fragile nature of the collections and the (occasionally) destructive nature of such works, it was decided to wrap the stacks in a special fire retardant sheeting. This would provide protection against physical damage and dust from the building works and limit the spread of any fire or smoke damage which might take place during the period of the works. As an additional benefit, the wrapping process protected items in the collections from removal by curious hands! Leaving the collections *in situ* clearly had an effect on the progress of the works, but the huge effort and dangers implicit in decanting, transporting and then reinstalling so many items could have added significantly to the cost of the project. The space necessary for temporary storage would also have been a difficult and costly resource to find.

Although disruption to services was significant, every attempt was made to minimize the effects on readers and staff. Wrapping the book stacks had the obvious consequence of making the books unavailable for use. As the rolling programme of sprinkler installation proceeded from floor to floor, readers had to be kept informed of stack restrictions which made books unavailable for use. When the time came to work on the public areas, it was necessary to transfer the reading rooms and reference stock (some 25 000 volumes) and Reference Services Division staff to the library's Causewayside Building (about one mile away) for a period of 18 months (October 1997 to March 1999).

THE FIRE SUPPRESSION SYSTEM

Apart from the sheer size of the fire suppression system, it is noteworthy for a number of reasons:

● Stainless steel pipework was used for the system. The decision to avoid the use of 'black' steel for pipework was not taken lightly. All the alternatives tend to be more expensive, but, when costed over the life of the system, and, in particular, when consideration is given to the problems of corrosion and sludge formation in black steel, it can be seen that the benefits of stainless steel are considerable. Indeed, taking into account reduced labour costs and the cleanliness of the installation, it has become increasingly clear that stainless steel is a viable alternative. Great care must be taken in the combination of materials to avoid, de-zincification, de-alloyization and galvanic corrosion. All materials must be compatible with stainless steel, that is, stainless steel sprinkler heads, valves, supports, and so on.

- Most of the system was prefabricated off-site. This offers many advantages, not least of which is the elimination of some dirty and dangerous processes which would otherwise have to be carried out in proximity to the collections.
- The huge number of joints in the smaller pipes used neoprene seals and were crimped, rather than being formed by brazing, making this element of the work both rapid and clean.
- In some locations the newest form of plastic pipe (specially fabricated for use in sprinkler systems) was used.

THE FINAL ANALYSIS

What has made this project unique is the fact that a major civil and mechanical engineering project has been undertaken in an occupied heritage building, which continued to operate during virtually the whole contract period. The NLS was faced with problems which had persisted for many years and which were not of its own making, but these were faced robustly. Utilization of the risk assessment technique has resulted in a safer, more effective building in which to safeguard Scotland's printed and written heritage.

The project was intended to ensure that not only could the library remain in occupation at the George IV Bridge Building, but also that the library's collection (and hence its whole reason for existence) was protected to the highest contemporary standards during the work.

The opportunity was also taken to improve certain life safety provisions by providing additional means of escape from the building which was occupied by staff during the whole contract period and which was open for business during most of that time.

LESSONS LEARNED

What was learned from the project can be summarized as follows:

- The project objectives must be clearly designed and planned before the main funding is sought and before consultants and contractors are commissioned.
- Clear allocation of responsibilities must be laid down.
- Great care must be taken in the selection of consultants and contractors.
- Attention to detail is important, there should be a higher than normal input from consultants and, therefore, fees will be higher than normal.

- Careful coordination and planning are necessary to ensure that there is minimal impact on the existing building's structure, fabric and operations.
- Those involved in, or affected by, the project must be fully briefed both before, and during, the project.
- Great efforts must be made to minimize the risk of fire during the works. All involved must receive training in the construction-stage fire safety plan, which must be updated as the work proceeds.
- The physical installation is only one part of the network of protection – maintenance, testing, staff training and policies also form an important part of the network of protection, which needs to be maintained.

MANAGING THE FIRE RISK: FIRE SAFETY STRATEGY

There are many components that make up the fire safety strategy needed to maintain a building in a fire-free environment. Figure 4.3 (which is based on a similar table in FIREPRO's 1990 report (FIREPRO Incorporated, 1990)) shows how these relate to each other and form a matrix of protection that needs to be managed effectively. The figure and the text which follows in this section are based on, and developed from, FIREPRO's *Thinking Total Fire Safety* brochure (FIREPRPO Incorporated, 1996).

MANAGEMENT POLICIES FOR FIRE SAFETY

Legal framework

Regulations set down minimum requirements for fire safety, but they are intended for safety of life and not protection of property which will require action that goes beyond the letter of the regulations. Fire and building regulations have traditionally been prescriptive, providing a codified approach to fire safety but this will often conflict with the library's objectives.

Modern regulations tend to allow an approach where librarians and fire engineers can work together to find methods of protection which both meet the regulations and suit the requirements of each library in terms of the assets they wish to protect. An engineered approach often offers solutions that more closely meet the needs of the organization. This is certainly the case for libraries.

Fire safety objectives

Objectives need to be established because they determine the level of protection that you require in *your* circumstances for *your* institution. The key is to focus your safety concerns on the protection of people and property and business

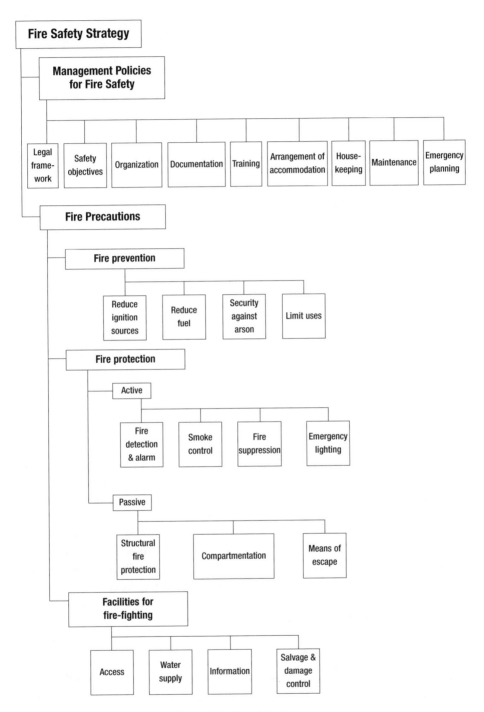

Figure 4.3 Fire safety strategy

continuity. Consider what is important to your library and what is not. How much damage and business interruption will you accept? What proportion of your collections, equipment or operation, if subject to *total loss,* would destroy the aims and objectives of your library? What is easily replaced? What is irreplaceable? By developing realistic statements reflecting the amount of fire damage you are willing to accept, you take a great step forward towards building a fire-safe library. Once established, these objectives must be included in the brief for the building consultants carrying out work in the future.

Organization

Clear lines of responsibility need to be set up for staff and consultants. Everyone in the organization should understand their responsibilities and who deputizes when others are not available, so that potential gaps and loopholes are covered.

Documentation

All systems, fabric and buildings contents need to be fully documented and this information needs to be available in an emergency. Such important records also must be duplicated and kept off-site to avoid the obvious risk of loss in the same fire that they are intended to combat. Similarly, collection catalogues and shelf catalogues will need to be duplicated, and computer systems backed up onto disks that are kept off-site if there is to be any hope of being able to establish what is missing in the event of a disaster occurring.

Training

A range of training from general induction to specific fire and safety training should be introduced to match the fire safety objectives. Remember that everyone needs to react in the appropriate manner to a fire situation. Staff and contractors must be involved in any fire safety programme and receive proper training because they need to understand why the work is necessary, and to understand what will be expected of them. They will then assist in reducing hazards and will act effectively during an incident. In particular, contractors must work to the Loss Prevention Council/BEC 1997 *Fire Prevention on Construction Sites – The Joint Code on the Protection from Fire of Construction Sites and Buildings Undergoing Renovation.*

Arrangement of accommodation

The arrangement of accommodation should be thought through carefully so that agreed fire safety objectives are not compromised. Accommodation functions that introduce a high risk of fire, such as furniture and stationery stores, workshops and plant rooms should be carefully sited to avoid placing sources of ignition next to collection areas.

Housekeeping

High standards must be maintained. All employees have a duty to keep their areas tidy and so reduce the risk of fire. Clear policies should be in place requiring the removal of rubbish at least daily. This will also apply to any construction areas.

Maintenance

Maintenance of the building's systems, plant and fabric must be to a high standard. Policies should lay down response times and there should be a forward maintenance plan. A well-maintained building will also deter vandals, thus reducing the threat to the collections from arson. Regular audits should be undertaken by the Chief Executive Officer (CEO), or equivalent, to ensure that the appropriate standards are being maintained. If reluctance to become involved is experienced, it is worth remembering that the CEO is legally responsible for the 'business' in all its aspects.

Emergency planning

It is important that there is a developed and tested business continuity plan. This must be clear and give concise instructions on how incidents are to be dealt with.

FIRE PRECAUTIONS

Fire prevention

- **Reduce ignition sources**
  Despite being an obvious precaution, it takes a degree of care to ensure that contractors do not introduce sources of fire into a building. Any *hot* equipment (that is, likely to cause a fire) must be subject to checking, and it is essential to introduce a strict permit system for *hot* work (for example, welding or cutting). Sparks from a grinder that fall into a duct and cause an outbreak of fire once everyone has left the area are a good example of why a permit system is needed. Generally, there should be a presumption against hot work within the collection building, because alternatives to hot work (for example, off-site prefabrication) can often be found. There should also be a system for monitoring portable equipment and appliances, turning off all computer terminals at night, repairing promptly all building services that can produce heat, and turning off lights that are not required.

- **Reduce fuel**

  As stated earlier, waste paper and old packing materials should be disposed of daily. Contractors must maintain a very high level of cleanliness and this must be an explicit requirement of their contract. Ideally, stationery stores should be maintained off-site and stocks of easily ignited materials like bubble-wrap and corrugated cardboard should be reduced as much as possible.

- **Security against arson**

  Security checks on staff and contractors should be carried out. Designers must consider the threat of arson when designing a new building; properly designed external lighting and landscaping around buildings can deter vandals. In the selection of a site avoid areas where vandalism is a problem.

- **Limit uses**

  Avoid uses for the building that are in conflict with the primary purpose of your organization. For example, hiring out public areas for functions may result in some income but could substantially increase risk to the collections, especially when the functions take place outside the normal working hours of the organization. It is essential to carry out risk assessments of any proposals to introduce uses that are in any way unusual.

Fire protection – active systems

- **Fire detection and alarm**

  Care is needed in the selection of the appropriate type of system and the sensitivity of its response to smoke. For example, with some sensitive systems it is possible to have a pre-evacuation alarm that will give time for security staff to investigate before the system sounds the evacuation alarm or further detectors detect smoke.

- **Smoke control**

  Smoke is a major concern for life safety and for property protection. Smoke can be generated at an alarming speed, and will fill a fire compartment in seconds. This could endanger life but will certainly result in damage to all of the contents of the space. Valuable books should be boxed to give protection from smoke, dust and (to a certain extent) water. Smoke evacuation and control is a major factor in property protection and requires specialist design, but it is important to understand that, generally, smoke can only be controlled if the fire that produces it can be controlled. A sprinkler system introduces this control.

- **Fire suppression**

  A sprinkler system will vastly enhance the security of collections by offering protection from the ravages of fire; because of this, insurance companies will generally offer substantial savings on premiums for a sprinklered building.

There are a number of types of sprinkler system, the most common of which are described in the Appendix 4A at the end of this chapter.

● **Emergency lighting**
There are two types of emergency lighting: self-contained units or fittings fed from a central battery position. The latter can be vulnerable to damage which will cause the loss of all emergency lighting, whereas the former can sustain damage to individual units without overall loss of lighting.

Fire protection – passive

● **Structural fire protection**
Steel-framed buildings must have structural fire protection added to prevent the steel from deforming. This will protect the building for a specific period of time in a fire. It is vital that the fire protection is not damaged during building alterations, since steel structures left exposed reintroduce the risk that the protection was designed to minimize.

● **Compartmentation**
Buildings are generally divided into fire compartments by means of fire resistant walls, doors, floors and ceilings. The smaller the compartment, the less the fire load, because the amount of fuel is less, and therefore the smaller any possible fire will be. Valuable contents should be housed in small compartments, but it is essential to accept that total loss of any material in one compartment can happen. The point to accept is that the smaller the compartment, the smaller the amount of material that will be lost. All holes between compartments must be fire stopped (that is, closed with material which prevents fire passing through an otherwise fire-resistant division) otherwise the integrity of the compartment will be compromised and fire can spread between compartments.

● **Means of escape**
It is a statutory requirement to maintain obstruction-free means of escape. Materials must not be stored in any part of an escape corridor or staircase. Checks should be carried out daily to ensure that the means of escape are freely available.

Facilities for fire-fighting

● **Access**
The fire service will need to be able to access the site. Are roadways clear? Do parked vehicles block access? Are gates wide enough? Once on-site, is access available all around the building? Is it clear where access for fire-fighting can be gained to the building? Is access possible at all times? Have checks been made out of hours to ensure that circumstances do not change?

Fire Protection Self-Inspection Checklist

The following checklist items can be adapted to local requirements to provide a daily/weekly or monthly inspection. The list is not exhaustive and is intended only to give an indication of the items that should be included.

Life Safety

❏ Exits clear, doors unobstructed and freely available for use when the building is occupied.

❏ Fire doors are closed and are not wedged open.

❏ Stairways, internal exit routes, fire doors and external paths leading to a place of safety are maintained in good condition.

❏ Emergency lighting operates when tested, exit signs are illuminated and are clearly visible.

❏ Fire brigade access routes are clear.

Fire Protection Equipment

❏ Fire extinguishers are in their proper location, fully charged and regularly inspected.

❏ Sprinkler heads are unobstructed.

❏ Fire detectors are unobstructed.

❏ Sprinkler control valves are open and locked/secured.

❏ Sprinkler tanks, piping, and supports appear in good condition.

❏ Lightning systems appear in good condition.

Housekeeping and Storage

❏ Rubbish is not left to accumulate and is removed daily.

❏ External rubbish storage is at least 12m from the building.

❏ Storage areas are kept clean and tidy.

❏ Combustible materials are stored safely.

❏ Inflammable and hazardous liquids are stored in appropriate containers and special cupboards.

Maintenance of Buildings and Systems

❏ Electrical systems are subject to regular inspection.

❏ Portable electrical equipment is registered and regularly tested.

❏ Drainage systems are operating efficiently, rainwater outlets are free from debris.

❏ Security systems are operational.

❏ External fences etc are properly maintained.

❏ Sprinkler and fire detection and alarm systems are subject to regular testing and records are kept.

❏ Building is maintained internally and externally in good decorative condition.

Exhibition Rooms

❑   Exhibition areas are not overcrowded and there is invigilation.

❑   Exhibition case lights do not show signs of overheating.

❑   Exhibits are not blocking exit routes and/or access to fire protection equipment.

Book Stack Areas

❑   All vertical/horizontal openings in fire barriers are fire-stopped.

❑   Salvage equipment and materials are provided and accessible.

❑   The fire department is familiar with and has access to these areas.

❑   Smoking regulations are enforced with employees and visitors.

Restaurants and Eating Areas

❑   Aisles and exit routes are unobstructed and illuminated.

❑   Extractor hoods, and exhaust ducts are clean.

Shops/Conservation Workshops/Packing Areas

❑   Laboratory wastes are disposed of daily, using appropriate precautions.

❑   Electrical equipment in areas near where flammable liquids are in use are explosion proof.

❑   Electrical appliances have warning lights and are unplugged when not in use.

❑   Employees are aware of special hazards and trained in any special precautions necessary.

❑   Entry is limited to authorised persons.

❑   Power tools are unplugged when not in use.

Personnel/Training

❑   All staff members know how to behave in a fire.

❑   All emergency team members have received training and are aware of their assigned duties.

❑   All staff members have received training in the use of portable extinguishers and fire prevention.

Figure 4.4   Fire protection self-inspection checklist – fire safety inspection forms
(adapted from NFPA – 909, National Fire Protection Association, 2001)
(Reprinted with permission from NFPA 909-2001. Protection of Cultural Resources, Copyright © 2001,
National Fire Protection Association, Quincy, MA 02269. This reprinted material is not the complete
and official position of the NFPA on the referenced subject, which is represented only by the standard
in its entirety.)

- **Water supply**

  Are there adequate supplies for fire-fighting? If there is no mains water supply, are there any watercourses nearby and can special arrangements be made to use these?

- **Information**

  The fire service needs to be given information on your priorities and plans and liaison should take place *before* an emergency situation arises. Laminated floor plans (plastic laminated for durability) should be available on-site for the emergency services use when called out.

- **Salvage and damage control**

  Involve the fire service in the development and testing of your business continuity plan, because the survival of your primary mission could depend on it.

The details above form a network of protection, which complements the structural systems of the buildings. Changing any aspect of this network of protection could result in unexpected consequences and requires careful coordination to maintain the fire-safe environment.

CONCLUSIONS

This chapter has illustrated that certain actions must be carried out in a routine manner to control a fire in a library effectively. Figure 4.4 provides a checklist which can be adapted for fire safety inspection.

The building's passive structural systems, active alarm systems, suppression systems and trained personnel must interact in accordance with a predefined plan so that they operate as a total system. Unless these have been thought through and planned in advance the situation will not be dealt with routinely.

Fires happen and no amount of planning can guarantee that a fire will not start. Our best defence against a subsequent disaster is preplanning, realistic assessment of risks and installation of defences. Above all we need a continued awareness that all these precautions might be needed in an hour's time – or might have been activated two minutes ago!

REFERENCES

FIREPRO Incorporated (1990), *National Library of Scotland Fire Defence Agenda*, report for NLS.

FIREPRO Incorporated (1996), *Thinking Total Fire Safety. Library Fire Protection*, Andover, MA: FIREPRO Incorporated.

FIREPRO Incorporated (2002), see <www.fireproincorporated.com> (accessed 29 August 2002).

Health and Safety Executive, UK (1994) *5 Steps to Risk Assessment*, London: Health and Safety Executive (Version current at May, 1999 available at: <www.hse.gov.uk/pubns/indg163.pdf>).

Historic Scotland (1997) *Fire Protection Measures in Scottish Historic Buildings*, Technical Advice Note 11, Edinburgh: Historic Scotland.

Historic Scotland (1998) *The Installation of Sprinkler Systems in Historic Buildings*, Technical Advice Note 14, Edinburgh: Historic Scotland.

Historic Scotland (2001) *Fire Risk Management in Heritage Buildings*, Technical Advice Note 22, Edinburgh: Historic Scotland.

Historic Scotland (2002) Scotland's Heritage – Listed Buildings, see <www.historic-scotland.gov.uk/index/wwd_whatwedo/wwwd_oubuiltheritage/wwd_listedbuildings/wwwd_listedbuildings-categories.htm> (accessed 4 September 2002).

Lewis, A. (1999) *The Prevention and Control of Arson*, London: FPA/Loss Prevention Council.

Lewis, A. and Dailey, W. (2000) *Fire Risk Management in the Workplace: A Guide for Employers*, 2nd edn, London: FPA/Loss Prevention Council.

Loss Prevention Council/BEC (1997) *Fire Prevention on Construction Sites – The Joint Code on the Protection from Fire of Construction Sites and Buildings Undergoing Renovation*, 4th edn, London: Loss Prevention Council/BEC.

National Fire Protection Association (2001a) *NFPA 909. Code for the Protection of Cultural Resources including Museums, Libraries, Places of Worship and Historic Properties*, Quincey, MA: National Fire Protection Association.

National Fire Protection Association (2001b) *NFPA 914. Code for Fire Protection of Historic Structures*, Quincey, MA: National Fire Protection Association.

National Fire Protection Association, NFPA Online, at <www.nfpa.org/Home/index.asp>.

PACE Central Advice Unit (1997) *Crown Fire Standards*, London.

PACE Central Advice Unit (1998a) *Fire Safety Guide*, London.

PACE Central Advice Unit (1998b) *Business Continuity Planning Guide*, London.

Parsloe, C.J. (1997) *Allocation of Design Responsibilities for Building Engineering Services – a Code of Conduct to Avoid Conflict*, TN 21/97, London: BSRIA.

Parsloe, C.J. (1997) *Allocation of Design Responsibilities – Example Drawings*, TN 22/97, London: BSRIA.

Scottish Executive/Home Office/NI Office/HSE (1999) *Fire Safety – An Employer's Guide*, London.

WEBSITES

The Fire Protection Association – The Fire Protection Association Online, available at: <www.thefpa.co.uk>.

Historic Scotland – Safeguarding the nation's heritage and promoting its understanding and enjoyment, available at: <www.historic-scotland.gov.uk/index>.

National Fire Protection Association. NFPA Online. Available at: <www.nfpa.org/Home/index.asp>.

Office of Government Commerce, available at: <www.ogc.gov.uk>.

PACE (Property Advisers to the Civil Estate), became an Agency of the Office of Government Commerce on 1 April 2000; more information about PACE and its services is available at: <www.property.gov.uk>. Details about Crown Fire Standards are available.

APPENDIX 4A: AUTOMATIC SUPPRESSION SYSTEMS

Sprinkler systems are not new. Throughout the nineteenth century sprinkler systems were patented on both sides of the Atlantic. Automatic sprinkler systems have a history of reducing fire losses. They are designed to:

- Detect fire at point of origin.
- Sound alarm/call for assistance if connected to a central monitoring service.
- Control or extinguish the fire (reducing the amount of water that otherwise would have been required to be used).

In a fire, water will have to be used, and the earlier it can be applied, the less damage there will be to material. Sprinkler protection reduces water damage by placing a small amount of water directly on the fire as the heat opens the sprinkler head closest to the fire and this also sounds the alarm. The sprinkler system controls the fire and reduces the need for the fire service to use large hoses.

Automatic suppression systems, mainly sprinkler systems, are increasingly used in libraries. Traditionally, librarians have resisted the use of sprinkler systems in their buildings because of a mistaken belief that water is worse for books than fire, and that installing a sprinkler system increases the risk of water damage when there is no actual fire.

Librarians have, however, accepted automatic fire detection systems, and have, therefore, accepted that there will be a delay in getting the extinguishant (water) on to the fire which has been detected. Under ideal conditions this may only be a few minutes, but even then the consequences can be disastrous. In the case of the Norwich Public Library fire (see pp. 191–211), the fire service was 30 seconds away from the building, but the damage by fire was catastrophic.

Fires in library collections develop rapidly (as the Norwich fire demonstrated) and will quickly reach a scale which means that fire-fighters will have to resort to using heavy water discharge from hoses that cause a great deal of damage to collections. Sprinkler systems deploy between 70 to 280 litres a minute depending on the design over a very precise area; by contrast a fire-fighter's hose will deliver up to 1000 litres of water a minute in a stream of considerable force. A sprinkler head will activate above the fire, and will begin to extinguish it immediately, whereas the much greater volume of water from a hose may not reach the actual source, and will affect much more of the building and its contents during its use.

Smoke detection *may* provide an opportunity for 'first-aid' action with portable extinguishers before the fire develops to a size when it will activate sprinkler heads.

Without automatic sprinkler protection a building with a fire-resistant construction can survive, but any combustible contents will perish.

Listed below are the three most common types of sprinkler systems.

1. WET-PIPE AUTOMATIC SPRINKLER SYSTEM

This system automatically detects and controls fire, it comprises a piped water system under pressure with heat activated sprinkler heads. In a fire the sprinkler head(s) nearest the fire are exposed to heat, open and discharge water to control or extinguish the fire. In most instances, the operation of only one sprinkler will control a fire until the arrival of fire-fighters. Often the operation of a sprinkler system will make the use of hoses by fire-fighters unnecessary, thus reducing the amount of water damage.

This type of system should not be installed in spaces that are likely to freeze. The design should ensure that sprinkler heads are protected from possible mechanical damage that could result in an accidental discharge.

2. DRY-PIPE AUTOMATIC SPRINKLER SYSTEM

Here, the piping system contains compressed air instead of water. When a sprinkler operates, the air pressure is reduced, thus allowing the dry-pipe valve to open allowing water to flow through the pipes to any opened sprinklers.

This system can protect areas subject to freezing, but the water supply to the system must be in a heated area.

3. PRE-ACTION AUTOMATIC SPRINKLER SYSTEM

The piping system contains air although, unlike dry pipe, it need not be under pressure. There has to be a fire detection system installed in the same area as the sprinklers. Actuation of the automatic fire detection system by a fire opens a valve that allows water to flow into the sprinkler system pipework and to be discharged from any sprinkler heads that are opened subsequently by the heat from the fire. In very large systems it may take some minutes for the water to reach the heads nearest the fire, during which time the fire may have grown larger than the system can cope with.

The system relies on the operation of the smoke detection system and will be subject to situations where the system will charge with water following a smoke detection signal. This will then need to be drained down and the system reset. The pipe-work design will need to allow for the complete removal of water, otherwise the piping could be subject to accelerated corrosion.

This type of system can be installed in areas subject to freezing. It minimizes accidental discharge of water due to mechanical damage to sprinkler piping or heads and could be useful in areas where system leaks pose a hazard. The system, unless charged with compressed air, will not detect damaged pipework or sprinkler heads and this could impair the system and/or damage the contents during a 'false' activation.

The pre-action system will cost considerably more and require a significantly higher level of regular maintenance, involving additional potential failure modes that reduces its reliability compared to a standard wet-pipe system.

5 Flood prevention and recovery

Christine Wise

INTRODUCTION

Flooding is as devastating as fire in a library or archive, but with prevention and preparation its effects can be minimized and collections protected. This chapter takes a cross-sectoral and cross-domain approach, with content equally applicable to multi- or single-site organizations, and to libraries and archives large and small. It concentrates on the specific factors relating to the management of flooding incidents, although reference is made throughout to detailed aspects of disaster planning and management covered elsewhere in this book, and to business continuity planning as an allied activity. It defines roles and responsibilities throughout the organization and is designed to assist the senior manager charged with the management of the disaster reaction and recovery and liaison with appropriate institutional departments in charge of estates, buildings and finance, the staff member researching disaster management, and anyone responding to a flooding incident. (In this case, it reinforces much of what has been said in Chapter 2, but in the specific context of flooding.)

DEFINITION OF A FLOODING INCIDENT

Examples of flooding incidents in a library and archive include a sudden but contained flood from a dishwasher, a pipe leaking over a longer period of time, water penetration through cracks in walls, or a sudden and widespread incursion of water from pipes above, below or beside the premises. The reason for this situation may be lack of maintenance, outdated equipment or facilities, or 'act of God'. Whatever the reason, the level of preparation and planning which has been carried out will contribute from the earliest stages to the success that the organization has in both predicting and reacting to the eventual impact on the library or archive service. It is, therefore, good management to consider these issues before any incident occurs, and to take steps to minimize both the risk and the impact.

IMPACT ON LIBRARY AND ARCHIVE SERVICES

The nature of the flooding incident will determine the impact on the library or archive service. A minor incident may mean the closure of a service point or a discrete area for several days while mopping up and relatively self-contained remedial action is taken; perhaps temporarily moving collections and quickly reinstating them in the affected area after thorough drying. A more serious incident may lead to closure of the service for a longer period of time while the premises are repaired and refurbished. In this instance, the collections may be transferred to temporary storage areas, while a partial enquiry service is offered from a temporary location; and the main service delivery and communication to users is via a virtual and interactive web presence.

The initial shock of the flooding incident may be severely disruptive and unforeseen, but, with data from current risk assessments and appropriate plans in place, it will be possible to appraise the situation at an early point, model the consequences and determine the steps for reaction and recovery. It is worth pointing out that even a relatively minor incident leading to the closure of a service point for a few days, or temporary unavailability of a particular collection during small-scale conservation work, may in fact be very serious for an individual researcher working to meet a particular deadline. Similarly, the impact of service disruption on externally funded project deliverables for the organization should be assessed and the funders notified at the earliest possible opportunity. When Collection Level Descriptions (CLDs) on websites are promoting access to previously lesser-known and used collections, and demand on services is high, the impact of any incidents on researchers should be carefully factored into the disaster planning process.

To illustrate the prevalence of flooding incidents, the findings of a search on Google conducted in March 2002 include several major flooding incidents in libraries worldwide, including Boston Public Library on 20 August 1998, <www.ala.org/alaonline/news/1998/980824.html> and in the Green Library at Stanford in 1998, <www.news-service.stanford.edu/news.april1/flood41.html>. A major incident occurred in the Morgan Library of Colorado State University Libraries on 28 July 1997, in which the lower level of the building, 77 000 square feet, filled with 10 feet of water, damaging more than 462 000 volumes. The university website describes this incident as follows: 'This tragedy ranked as the fourth largest disaster of any library in the world in the 20th century' (Morgan Library of Colorado State University Libraries, <www.lib.colostate.edu/library_history/overview.htm>). In the UK, the Lewes Depository of the University of Sussex Library was flooded in October 2000, causing severe damage (University of Sussex, 2000). More recently, the website of the National Library of Canada reported a flood on 23 June 2002, <www.nlc-bnc.ca/1/1/n1-334-e.html>.

Mindful of these ever-present threats to library and archive services, the M25 Consortium of Academic Libraries formed its Disaster Management Group, bringing together colleagues in academic libraries and archives with experience of and/or responsibility for disaster management within their own institutions in the London area. (The M25 is the orbital motorway around London.) Highly valuable practical information is contained and kept updated in the Disaster Management Group's website at <www.m25lib.ac.uk/ M25dcp>. The website includes a model disaster control plan template and linking commentary, essential for tackling fire, flood and other emergency situations, alongside a detailed bibliography.

THE BUSINESS CASE FOR A DISASTER CONTROL PLAN

In the light of the impact of flooding incidents, with the unavoidable disruption to services, there is a clear strategic and operational imperative to devise a Disaster Control Plan (DCP) to prepare for and deal with flooding and other incidents. The DCP will, therefore, itemize the steps in risk assessment, preparation, reaction and recovery which have been or will be undertaken by the library and archive service to deal with the immediate incident and to re-establish and restore longer-term credibility (see Chapter 2, pp. 13–40). The creation of this plan will also strengthen the case for a Business Continuity Plan (BCP).

THE CASE FOR A BUSINESS CONTINUITY PLAN

Business continuity planning involves a hard-headed assessment of the likely outcomes of, in this instance, any flooding incident, or any unexpected incident which leads to disruption to normal services. Following this assessment, an agreed set of policies and actions will be pulled together to form the best possible set of actions in the circumstances to minimize the impact on researchers and staff. There is an additional imperative to ensure that services suffer minimum disruption in a funding environment where organizations derive proportions of their funding from external income streams.

It is possible that one, either or both of these plans may be a specific requirement of an organization's insurance arrangements, and may be subject to on-going scrutiny to ensure that specific areas are addressed. If a DCP or BCP is not in place, then a timescale may be set by the external agencies involved for suitable plans to be drawn up and approved. It is therefore worth investing staff time and effort in these activities as insurance against future risk and an unexpected turn of events which leaves an organization exposed to greater risk.

As stressed in Chapter 2, a necessary consequence of work on DCPs and BCPs is the fostering of a disaster awareness culture throughout the organization at all levels so that everyone, not just those directly involved in the development and implementation of such plans, is aware of their responsibility in monitoring the fabric of the buildings and the condition of their collections and how to respond and react when a flooding incident occurs. The disaster awareness culture is an extension of the stewardship and curatorial responsibility throughout library and archive services.

FLOOD PREVENTION

RISK ASSESSMENTS

Risk assessments should be carried out regularly in the workplace (see also Chapter 3). Formal guidance on procedures may be obtained from such organizations as the UK's Health and Safety Executive, which publishes literature on its website (see, for example, *A guide to risk assessment* <www.hse.gov.uk/pubns/indg218.pdf>) and provides links to relevant organizations and literature. Some risk assessments may involve both visual inspections of premises and equipment and testing of equipment by suitably qualified professional staff. In all cases, the results should be documented in an appropriate form, noting any remedial action required. The documentation may be held locally and, in larger organizations, additionally by the Building Department. In all cases, there is an expectation that any remedial work uncovered by a regular risk assessment should be undertaken to minimize any such risk, for example, from leaking pipes, dripping taps, blocked gutters or drains. In some cases, work may be considered essential if required by health and safety legislation, and may need to be completed within a given timescale. Some work may be considered desirable, for example, re-siting of waste or soil pipes away from collection storage areas, and may be undertaken over a longer timescale. When undertaking a risk assessment, the requirements of the Historical Manuscripts Commission's (HMC) *Standard for Record Repositories* (Historical Manuscripts Commission, 2001) and *BS 5454: 2000 Recommendations for the Storage and Display of Archival Documents* (BSI, 2000) should be consulted (or the appropriate national equivalent for non-UK readers).

The provisions given in such documents are very detailed. For example, the HMC *Standard for Record Repositories* recommends, among other things, that 'The repository and most especially its storage accommodation must be of robust construction of brick, stone or concrete, with adequate protection for all roofs, walls, floors, ceilings and openings against unauthorised entry, fire, flood and damp' (Section 5.3.1) and 'Plumbing, plant and drains in, above or adjacent to the strongrooms should be avoided, and services should not pass through a strongroom unless required within it' (Section 5.3.3). *BS 5454: 2000* recommends that for ventilation purposes 'There should be a distance of at least 150mm between the floor and the lowest shelf' (Section 7.4.2) – in itself initial protection against flooding. This documentation will assist in making a business case for building improvements.

The position may be more complicated where different organizations share premises, but the various responsibilities for maintenance of shared premises and equipment should be known and documented. It is possible that the same risk of flooding applies to both or all organizations, in which case it will be important for all parties to investigate, cooperate and collaborate. In this instance, consideration should be given to shared minimization of risk and collaboration to achieve this via a cross-organizational disaster management committee. Risk assessments should also look at patterns of access to buildings, including security cover and cleaning. Are the premises left unattended overnight or for long periods over public holidays, Christmas and Easter? Is there monitoring of the premises out of hours? The consequences of these arrangements should be fed into scenario and contingency planning.

SCENARIO AND CONTINGENCY PLANNING

After the complete risk assessment of premises and equipment regarding flooding, any remedial works or replacement equipment should be undertaken or ordered according to an agreed list of priorities. Concurrently, scenario and contingency planning should be undertaken – in effect, to think the unthinkable. Only then can a robust DCP be drawn up. Contingency arrangements should form a regular part of the senior management agenda, as this provides an opportunity to consider risks and scenarios as part of the wider strategic planning process for service development. Responses to temporary and limited disruption caused by a leaking pipe, radiator or skylight onto a reading room, collection or equipment should form part of forward planning.

As a consequence of a flooding incident, one of a number of scenarios is likely and should be planned for over a period of time:

- temporary, but short-term disruption to library and archive services through fetching items from collections for readers, and striving to maintain a front-line enquiry service, whilst simultaneously dealing with the incursion in the affected area
- closure of the library and archive service for a short period and displacement of some or all staff

- closure of the library and archive service for a longer period and displacement of some or all staff
- some of the collections going into store
- all of the collections going into store
- replacement of some of the collections
- replacement of some of the furniture and equipment
- replacement of all of the furniture and equipment
- partial repairs and refurbishment of the premises
- full repairs and refurbishment of the premises
- conservation of some of the collections
- conservation of all of the collections.

If the library and archive service must be closed for any length of time, consideration should be given for key items from the collections, finding aids, furniture and equipment, working files (including project files) papers and other administrative documents such as collection agreements, to be collocated in temporary working areas. Other lower-priority materials may be placed in storage if flooding has damaged the collections and service areas to such an extent that the premises must be cleared. Such a scenario may involve hiring of key IT equipment, if current equipment has had to be moved, disposed of, or is otherwise unavailable. Much productivity may be lost at an operational level if servers, PCs and printers are not available, in addition to lack of access by researchers to electronic sources of information in the hybrid library and archival environment. The library and archive service may be a member of a national or regional organization, such as the M25 Consortium of Acaedmic Libraries, which, among other things, offer a mutual support agreement to members in the event of any emergency. Arrangements such as researcher reference access to adjacent library and archive services during a temporary closure period can be explored as part of scenario and contingency planning.

A set of criteria for defining essential collections, material and equipment in contingency planning may be:

- essential in maintaining a virtual reading room enquiry and referral service elsewhere
- essential for future planning for resumption of full library and archive services
- essential in maintaining project work for staff
- essential in planning for library and archive services well beyond re-opening of premises.

THE DISASTER PLANNING COMMITTEE

Once the policy for an organization's DCP has been defined by senior management, a Disaster Planning Committee can be set up to draw it up and develop it. The committee will operate within the parameters defined by the senior management team and will involve specialist staff members from across the organization. If there is a Building Department, it may be appropriate to have their representation and input at an early stage.

The Disaster Planning Committee (see Chapter 2, pp. 18–20) should be empowered to seek out examples of good practice elsewhere, both cross-sectoral and cross-domain. If curatorial experience is not available in-house to advise on the consequences of flooding incidents on collections, then it is advisable to obtain this advice from external experts. A conservator can provide hard data to enable staff to assess scales of damage to collections through water penetration (even through sturdy archival-quality boxes) and mould growth, and advise on measuring equipment and standards for their performance. They will advise on labelling storage media with water-resistant archival quality ink and using brass paper clips (which do not rust). They can illustrate the early stages of mould growth, demonstrating that it can appear on water-damaged collections within 48 hours, earlier if in particularly hot conditions, and advise on which treatments can safely be applied in-house and which require external specialist help. They can source equipment such as wet and dry vacuum cleaners, mobile and static dehumidifiers, fans, suction pumps and hand-held thermohygrometers. These tasks, actions and equipment will all require costing, leading to management decisions about the best way to fund preparedness for a flooding incident, either from existing budgets or from contingency sources, and, in the event of an incident, how these budgets may be drawn down. Further practical detail on collection handling and treatments can be found on the M25 Consortium of Academic Libraries Disaster Management Group's template and commentary.

INSURANCE AND LOSS ADJUSTMENT

The organization's insurers will have a major role in ensuring preparedness for flooding and other incidents. It is essential to update premiums regularly in respect of the value and location of collections, so that new collections received into the organization are included and any adjustments to cover are made. The insurance company representative, sometimes an independent expert, may on occasion visit the organization to inspect the location of collections, the condition of the premises and practical safety measures. Such inspections may lead to the insurance company specifying further work. The insurance company may also request a valuation of the collections in respect of recovery and the treatments which would be required in the event of a flooding incident. At the point of the inspection the organization may be required to designate collections which are irreplaceable, and therefore must be conserved, for example, the whole of special collections, and to designate those which may be discarded and replaced, for example, undergraduate teaching collections. The conservation costs resulting from a flooding incident to make good the damage in special collections will be high, and the insurance premiums will be correspondingly high (see also, Chapter 2, pp. 127–28).

CONTRACTS WITH DISASTER RECOVERY COMPANIES

At this stage of disaster preparedness, senior management will have considerable amounts of hard data to hand on its organizational response to flooding. It may then wish to consider an annual contract with an external disaster recovery company. There is no doubt that the impact of a flooding incident may be significant, and a timely and fast response may be worth paying for. Some suppliers offer different levels of contract depending on cover required. Such a contract may already have been identified as a priority as part of the risk assessment exercise, or be a requirement of institutional insurance.

In any case, specialist focused assistance is needed at the critical point when response time must be swift and greatest resources are needed. It may be more cost-effective to buy in this blanket support on a 24/7 basis, including holiday periods, than to draw on internal staff, some or all of whom may be needed after the critical response time to move collections to safe areas and set up and maintain physical and virtual service points elsewhere. The level of support offered by the external disaster recovery contractor may be determined by the type of contract, so it is important to check at the outset whether the contract includes on-site access by a conservator familiar with the conservation needs of, for example, wet fifteenth century documents (if that is your concern), or can supply access within 24 hours to freeze-drying facilities for moist documents pending further treatment, or can provide large temperature-controlled spaces for condition analysis of many documents.

It is uneconomic to keep large disaster supplies at maximum levels for an event which may never happen. Certain supplies (for example, latex gloves) have expiry dates. It is better to budget materials for a small-scale flooding incident which can be handled on a local basis, and to leave the large quantities of supplies for a major incident to the contracted external supplier. Disaster boxes stored on the premises should typically contain practical items such as disposable rubber and cotton gloves; blotting paper; unbleached cotton typing tape; acid-free boxes and envelopes for wrapping; plastic sheeting, buckets and mops. Their location will be determined by the physical layout of the building and the perceived risks, but priority should be given to locations close to unique and irreplaceable collections.

The disaster recovery company can call on external specialists to advise on flooding situations, which may be particularly valuable or important where premises are shared and negotiations may be complicated. Finally, it is likely that the disaster recovery contractor will wish to feed into the DCP at the planning stage and may have comments from experience elsewhere relevant to the BCP.

DISASTER PREVENTION

CIRCULATION AND IMPLEMENTATION OF THE DISASTER CONTROL PLAN

As advised in Chapter 2, once the DCP has been drawn up and agreed, it is important to ensure that its contents are kept up to date. This should be the responsibility of a particular member of staff, and it is recommended that the DCP should be reviewed at minimum every four months, and more frequently in larger organizations where there are frequent staff and collection changes. The DCP should be circulated to senior management within the library and archive service, and to key individuals as appropriate in the Building Department, and any other stakeholders in shared premises. The external recovery contractor should also receive a copy. One single member of staff should be empowered as Disaster Recovery Manager, to implement the plan should a flooding incident arise, with the backing of senior management and appropriate deputy cover when that individual is on annual leave or otherwise unavailable. The Disaster Recovery Manager should carry a copy of the DCP at all times and copies should be kept in agreed secure locations both on and off the organization's premises.

The communications 'tree' within the organization, in the event of a flooding incident, should be clearly defined. This may involve a telephone or pager tree, with individuals forming part of an out-of-hours rota, and with a responsibility to be within ready distance of the library or archive service should an incident occur. Such arrangements may have a financial implication for the institution. In order to facilitate communication during an incident, the organization may wish to assign mobile telephones, chargers and batteries to a secure disaster box location.

SUPPORTING DOCUMENTATION TO THE DCP

The DCP should be written in such a way that if the Disaster Recovery Manager is not available, any deputy or indeed any member of the organization's staff should be able to implement it without difficulty. In addition, the following supporting documentation is essential:

- a separate listing of the external disaster recovery contractor's details and a copy of the current contract

- a copy of *BS 5454:2000: Recommendations for the Storage and Display of Archival Documents* (BSI, 2000)
- a copy of *HMC Standard for Record Repositories* (Historical Manuscripts Commission, 2001)
- Inventories of collections, administrative files, furniture, equipment, and IT equipment not included in the DCP
- details of passwords and authorizations from those with responsibility to activate or disable IT systems
- separate listings of the communications tree information
- lists of specialist removal firms
- locations of local libraries and archives, with their contact details and a note of the assistance they are likely to be able to provide in the event of a flooding incident
- details of national organizations such as the UK's National Preservation Office, and the M25 Consortium of Academic Libraries Disaster Management Group who may be called upon for advice
- details of conservators and other external specialists familiar with the collections.

STAFF TRAINING AND AWARENESS

It is essential to nurture the disaster awareness culture. In addition to regular discussions and updates at staff meetings, one practical method of doing this is to organize an on-site training session. This can be drawn up by the Disaster Recovery Manager, or an external disaster recovery company can devise and run a simulated response to an imaginary flooding scenario on the premises. Various factors can be built into this, for example, scenarios where the public are on the premises, at weekends or out of hours, in the special collections reading room or at the main enquiry desk. Such rehearsals are a good team-building and training exercise. The external disaster recovery company is often able to provide illustrative material about actual floods elsewhere, which emphasize the severity of the events and the painful after effects.

OPERATING STATEMENTS

One output of the scenario and contingency planning work by senior management will have been an analysis of the various options available to the library and archive service in the event of a flooding incident, once its implications are known. These operating statements may define alternative locations and communications within the premises or a completely alternative location elsewhere. One such statement might be:

In the event of a serious flooding incident in the entrance area affecting the circulation desk and the short loan collection, this area will be closed to the public. An alternative service will be offered from the Information Room, and all available staff transferred there, until such times as the library entrance area is available for public use. Please refer to the website or telephone for the latest information.

Examples of such operating statements should be included in the DCP, and discussed with the external recovery contractor. They will also assist with managing the publicity and public relations aspects of the flooding incident.

FLOOR PLANS AND COLLECTION LOCATIONS

Floor plans and collection locations will be available from institutional collection management and development plans. They can be amended to meet the needs of disaster control planning, by adding details of collections to be moved first in the event of flooding and the location of disaster boxes. As a consequence of analysing these plans in a risk assessment, collections may be moved from areas defined as at medium risk of flooding to low-risk situations. Disaster control planning provides an excellent opportunity to update existing plans for incorporation in the DCP, marking on them known locations of pipework, both clean and soil, radiators, drains, grates, gutters, windows, domestic equipment, sprinklers, and any hazards.

DISASTER RECOVERY

IMMEDIATE DISASTER RESPONSE

The key message on discovering flooding is not to panic. If the water is rising steeply (say by centimetres per minute), the affected area of the building should be evacuated without delay and the disaster response implemented as outlined in the DCP. A water incursion can come from overhead as well as below, so if possible the source of the flooding should be identified at the outset. If the water level is not rising steeply, the Disaster Planning Manager should start to implement the agreed disaster response, summoning assistance using the emergency contacts list in the DCP.

The DCP will have defined a priority order in which to remove key collections from affected areas. These should be removed from vulnerable areas, for example, in the locations where the water is rising, flowing or cascading. The nature of such water incursions should be noted at the time, for example, whether it is visibly clean or soiled. It is essential to document transfers of collections carefully.

The Disaster Planning Manager should take the lead, responsible to senior management, for the operational implementation of the plan. It is essential to keep in touch with colleagues, while maintaining control of the disaster response. The Disaster Planning Manager should brief senior management at regular intervals and work with other colleagues in the team. Other colleagues should be working to pre-defined responsibilities, for example, retrieving collections, wrapping, monitoring and recording temperature and relative humidity readings, monitoring dehumidifiers and pumps, operating wet and dry vacuum cleaners, re-boxing, labelling, or documenting. Everyone should be kept informed and involved at every stage of the disaster response.

It is useful to bear the following in mind: after the security of staff members, the preservation of collections according to agreed priority is the topmost concern. The organization may have already decided not to assign resources to saving furniture or equipment.

Undamaged items should speedily be removed from the affected areas, either to another area or outside the premises. Damaged collections, or those judged to be in danger of mould growth, can be removed by the external disaster recovery company to be freeze-dried prior to conservation, unless it is possible to undertake this work in-house. A decision to stabilize damaged collections by freeze-drying them will make time to decide on a priority order or treatment, or to discard individual items. However, care should be exercised, as freeze-drying is not suitable for all items, for example, documents with seals, parchment or vellum. Vacuum-drying is another possible treatment, but as it can lead to distortion of documents advice should be sought from an experienced conservator. On their advice, certain vulnerable items may be kept back from storage if it is essential that their condition is inspected on a daily basis, and special provision may be needed for this.

Dehumidifiers, fixed or mobile, can be used to reduce the moisture content of the air in the affected area. Any damaged stationery, either for collections or administrative use, should be disposed of immediately, as it may harbour future mould growth, no matter how slightly damaged, and present a future risk to the collections. Any discarded material should be documented, as it may be possible to make a later insurance claim.

Trolleys and tables can be used in the short term to store collections, but rented crates may also be necessary. One-metre crates are essential, as they can safely store an entire standard shelf of books or several archive boxes with appropriate archival quality wrapping. Crates may be sourced from the Building Department if not held on-site, or from the external disaster recovery contractor. The contents of each trolley, table and crate should be carefully documented, including on the storage medium itself.

As necessary, arrange for undamaged furniture and equipment which is impeding remedial work on the premises to be removed to a secure location, and for any damaged items to be disposed of after due authorization. The objective is to leave the premises as clear as possible for any necessary works to be carried out. The DCP should itemize alternative storage and operation space or detail off-site storage which may be used. If any collections are left *in situ* while repairs are carried out, ensure that they are carefully covered and protected against damage, and that the temperature and relative humidity readings are constant and within acceptable parameters. In case of doubt, *BS 5454: 2000* (BSI, 2000) indicates acceptable parameters for temperature and relative humidity for collections. Weigh up very carefully the pros and cons of moving collections off the premises and keeping them *in situ*, in terms of risks, further damage by flooding and costs.

Once collection moves have been completed, collate all the information into a document – creating a spreadsheet is a good way of doing this. This document is a vital part of the audit trail for the flooding incident, and can be used for planning how to return the collections to their original, or alternative, locations in due course.

It is essential to have video or photographic records of the actual flooding event and its aftermath, for documentation, insurance and publicity purposes. If no such in-house capacity is available, the DCP should give details of how such resource can be drawn upon in an emergency. Photography and filming should take place on the first day of the incident, to demonstrate its extent and impact, and at regular intervals thereafter. This evidence may also be helpful in discussions with the Chartered Loss Adjuster appointed by the organization's insurance company.

It is likely that senior management will meet with the Chartered Loss Adjuster appointed to the incident within twenty-four hours. The Chartered Loss Adjuster is an objective assessor of the situation and will receive information about the incident and regular updates on the consequences. The role of the loss adjuster is:

- to identify the reasons why the flooding incident occurred
- to seek to minimize the loss
- to negotiate the total cost of the loss with the insurers
- to investigate the possibility of third-party mitigation.

It may be helpful to prepare to answer the loss adjuster's questions about the flooding incident along the following lines:

- the nature of the flooding incident, when it happened, who discovered it, what action was taken initially and subsequently
- the history of the library and archive service, its collections, stock arrangement, disposition of functions on a floor by floor basis

- disaster response procedures, including the DCP and BCP
- who uses the building, how often, why and what for
- the likely short-, medium- and long-term impact on the library's functions (if these can be determined at the time).

Senior management may find it helpful to have a representative from the Building Department and a representative from the disaster recovery firm present for specialist input. Reports at the early stages can only be interim, pending a full assessment of the impact of the flooding incident and its consequentials.

During this period, it should be possible to begin to assess the impact of the damage to the collections and the premises, and the consequentials. The Disaster Planning Manager should already, for example, be prioritizing conservation treatments, sourcing replacement copies for discarded material, or new equipment, on the basis of the policy guidelines in the DCP. Further guidance from senior management may be sought if the recommendations, with good reason in these special circumstances, are at variance with the DCP.

MANAGEMENT OF REPAIRS AND REFURBISHMENTS

At the same time as the Disaster Planning Manager is managing the disaster recovery process, and steps have been taken to safeguard the damaged and undamaged collections in the short to medium term, senior management should be using available information and expert advice to determine the extent of repairs and refurbishments required as a result of the flooding incident. The timescales for these will be determined by their extent. What seems like a relatively contained incident, for example, a burst pipe, may require replastering, new shelving and flooring in the affected area, including re-sealing of floors and walls to guard against future mould growth in the premises, and a period of monitoring to ensure stable temperature and relative humidity readings within acceptable parameters, before the collections can be moved in once more.

This may also prove an opportunity to carry out refurbishment work during a period when services are already subject to disruption. A cost–benefit analysis may have to be drawn up at this stage, to measure the effect on service delivery in the short term against longer-term benefits, alongside sourcing funds to implement work acquiring items on the 'desiderata' list.

Some working definitions for this process are:

- *Repairs* – the works which need to be carried out to the premises to make them safe, secure, wind and weather proof, and conform to all health and safety legislation. Generally, the cost of this work may be covered by the organization's insurance claim, although specialist advice should naturally be sought.

- *Refurbishments* – the works which can be carried out in tandem or subsequently to upgrade the existing premises. For example, during a longer period of disruption and closure, it may be advisable to upgrade to more modern ventilation, heating and cooling systems, alarms and electrical power points. These may facilitate flood prevention and monitoring and minimize future risk. Some of these works may be covered by the insurance claim, and again specialist advice should be sought.

Further, more detailed, definitions of terms such as *preservation* and *conservation* may be obtained from *BS 5454: 2000 Recommendations for the Storage and Display of Archival Documents* (BSI, 2000) and *HMC Standard for Record Repositories* (Historical Manuscripts Commission, 2001).

A programme of repairs and refurbishments may be project managed or coordinated by the library and archive service, by the Building Department, or by a specially appointed external project manager; senior management will manage the briefing process. It is inadvisable for works to be started before appropriate authorizations have been received from the organization's insurers. A generic brief for the repairs programme could be 'to minimize further flooding risk to the collections' and the programme may be approved by the organization's insurers and assessors from other external agencies such as funding bodies. It may also contain elements of work deemed essential by the organization's insurers. For a programme of refurbishments, it is advisable for senior management to specify essential and desirable features of the works in order to form a feasibility plan for costing and internal authorization. Briefing, such as better temperature control in the collection cages, should result in the specification for an improved air handling and ventilation system or air conditioning system in this area, informed by the requirements of BS 5454 (2000) and Historical Manuscripts Commission Standard (2001).

COST CENTRE MANAGEMENT

Specimen ledger forms for spreadsheets with appropriate nominal forms should be included in the DCP to ensure that an on-the-spot record is kept of all purchases so that necessary records can be generated. Copies of all purchase order forms should be kept. Figure 5.1 shows a sample record for transfer into a spreadsheet.

TIMESCALES FOR RECOVERY

Prior to returning the collections to their original locations, the exact order of operation needs to be determined, to ensure a smooth transfer. This planning

31 March 2002

- 10 hours of specialist advice time from external disaster recovery firm @ £n plus VAT (government valued added tax) per hour
- hire of two dehumidification units from external disaster recovery firm (estimated initial cost £n plus VAT)
- purchase of large plastic sheeting (£n to reclaim on expenses form)
- two security staff on overnight duty to 06h00 31 March 2002 on standard overtime rates at £n per hour
- lost revenue during the closure period itemized by individual income stream (based on a comparative analysis of an identifiable equivalent period)
- emergency inspection and service of photocopier to rule out water damage at £n plus VAT (if not covered by service plan)

Figure 5.1 Sample record for transfer into a spreadsheet

process should also include relocation of furniture and equipment in priority order. During the closure period, there may be an opportunity to re-plan locations of collections, furniture and equipment to minimize further risk from flooding. Using the resources of a removal company on returning collections from storage, it may be possible to re-plan their locations with minimal physical input from staff. This re-planning may be informed by experiences of the flooding incident and the timescales governed by the consequent repairs and refurbishments. For all of these reasons, there can be no set timescale for recovery; it is determined by the individual circumstances of the flooding incident.

NEWS MANAGEMENT

As soon as the likely short-, medium- and long-term impact on the service becomes clear, a press statement should be issued to inform the user community and stakeholders when services are expected to return to normal. In such circumstances, some news is better than none as there will be understandable concern about the effects of flooding. Stakeholders such as donors and funders should receive regular bulletins, while the user community will need advice on alternative sources for their studies. Much information can be communicated effectively via an organization's website, if there is one.

THE IMPACT ON STAFF

Colleagues will be deeply upset by a flooding incident, especially if there is damage to the collections. They will appreciate information about the progress of events, messages of support received, donations of time, replacement copies, funding and offers of alternative facilities. As the disaster responses continue, it is helpful to bring colleagues together at regular intervals, for example, at lunchtime or at the beginning and end of the day, to update them and to provide refreshment. It is also essential that the Disaster Planning Manager has the opportunity to refresh their energies and to keep an overview of the operations.

Provide protective clothing, headgear and footwear if necessary to ensure that colleagues do not spoil their own clothes; otherwise expect to include costs of clothes in insurance claims from members of staff.

DOCUMENTING THE FLOODING INCIDENT

At all times, keep a running note of events, actions and decisions, including the exact sequence of events and why and when decisions were made and actions taken. This will be essential in piecing together what actually happened, in providing the definitive record of the event for the organization's insurance company and loss adjuster, for future publicity about the event, and for ultimate revision of the DCP and BCP to incorporate lessons learned. At the very least, update the record at the beginning and end of each working day. Do not hesitate to record the minutiae of the event, as so many incidents will take place that it will be hard to recall a particular incident, or why a certain decision was made, although they were memorable, explicable and obvious at the time. Open a special file, with material filed by subject category in date order, to keep track of the documentation that will contribute in hard copy and electronic format to the organization's official record.

The basic documentation should include:

- the nature of the flooding incident, when it happened, some explanation as to why, who was contacted, and when
- reports of visits by specialist advisers and their authorization as necessary to carry out various works
- reports of discussions with colleagues both within the organization and externally
- a running tally of costs incurred
- key points for internal and external briefings
- specialist summaries by the Building Department, suppliers or contractors of any repairs or refurbishments carried out, floor plans, specifications, equipment replaced or renewed, and so on
- summaries of stock moves, crate-by-crate, or shelf number-by-shelf number
- conservation treatments carried out
- items disposed of and replacement copies obtained
- preliminary steps taken to ensure that a similar incident does not happen again

- lessons learned from the experience to pass on to colleagues as part of the corporate memory and for the basis of the eventual insurance claim; this will include revised inventories of collections, furniture and equipment.

Finally, the DCP and BCP should be revised to take account of lessons learned.

FUTURE RISK ANALYSIS

And so the process begins again, at the strategic and operational level. There will be a revision of all plans, documentation, new risk analyses, adjustments to insurance cover, and staff training to undertake. All collection plans will need to be revisited. Once again, disaster control planning will form a standing agenda item for senior management and for an appropriate committee forum for collection management and development.

A CASE STUDY: THE FAWCETT LIBRARY, LONDON GUILDHALL UNIVERSITY, 11 AUGUST 1994

To conclude this chapter, it is appropriate to provide a case study illustrating the impact of a flooding incident on one particular library. The Fawcett Library, London Guildhall University, which houses the most extensive collection on women's history in the UK, was flooded in the early morning of 11 August 1994.[1] On that day there was unprecedently heavy rainfall across London and the storm drains to the rear of the building in which the library was located were unable to cope with the amount of water which rose across the basement to a level of 2 to 3 inches. Fortunately, the flooding was discovered early in the morning and staff were alerted to deal with the situation. By 08.00, staff from right across London Guildhall University were moving the collections from bottom shelves as well as unique items, such as the library's collection of suffrage banners, upstairs into empty teaching space under the direction of the then Archivist. It was fortunate that large empty rooms were available during the vacation to spread out, document, assess and temporarily store the displaced collections.

Specialist advice from disaster recovery firms was obtained at a very early stage, and pumps, fans and dehumidifiers were installed to stabilize the environment, now hot and damp, within acceptable limits, and to begin drying out the premises. Conservators from the Guildhall Library also inspected the collections in the initial stages of the disaster response, and advised that major mould growth had been avoided by a few hours due to prompt staff action. As a consequence of moving the collections out of the affected area so quickly, only a few items were damaged by moisture. These were subsequently conserved and made available to researchers when the library re-opened.

The situation was assessed by the Chartered Loss Adjusters appointed by the university's insurers, and it rapidly became clear that the entire library space, measuring some 320 square metres, would have to be cleared in order to carry out major repairs, including the laying of a new floor layer, prior to substantial redecoration. The collections, furniture, equipment and wooden compact shelving therefore went into environmentally controlled, secure, off-site storage, into conditions approved by the university's insurers. Arranging this operation, to effectively clear the entire library for the first time since it had been received into the then City of London Polytechnic in 1977, was no small undertaking.

The university also decided to take the opportunity to carry out refurbishments to the premises, with the overall brief of minimizing further risk to the collections. The work carried out included relocating service pipes away from the collections, and installing security devices, including a video entry system. These repairs and refurbishments resulted in the closure of the library to personal visitors for some 11 months.

While the repairs and refurbishments were being carried out, library staff continued to offer an enquiry service to readers from a temporary office, while taking the opportunity to work on housekeeping and other projects funded by external bodies such as the Corporation of London Education Committee, and on funding applications. Successful applications during this time included a total of £255 000 over four years from the Higher Education Funding Council for England (HEFCE) under the Specialized Research Libraries in the Humanities Programme, popularly known as Follett. Library staff also undertook the time-consuming business of re-planning the entire disposition of stock, to enable particularly rare and precious items to be moved promptly out of the basement in the event of any future incident, and to make the arrangement more intuitive for researchers. During the closure period, members and Friends of the Library, funders and other stakeholders, relevant journals, organizations and associations and the wider library, archival and museum community were kept informed about progress towards re-opening on 3 July 1995.

Many practical lessons were learned. As already indicated, the collections were re-arranged to ensure that the rare book collection, the Cavendish-Bentinck Library, were situated close to the exit for fast retrieval in the event of an emergency. More than ever, the importance of having a detailed, tailor-made and up-to-date DCP was realized. The DCP was being compiled at the time of the flooding incident, following an early conservation survey of the collections and inspection of the premises. The DCP was subsequently completed and revised from time to time to take account of changing circumstances. It was also written in such a way that any member of staff could react promptly, with sufficient information and authority, to an incident. The importance of having adequate insurance cover to undertake conservation work and to cover repairs was highlighted, along with the importance of having regular valuations when such a large proportion of the collections was irreplaceable. Finally, the disruption of being separated from collections which are in the daily stewardship of staff, and which are in constant use by researchers, for some 11 months, should not be under-estimated. Finding aids and collection guides are indeed valuable, and, since that time, the creation of Collection Level Descriptions (CLDs) provides welcome introductory and explanatory material for researchers. But in many cases there is no longer-term substitute in a research-based arts and humanities collection for physical access to unique items.

The postscript to this story is a happy one. Shortly after this event, London Guildhall University announced its intention to re-house The Fawcett Library in a new purpose-built building near its former basement location in east London. Considerable effort right across the university was invested in a series of funding applications to enable the library to leave its basement premises and move to the nearby wash houses site. Thanks to £4.2 million capital funding from the Heritage Lottery Fund and many other capital and revenue funders, a new building for the library, now renamed The Women's Library, was formally opened by the Rt Hon. Tessa Jowell, MP, Minister for Culture, Media and Sport, on 31 January 2002. The new building has exhibition and café facilities, as well as a reading room and collection storage. Many of the lessons learned in the flood of 11 August 1994 and its aftermath were transmitted in the briefing process for this building, now reflected in the security features to protect the collections in the exhibition, reading room and collection storage areas, and naturally in its DCP.

CONCLUSION

This chapter has been written from a practical perspective. It covers both the strategic and operational steps required to anticipate, prepare for and react to a flooding incident of any magnitude in a library and archive service. Even in the best-regulated and monitored organization, the possibility of a flooding incident can never be ruled out, for water, sewers and drains form integral parts of the fabric of buildings. As a consequence, risk assessments, DCPs and BCPs should be in place to cover eventualities. The author's personal experience underlines how disruptive a flooding incident can be. Its impact should never be under-estimated; but it is heartening to know that a stronger service can emerge from it.

NOTE

1. This case study is a revised and updated version of an article written by the author, 'The flood and afterwards: a new beginning for the Fawcett Library', which appeared in *Library Conservation News* (48), 1995:1–2, published by the National Preservation Office based at the British Library.

REFERENCES AND SELECT BIBLIOGRAPHY

STANDARDS

BSI (2000) *BS 5454:2000 Recommendations for the Storage and Display of Archival Documents*, London: BSI.
Historical Manuscripts Commission (2001) *HMC Standard for Record Repositories*, third edition, London: Historical Manuscripts Commission.

BOOKS

Matthews, G. and Eden, P. (1996) *Disaster Management in British Libraries: Project Report with Guidelines for Library Managers*, Library and Information Research Report 109, London: British Library.

THE M25 CONSORTIUM WEBSITES

The M25 Consortium of Academic Libraries Disaster Management Group. Available at: <www.m25lib.ac.uk/m25sec/business/disaster/disasterwghome.html>
The M25 Consortium of Higher Education Libraries Disaster Management Group Disaster Control Planning Site. Available at: <www.m25lib.ac.uk/M25dcp/>.

LIBRARY WEBSITES

Boston Public Library on 20 August 1998, available at: <www.ala.org/alaonline/news/1998/980824.html> [dead link].
Green Library at Stanford in 1998, available at: <news-service.stanford.edu/news.april1/flood41.html>.
Morgan Library of Colorado State University Libraries, available at: <lib.colostate.edu/library_history/overview.html> [dead link].
National Library of Canada, available at: <www.nlc-bnc.ca/1/1/n1-334-e.html>.
The Women's Library, London Guildhall University, available at: <www.thewomenslibrary.ac.uk>.

Following recent (August 2002) flooding in Europe, see
UNESCO, 'Floods in Europe: damages to libraries and archives' available at: <www.unesco.org/webworld/floods_europe>.
University of Sussex (2002), 'Library salvage operation underway', *Bulletin: The University of Sussex Newsletter*, 1st December. Available at: <www.sussex.ac.uk/press-office/bulletin/oldecoo/articles.html>

ORGANIZATIONS

Health and Safety Executive, <www.hse.gov.uk/>. For example, see, Health and Safety Executive (2002), 'A guide to risk assessment requirements. Common provisions in health and safety law', available (July 2002) at: <www.hse.gov.uk/pubns/indg218.pdf>.

National Preservation Office, whose aim is to provide an independent focus for ensuring the preservation and continued accessibility of library and archive material held in the UK and Ireland. Available at: <www.bl.uk/services/preservation/national.html>.

Institute of Paper Conservation (IPC), which is an organization devoted solely to the conservation of paper and related materials. Available at: <www.ipc.org.uk/introframe.htm>.

6 Cooperative activity in the USA, or misery loves company

Sheryl Davis and Kristen Kern

The USA has some interesting models of libraries cooperating to help each other manage disasters. The most extensive and varied examples are from the state of California, but there are many from other states. We address both of these, and then suggest some lessons which might be learned.

THE CALIFORNIA EXPERIENCE

Sheryl Davis

Currently, California has four regional networks that are devoted to preservation activities, all with a large component of activities dedicated to disaster management. These networks form the basis for achieving the goals of the California Preservation Program. One of the Program's highest ranked goals is to develop the ability of cultural institutions to prepare for and recover from disaster.

I am occasionally asked how Californians have been able to start, sustain and even increase regional disaster preparedness activities. To which I often respond: 'It helps to have an earthquake every now and then.' Sad, but true. While individual libraries and archives in the state have had devastating losses, it is the frequency with which California earthquakes occur that keeps the interest in disaster management alive. There is nothing like a small earthquake a few weeks before a disaster workshop to double the attendance.

THE LOS ANGELES CENTRAL LIBRARY FIRE

But it was not really an earthquake that got Californians started in cooperative disaster activities. It was the shocking arson at the Los Angeles Central Public Library (LAPL) in April 1986 that got our attention. The fire destroyed 400 000 of its 2.1 million volumes, making it the most destructive library fire in American history. An additional 700 000 books were wetted to varying degrees and the entire contents of the building had smoke damage. In all, more than 1.3 million volumes were damaged by water and smoke. The building, in essence, became a hothouse: heat from the fire, water from the fire hoses, and lack of ventilation made the perfect environment for mould and mildew, putting the entire collection at risk. It was quickly apparent that there were not enough internal resources (especially staff) to handle the removal of materials from the building. A call was put out for volunteers.

1500 people responded from all over the Los Angeles basin over three days. They worked in six-hour shifts around the clock; it took 44 000 cardboard boxes to pack out 600 000 items.

> The lack of a disaster plan did hinder the salvage operation. While most resources were managed well, this was not always true of people and their actions. Lack of preparation appears to be the consistent factor running throughout most of the problems encountered. The need for preparation and training is perhaps the most important lesson to be learned from this catastrophe. (Butler, 1986)

REASONS TO COOPERATE[1]

It was working in the aftermath of the LAPL fire that it became obvious that most organizations would not even be able to handle a disaster of far lesser magnitude unassisted. The volunteers were wonderful, but how much better it would have been to have people trained in how to handle and pack wet materials. Even a minor disaster can seriously disrupt day-to-day activities. It demands staff time and drains resources. A major crisis magnifies this impact.

A cooperative network is one of the most efficient strategies for maximizing library strengths *before* a disaster occurs. Networks vastly improve each library's ability to *respond* to and *recover* from disaster, while saving members time, money, and effort. Once a network is activated, benefits can multiply across the board. For instance, the work of locating vendors of disaster supplies and emergency equipment can be spread out among member libraries.

The network can spread out the work of developing a list of supplies and suppliers and make agreements with local vendors for items that cannot be stocked by individual libraries but would be needed during salvage efforts, such as fork-lifts, portable toilets, food and water, as well as freezers and freeze-dry facilities. While each library is responsible for maintaining a cache of basic emergency supplies, such as plastic sheeting, boxes, mops and flashlights, few libraries have enough money or space for on-site storage of enough supplies to cope with a major disaster. Even if space were available, in an emergency of great magnitude, supplies stored on-site might be inaccessible or damaged.

There are other less tangible benefits from participating in a network that are not so obvious. Network activities often attract the interest of the media, thus creating a lot of favourable publicity for network members. They also foster closer ties with neighbouring institutions and lead to cooperative efforts in other areas of mutual interest. And, there is nothing like going through a disaster together to create a bond.

Indeed, as one member of the Inland Empire Libraries Disaster Response Network will attest, the psychological support she received from the network members following an earthquake was the most important service. A disaster takes a tremendous emotional and physical toll, especially on the home staff. Some become emotionally devastated and unable to work at all; others push themselves to the point of exhaustion and may make errors in judgement. In such an emergency, colleagues from the network help the disaster officer think of the myriad details that need attention: they make phone calls, handle volunteers and supervise salvage crews. The network of disaster officers, with trained volunteers from their libraries, stand ready to aid the stricken library before its own staff reaches its limit. Because of the preliminary work done by the network, time is not lost trying to locate supplies and decide on the best plan of action.

After it is all over, the recovering library also has the strength of many added to its own, to put it all back together. Whether the need is air drying or reshelving volumes, the network will be there assisting in the aftermath, often providing temporary reference services to the clientele of the afflicted library.

The section that follows describes cooperative networks that have been set up in California under the umbrella of California Regional Preservation Networks: IELDRN, SILDRN, LAPNet, BAPnet and other challenging acronyms!

INLAND EMPIRE LIBRARIES DISASTER RESPONSE NETWORK (IELDRN)

<http://www.ieldrn.org/>
Library of California – Tierra Del Sol region

About 50 miles east of Los Angeles in Southern California is a large central valley known as the Inland Empire. It was here, in 1987, that IELDRN was established by libraries in Riverside, San Bernardino, and part of Los Angeles counties to provide mutual aid in response to any type of library disaster.

The University of California Riverside (UCR) Library, with the only trained preservation librarian in the region, took the lead in forming the network. The university librarian proposed the network to the directors of academic libraries in the region. Each was asked to send a representative – hopefully the person in their library who would be responsible for organizing disaster response activities – to meet with UCR's Preservation Officer to explore the idea further. The major public libraries in the region were contacted and invited to attend.

Representatives from five academic libraries, three city libraries, two county libraries, and the already existing multitype library cooperative providing interlibrary loans and reference support for the region attended the first meeting.

This group became the IELDRN Steering Committee. Over the years, three more academic libraries and another city library have joined the Steering Committee. In all, this group represents more than 90 libraries, from major academic to 'storefront' public.

The most frustrating and challenging task a network may confront (one hopes) is finding agreement on a name to call itself. It took the Inland Empire Libraries Disaster Response Network (IELDRN) three meetings to come up with that long-winded name!

Over the first few meetings, the group also developed the following mission statement:

Mission:

The Inland Empire Libraries Disaster Response Network (IELDRN) is a cooperative organization established for the purpose of mutual aid in preparing for and coping with disasters.

It seeks

1) to assist member libraries in the development of their disaster and collection salvage plan;
2) to organize workshops and seminars in order to acquire the expertise needed to cope with disasters;
3) to acquire, on a cooperative basis, supplies and equipment to support the disaster preparedness and collection salvage programs of member institutions;
4) to prepare and disseminate to any interested library, lists of preservation and disaster services, supplies and suppliers, and resource persons, etc.; and bibliographies on disaster preparation and recovery;
5) to set up subcommittees and task forces to deal with specific, identified problems;
6) to serve as a model and encourage the development of similar networks.

(Inland Empire Libraries Disaster Response Network, 2000a)

The first Steering Committee project was to write a grant application to obtain funds from the California State Library for fiscal year 1988–89. The grant was to sponsor three workshops on earthquake preparedness, fire safety, library disaster plans, and the handling of wet books. It was also to explore whether it was possible to develop a mutually owned set of disaster supplies and equipment and the feasibility of a written mutual aid agreement. The grant application was welcomed as a groundbreaking model of multi-type library cooperation.

The Mutual Aid Agreement

If IELDRN thought finding a name was challenging, the Mutual Aid Agreement took three years and nine lawyers to hammer out (see Figure 6.1). Drafted by the

University of California lawyers, each member of IELDRN had it reviewed by its own institution's lawyers. The back and forth seemed endless until we were satisfied with a document that basically says that the libraries can give each other help as each of them wish and are able. The lack of precedent for this type of agreement was what delayed the process.

Co-owned disaster supplies

A second grant was applied for and received from the State Library for 1989–90. This grant provided US$8400 to purchase disaster response supplies to be co-owned by all the member libraries.

Originally the plan was to store the supplies in a rental facility, but the idea of the on-going financial commitment of rental fees seemed daunting. Instead, the State Library agreed to modification of the grant to allow the funds to be spent for the purchase of two storage containers to be placed in widely spaced areas in the Inland Empire. The California State Polytechnic University in Pomona, offered space for a small container on their Library's loading dock. A much larger one was placed on the UCR campus. IELDRN members agreed to contribute enough funds to fill the containers with supplies sufficient to pack 20 000 wet books.

The supplies include a dehumidifier, paper towels and blank newsprint paper to wick moisture out of books, boxes in which to pack books in preparation for freeze-drying, natural rubber sponges to wipe soot from books, and so on. Figure 6.2 is the list of shared supplies in one container. Every IELDRN member library has a key to the nearest container. Any member can draw from the supplies to assist in recovery from a localized disaster, with the requirement to replace them within 90 days. Payment of a joining fee by the membership allows the cache inventories to be enhanced and outdated supplies to be discarded and replaced.

On two occasions libraries needing help following an earthquake have invoked the agreement.

The Libraries of the Claremont Colleges requested help after the 28 February 1990 Upland earthquake, when they sustained significant shelving damage during a 5.5 earthquake. IELDRN responded to the Claremont request for help even though the member libraries' directors had not yet signed the final version of the agreement. The Steering Committee toured the site 42 hours after the earthquake (and during some significant after-shocks). Over the subsequent ten days IELDRN libraries sent staff to assist in reshelving more than 300 000 books. The Los Angeles Preservation Network (LAPNet), with whom IELDRN has a close relationship, also assisted in the recovery. It may sound callous, but helping at someone else's library's disaster is one of the best training techniques for staff in disaster response – far better than any planned workshop.

Inland Empire Libraries Disaster Response Network [IELDRN]

Mutual Aid Agreement

This AGREEMENT is made and entered into by and between the libraries [whose chief executive officer, or the chief executive officer of the institution or agency to which the library belongs, has signed the AGREEMENT], hereinafter referred to as 'parties' and is effective on the date executed.

RECITALS

Whereas, the parties hereto are libraries of agencies or institutions generally located in, or near, the Inland Empire; and

Whereas, the expertise and authority of the Disaster Recovery Coordinators and Disaster Recovery Teams of each party hereto to perform such services and to exercise such functions are limited by and may be performed only within the institution or agency employing them; and

Whereas, it would not be economical for any library, institution or agency, to purchase and store all of the supplies and equipment which would be needed to cope with a major disaster; and

Whereas, the parties hereto are desirous of providing mutual disaster recovery assistance beyond their own institution or agency; and

Whereas, it is contended that mutual disaster recovery assistance would be beneficial to all parties hereto:

NOW THEREFORE it is agreed as follows:

1. The contracting parties will share the purchase of emergency supplies and equipment, needed for salvaging library materials following a localized emergency. These contributions would be through providing funds for purchase, through donation of previously purchased supplies/equipment, or through other in-kind contributions equivalent to funds as determined by the Steering Committee. These supplies will be considered the common property of the parties solely for emergency purposes.

2. Any party to this AGREEMENT may withdraw at any time, upon a thirty day written notice to each of the other parties, and thereafter, such withdrawing party shall no longer be a party of the AGREEMENT, but this AGREEMENT shall continue to exist among the remaining parties. None of the parties hereto shall incur any liability to the other by reason of such termination, nor shall the withdrawing party have claims to the supplies/equipment contributed through funds, purchase or otherwise.

3. The contracting parties are responsible for the cost and maintenance of two storage containers. If a Network member housing a container withdraws from the Network, the container will be moved at the Network's expense. If the Network disbands the containers will be sold and the money pro-rated [based on size of the collection] and dispersed among the members.

4. In the event of any natural or man-made disaster which cannot be conveniently or expeditiously met with the emergency supplies held locally, upon request from its designated administrator or from its Disaster Recovery Coordinator, the affected party shall be given immediate access to the supplies in the store. And following the emergency, the party withdrawing supplies from the store will replace in kind within 90 days of removal.

5. Similarly in the event of any natural or man-made disaster which cannot be conveniently or expeditiously met with local emergency personnel, the other contracting parties hereto agree, upon request from the designated administrator or Disaster Recovery Coordinator, to furnish the aid of their Disaster Recovery Teams in coping with such situation to the party requesting such aid upon either an actual or standby basis. Such personnel will be provided at the option of the lending agency and may be denied without recourse to the requesting agency. The extent of the aid to be furnished under this agreement shall be determined solely by the party furnishing the aid, and it is understood that the aid so furnished may be recalled at the sole discretion of the furnishing party.

6. Disaster Recovery personnel of one party performing services at another library under this agreement shall be subject to the control, supervision and direction in such performance of administrative personnel designated for such purpose by the party for whose library the performance is rendered. Nothing herein, however, shall be construed as giving any authority to personnel of one party over personnel of another party with respect to standards of performance, advancement, compensation and discipline of personnel or similar administrative matter.

7. Employees furnished by a lending party pursuant to this AGREEMENT shall be considered to be acting for their employer in pursuit of lawful duties, and any wages, salaries, compensation claims or other costs relating to their employment will be borne by the lending party.

8. No party to this agreement shall be required to pay any compensation to any other party to this AGREEMENT for services rendered hereunder, the mutual advantages and protection afforded by this AGREEMENT being considered adequate compensation to all of the parties.

9. Nothing contained in this AGREEMENT shall be construed to make any party hereto or any of its employees, the employee of any other party.

10. Any party to this Agreement shall defend, indemnify and hold harmless all other parties to this Agreement from and against any and all liability, loss, expense, attorneys' fees, or claims for injury or damages arising out of the performance of this Agreement, but only in proportion to and to the extent such liability, loss, expense, attorneys' fees, or claims for injury or damages are caused by or result from the negligent or intentional acts or omissions of the party, its officers, agents, or employees.

Contract expires in five years from date of signing.

If all the parties to the AGREEMENT determine that IELDRN should be dissolved, the store of supplies will be disbursed to the parties involved in the same proportion as their respective contributions over the lifetime of the agreement, both in equipment and supplies, and in storage costs. All equipment and supplies contributed in kind in lieu of purchase will be returned to the parties which provided them originally, with their assumed value being the fair contribution. All remaining jointly purchased equipment and supplies will be distributed on a pro-rated basis, with the values of in-kind contributions being included in the distribution determination.

IN WITNESS WHEREOF, the parties have executed this AGREEMENT as of the date the first herein above written.
Executed by:

this _____ day of _____ 19___, _____
                                                                            Library Director
Executed by:

this _____ day of _____ 19___, _____
                                                                            Library Director

April 26, 1989
Revised: April 16, 1990
This page last changed: January 27, 1997

Figure 6.1   IELDRN Mutual Aid Agreement
(Reproduced with permission of Administrator, IELDRN. Available at: <www.ieldrn.org/mutual.html>).

**IELDRN CARGO CONTAINER SUPPLIES Location: Corporation
Yard, UC Riverside**

ITEM	AMOUNT
Boxes (flattened), lids separate	
12x15x10	725 each
18x18x18	200 each
Clear 3M Plastic Sealing Tape	57 rolls
Clip Boards	6 each
Dehumidifier	1 each
Document Cleaning Pads	190 (approx)
Felt Tip Markers (Black)	5 each
Flashlight (inside door right wall)	1 each
D size batteries (last checked 9-6-91)	2 each
Freezer Paper (1811 x 30′)	2 pkgs (500 in each pkg)
Gasoline Container (Galvanized Steel, 5 gallon capacity)	1 each
Generator, Medium Duty **	
(MAX VA 4400, 8HP, 120V 20AMP, 25x18x18.3″)	1 each
Wheel/Handle Kit for Generator #GA100	1 each
Gloves	1 pair
Hard Hats	
Red	8 each
White	47 each
Index Cards (3 x 5)	1 pkg
Lamps, Philips Rough Service (100 watt, 120v)	20 each
Lantern (beam), with battery <Industrial-6volt-Sealed>	1 each
Lights, Light-A-Sight Temporary Construction String 100 ft with 10 ft guards and sockets at 10 ft intervals	2 each
Moisture Content Reader and Electrode**	1 each
Newsprint Paper (24″ x 30″)	2 pkg (100 lbs)
Pallets (flattened boxes on top of them)	3 each
Polyethylene Tarp (8 x 10′)	3 each
Reinforced Paper Gummed Tape	8 rolls
Scissors (6″)	4 pairs
Sealing Tape Dispensers	9 each
Shrink Wrap	4 rolls
Shrink Wrap Dispenser	1 each
Simple Green (1 gal)	2 each
Smoke Off Sponges	2 cases (36 in each case)
Spray Bottles (empty)	8 each
UCR Plastic Crates	59 each

Date checked: _____

**Stored with Sheryl Davis at Rivera Library.

Figure 6.2 IELDRN list of shared supplies
(Reproduced with permission of Administrator, IELDRN. Available at: <www.ieldrn.org/supplies.html>.)

The second instance was following the 1992 Big Bear-Landers earthquake. The earthquake caused tens of thousands of books to fall throughout the region's libraries and collapsed stacks at the San Bernardino County Library Big Bear branch.

When a disaster affects the entire region those libraries closest to the location of the stored supplies are the most likely to be able to reach and use the supplies. Since only books were down in every library, and there was no water or fire damage, the only request for supplies from the storage containers was for the hard hats for nervous staff working in book stacks during aftershocks. The same earthquake did substantial damage to the University of Redlands library. While not a member of IELDRN at that time, they requested and received advice and consultation. (For illustrations showing the effect of earthquakes on libraries, see the IELDRN website at: <www.ieldrn.org/PhotoAlbum/photos.htm>.)

There have been many small-scale water-related disasters among the member libraries but they are now able to cope with minimal need to consult with other members or use the storage container supplies.

The IELDRN generic disaster plan

As part of the 1989–90 grant, IELDRN wrote a 'fill-in-the-blanks' disaster plan and made it available on diskette. It is designed for use by libraries who wanted a basic framework to assist them in writing their own plan. 'Fill-in-the-blank' disaster plans are more common now, but the use of word-processing software that institutions could tailor the files to their own needs and allowing for easy revised and updated was an innovation then. It is now available on several websites (including <www.palimpsest.stanford.edu>, <www.cpc.stanford.edu>), as well as IELDRN's website (Inland Empire Libraries Disaster Response Network, 2000b).

The disaster plan is divided into four units: Disaster Preparedness and Prevention, Disaster Response, Disaster Recovery Restoration Methods and Disaster Recovery and Completion. It contains forms that can be printed to take on a building inspection and to provide a paper trail for fixing, replacing, ordering, and so on. The plan is also intended to serve as a training document to familiarize staff with the actions they need to take during and immediately following a disaster. Most importantly, it becomes the action document to guide people through the steps they must take in response to and recovery from a disaster.

Education and training

IELDRN's commitment to education and training for disasters has resulted in an effort to present two programmes a year on some aspect of emergency preparation, response or recovery. One of the most requested programmes is a full day's training on the major parts of a disaster plan and a simulated wet books pack-out. Other regularly repeated programmes include air-drying and other recovery methods, seismic bracing and building assessment.

The programmes consistently receive very high evaluations by attendees, but perhaps the best measure of IELDRN's effectiveness came from a 1998 survey. The California State Library commissioned a survey of the preservation needs of libraries throughout the state. The survey showed that more libraries in the Inland Empire had disaster plans and felt better prepared than any other region of California. This is not to say that the work is done, but past training efforts have been effective.

As IELDRN has become increasingly part of the California Preservation Program (see below) it has taken on the role of promoting that statewide initiative.

Becoming a member

To join IELDRN, the director or head of the library applying for membership must agree to the terms of the Mutual Aid Agreement and sign it. A one-time fee of US$150 is currently required. Then, the library must appoint a person to be its representative on the IELDRN Steering Committee. The person need not have prior knowledge of disaster planning, but must be willing to participate in and be in support of the Network's activities.

The Steering Committee meets once a quarter for regular meetings, and more often when a programme is being planned. Meetings are scheduled at least once in every member's library. After the meeting, the Steering Committee tours the library to understand its layout in case they are called in to help in a disaster. The group also does a cursory building survey as they walk through. It is often helpful to have fresh eyes view your work environment and 10–15 pairs of eyes can see a lot in a short time, especially with experience.

THE LOS ANGELES PRESERVATION NETWORK (LAPNet)

<www.lapnet.org/AboutUs.html>
Library of California – Arroyo Seco region

LAPNet started a few months before IELDRN in 1987 and has included disaster training among a full range of preservation training:

> The Los Angeles Preservation Network (LAPNet) was established in January 1987 to meet some of the preservation needs of librarians, archivists, conservators and records managers working in Los Angeles City and county. Its affairs are managed by a Steering Committee of ten to fifteen members drawn from libraries and other record depositories in the Los Angeles area. The Committee hopes to involve a wide range of

interested professionals in the activities of the network by inviting them to serve on subcommittees and task forces and to participate in workshops and seminars. LAPNet aims to foster the development of cooperative preservation programs among all the libraries in Los Angeles, irrespective of size or type, and to serve as a forum of information exchange between librarians and others concerned with preservation and conservation. (Los Angeles Preservation Network, 2002)

LAPNet list of disaster supplies and suppliers

A wonderful resource developed by the University of California Los Angeles Library's Preservation Office and mounted on the LAPNet website is a list of disaster supplies and suppliers. 'Although the List attempts to include all the necessary supplies and services for disaster response, it is not a comprehensive directory for their sources. In the choice of suppliers there is a bias in favor of those situated in and around Los Angeles, or national suppliers with local outlets' (Los Angeles Preservation Network, 2001).

The well-designed website offers a number of documents useful to disaster management.

SAN DIEGO IMPERIAL LIBRARY DISASTER RESPONSE NETWORK (SILDRN)

<www.orpheus.ucsd.edu/sildrn/>
Library of California – Tierra del Sol region

The Preservation Officer of University of California San Diego Library (Julie Page) started SILDRN in 1995. It was modelled on IELDRN with a similar mission and goals. SILDRN's region is the San Diego and Imperial counties of California. SILDRN adopted the Mutual Aid Agreement, has shared supplies in four storage containers and gives programmes and workshops for their region. SILDRN also has a Steering Committee of 12 to 15 members. Yearly membership dues of US$150 were assessed for the first five years of its existence.

SILDRN's website has useful information on disaster preparedness (San Diego Imperial Library Disaster Response Network, 2002).

THE BAY AREA PRESERVATION NETWORK (BAPnet)

<www.palimpsest.stanford.edu/byorg/bapnet/>
Library of California – Golden Gateway region

BAPnet's plan was to emulate both the LAPNet and IELDRN models in Northern California, especially the area around San Francisco. It applied for and received a grant from the California State Library; it had byelaws and has a website; it gave five training programmes on disaster management. Then, in early 1998, all activity stopped. There are patterns and life cycles to a cooperative network, reasons for failure and success which will be discussed briefly later in this chapter: Why Networks Fail (pp. 138–9). One hopes that this network is merely dormant and will come to life again. Some members of BAPnet are active members of the California Preservation Task Force (see below).

UNIVERSITY OF CALIFORNIA PRESERVATION ADVISORY GROUP (PAG)

<www.library.ucsb.edu/ucpag/ucpag.html#charge>

The existing California Preservation Networks, especially the three in Southern California, have always been close, sharing workshops, materials, speakers and ideas. Undoubtedly this is because they were all formed by University of California Library Preservation Officers.

The University of California Berkeley Library Conservation Department trained one person from each of the nine (soon to be ten) campuses over 1988–89 and 1989–90. This formed a systemwide committee, called the Preservation Advisory Group (PAG), which meets twice a year to discuss areas of mutual concern. The Chair is selected by the membership for a two-year term. While a number of the original Preservation Officers have left, they have always been replaced – often by a person without training but with an interest and desire to serve.

In the area of disaster management PAG members all have disaster plans and a shared cache of disaster supplies stored at the university's two (north and south) Regional Library Storage Facilities.

Its charge to the University of California (UC) PAG is to:

- Advise the UC Collection Development Committee on preservation issues.
- Coordinate systemwide preservation activities related to the California Digital Library's (CDL) responsibilities for preservation of digital collections.
- Coordinate preservation policies among the campus library systems and the CDL.
- Develop preservation services with the broadest possible cost-savings for UC libraries.
- Serve as an education and discussion group for its members on preservation issues and innovations.
- Serve as a focus for information dissemination on preservation issues for the University of California and the State of California.
- Communicate with all other campus groups, University task forces and other common interest groups on preservation issues.
- Serve as a liaison group to other state agencies, and library or preservation

consortia for developing cooperative and cost-effective approaches to preservation.
(University of California Preservation Advisory Group, 1999)

CALIFORNIA PRESERVATION PROGRAM AND THE LIBRARY OF CALIFORNIA

<www.cpc.stanford.edu/library/calpresprog/>

California Preservation Program was first designed in 1991 under the auspices of the California State Library. Following a survey of the preservation needs of cultural institutions throughout the state and a series of statewide meetings of librarians and archivists, a California Preservation Task Force was assembled to design the components of the state Preservation Program.

The mission of the Program is to identify and preserve important archival and library materials in information agencies of all types and sizes in California to ensure continuing public access. The initiatives designed to accomplish this were to:

- develop and provide a broad programme of education in training in preservation
- assist information agencies of types and sizes to develop and implement preservation programmes
- promote cooperative and coordinated preservation efforts in order to maximize the effective use of finances, personnel, materials and other resources.

From the beginning it was planned that the California Preservation Program (CPP) would become part of the Library of California (LoC). The Library of California is a statewide programme

'to provide equitable access to library materials and information resources for all Californians. Administered by the California State Library, under the policy direction of the Library of California Board, this program has both a statewide component for infrastructure support and development, and a regional component for direct service delivery to and through libraries. Seven regional library networks provide the regional services specified in the Library of California Act' (Library of California, 2001).

Those services currently funded are Interlibrary Loan and Direct Loan, Reference, Resource Libraries, Statewide Information Databases and Young Adult Services. The preservation component of the LoC has not yet received permanent funding.

The lack of funding has not deterred members of the California Preservation Task Force (CPTF). The CPTF is composed of a committed group of individuals striving to meet the preservation needs of their regions and reach out to the rest of the state until permanent funding for preservation is available.

With the encouragement of the State Library, the Task Force developed an action plan for 1998–2000 and received grant funds to support some of the high priority action items originally identified in a 1991 document and confirmed by a 1998 survey.

The CPTF determined that the most effective way of making information available to a broad audience would be through a website. To that end, the California Preservation Clearinghouse (CPC) was created.[2]

CALIFORNIA PRESERVATION CLEARINGHOUSE

www.cpc.stanford.edu/

Mission:

To preserve the collections of California's cultural institutions by providing preservation information for the staff of those institutions. It is intended to be an online resource for the staff of libraries, archives and other cultural institutions who recognize the need for preservation and disaster preparedness, book repair, training and more.

Goals:

To assist staff working in cultural institutions who are concerned about preserving their collections but lack the specific knowledge and information resources necessary to preserve their collections by helping them:

- to become more knowledgeable about preservation;
- to be able to identify needs and concerns;
- to prepare for and properly respond to disasters;
- to, in turn, help educate others.

A website to help cultural institutions and people who want a basic, practical understanding of what steps they can take to:

- Repair circulating books and documents
- Prepare for a disaster affecting buildings and collections
- Educate staff and users on how to handle material in a non-damaging way
- Deal with mold and bug infestations
- Conduct preservation assessments of collections

An online mailing list, *California Libraries and Archives Preservation* (CaLibArc-Preserve@lists.stanford.edu) is monitored by preservation librarians to answer questions and concerns on preservation topics of interest to California librarians, archivists, records managers and other information professionals. (Davis and Page, 2001)

OTHER ACTIVITIES

A 1998 survey indicated that one-third of all California libraries and cultural institutions have experienced a disaster, natural or man-made, but that the majority do not have a written disaster plan. Therefore, one of the first sections developed for the Clearinghouse was on disaster management.

Disaster management was also the focus of the first workshops developed for the state by the CPTF. Two-day disaster preparedness and recovery workshops were designed and the first four were held in May 2002. Attendees are taught about risk assessment and what to do to begin to prepare a disaster plan for their institution (day one). In the intervening weeks, before day two of the workshop, they receive personal mentoring/consulting services from their trainers as they attempt to complete their plan. Day two of the workshop focuses on basic training in disaster recovery through hands-on salvage exercises.

A group of consultants has been trained to conduct building surveys for collection management.

Through workshops and other means, the CPTF identifies potential trainers and consultants. It is planned that a core of consultants will be available throughout the state to perform building and collections assessments, assist in grant writing, and writing disaster plans. Further, it is hoped that staff trained in disaster response will eventually be so widespread that any cultural institution suffering a disaster will have a number of people within easy reach to assist it.

The long-term goal is to have a fully functioning California Preservation Program within the Library of California supported by permanent state funding. Such an entity would have a Preservation Information Center providing training and education; preservation information resources; grant writing assistance; site surveys and needs assessments; disaster response and recovery information; outreach to underserved areas; and advocacy for preservation within the state.

Until that funding occurs, the CPTF is determined to set up and support as many aspects of the California Preservation Plan as possible (Davis and Page, 2002).

CONCLUSIONS

Looking at the many different ways Californians are trying to network disaster management activities one might conclude we are a little paranoid. Our climate is envied for its moderation and its many sunny days. However, those of us who live in the state know that there are really three distinct seasons: flood, fire and earthquake.

In the states and regions where they have real weather there are also models of cooperation; some even pre-dating California's earliest networks. The next section describes some of them.

COOPERATIVE ACTIVITY: OTHER US MODELS
Kristen Kern

Models for cooperative disaster management between libraries have also developed in states other than California. There follow three examples of cooperative efforts in Oklahoma, New Mexico and Oregon. In other parts of the country, library networks providing a number of library-related services can also offer assistance in the event of an emergency striking a member institution. These networks are members of the Regional Alliance for Preservation which is described following these examples.

Cooperative disaster management initiatives in California have set a high standard for others elsewhere to follow. Members of a library consortium in the Portland, Oregon, metropolitan area undertaking cooperative disaster planning have looked to the California model for successful ideas to implement. In other parts of the USA, preservation or conservation alliances, connected formally or through individuals to the state library, have organized cooperative disaster management enterprises. Examples of the group in Oregon following California's lead and those more closely aligned with state library organizations in New Mexico and Oklahoma are described below.

In addition, there are numerous governmental and non-profit agency sites on the internet that provide excellent general and site-specific information on disaster response and recovery. For example, the Colorado Preservation Alliance lists local agencies and response companies that can offer immediate assistance (Colorado Preservation Alliance); FEMA, the Federal Emergency Management Agency and Heritage Preservation (Federal Emergency Management Agency), an organization of the nation's leading museums, libraries and archives, historic preservation organizations and historical societies have co-sponsored The Heritage Emergency National Task Force that helps individuals and institutions protect their collections in times of disaster (Heritage Emergency National Task Force).

OKLAHOMA DISASTER RECOVERY ASSISTANCE TEAM (O-DRAT)

One of the most venerable models of cooperative disaster management in the USA is the Oklahoma Disaster Recovery Assistance Team (O-DRAT). O-DRAT began as part of the Oklahoma Chapter of the Western Council of Conservation, which in 1983–84 changed its name to the Oklahoma Conservation Congress (OCC). This small organization holds periodic meetings of its executive board, comprising officers and member representatives from O-DRAT, as part of the disaster preparedness committee, and the education committee and publications committee. The congress collects dues from its membership of around 20, which includes interested individuals and corporate entities such as the state library, universities and colleges. The Oklahoma Conservation Congress centres its efforts on preservation and holding educational workshops.

Because of the state library support for the Oklahoma Conservation Congress, a mutual aid agreement has not been established between members. Disasters at institutions in Oklahoma are typically reported first to the State Library, then referred to the Administrative Archivist and Preservation Officer for the Oklahoma Department of Libraries. While disasters can strike all types of institutions, his primary responsibility is to state agencies affected by a disaster. Depending on the severity of the emergency, other institutions may need to contact Amigos, a regional clearinghouse of library services (Amigos, 2002) and a member of the Regional Alliance for Preservation (see pp. 137–8), including disaster salvage and recovery information.

The State Library maintains a cache of disaster response supplies that can be shared with other institutions at the consent of the Administrative Archivist and Preservation Officer. For large emergencies, outside firms are contracted for salvage operations. The State Library possesses a disaster plan that assisted in the smoother response to a water damage disaster occurring to the State Archives. A broken tap resulted in the building being closed for four days while floors and vents were cleaned, carpets dried, and over 1600 boxes of library and archival material was prepared and sent offsite for vacuum freeze drying.

The State Administrative Archivist delivers record management training. He uses this as an opportunity to emphasize the need for agencies to proceed with writing a disaster plan if they have not prepared one already (Harrington, 2002). Due no doubt to his efforts, a number of state agencies, colleges and universities in the state have completed disaster plans.

NEW MEXICO DRAT

This is another model of cooperative disaster management developed in the state of New Mexico through the efforts of the New Mexico Preservation Alliance. The New Mexico Preservation Alliance was formed over ten years ago, and became an official interest group of the New Mexico Library Association in the mid 1990s. University and public librarians, archivists from the state, universities and museums, county clerks, government organizations, historical societies and tribal archivists are members of the informally organized alliance. Training has been a positive outcome in the late 1990s for the New Mexico Preservation Alliance. Three years ago, the Alliance sponsored a well-received emergency preparedness and recovery workshop presented by a member of Amigos. Two years ago, in 2000, the Alliance sponsored an archival holdings maintenance training that was also well attended. The Alliance has made a conscious effort to address the geographic disparity in New Mexico, holding most of its meetings in the middle of the state, and the archival holdings maintenance workshops in four different locations.

In 2000, wild fires devastated parts of northern and southern New Mexico, particularly in Los Alamos, near Santa Fe. The city was evacuated, including the local historical society and public library. The State Archivist in Santa Fe, the Southwest Studies Librarian and then chair of the Preservation Alliance at the palace of the governor's history library, and others were concerned and determined that a network of contacts should be established to provide emergency response assistance. The potential for serious fire outbreaks for 2002, the time of writing this, is high. This network is in the initial stages of formation.

The New Mexico disaster team is modelled after the O-DRAT. The State Archivist and the State Librarian, located in the same building, in Santa Fe, volunteered to be the central contact point for the state disaster recovery effort. The idea was that agencies coping with an emergency would call the State Archives or State Library that would then provide a list of contacts who could offer local assistance.

A disaster team steering committee of six or seven people was established. A priority for the committee was developing a brochure for disseminating the emergency response contact information. A member of staff from the State Archives was enlisted to design the flyers, which were completed in summer, 2001. The committee determined several crucial distribution points. Archival workshops, funded by the New Mexico Historic Records Advisory Board, and the New Mexico Library Association annual meeting are logical places to distribute the brochure, now in need of revision.

Ann Massman, the Southwest Studies Librarian and former Chair of the Preservation Alliance, cautions that in the case of a volunteer effort, such as the disaster recovery assistance team, volunteers providing needed outreach services face the challenge of their efforts being in addition to their normal jobs, and that the voluntary activity may become too sporadic or even grind to a halt. What formal entities such as Amigos, state libraries and archives can accomplish is important for sustaining initiatives (Massman, 2002).

A fortunate situation in New Mexico is that the core group of Preservation Alliance participants come from varied backgrounds. The broader group of people interested in preservation who have been reached by the alliance include librarians, archivists, and staff from a wide variety of the state's archives, records, and library institutions. The Preservation Alliance's affiliation and contact with the New Mexico State Library and the New Mexico Historic Records Advisory Board (a part of the National Historical Publications and Records Commission) are to be credited for much of this broad support. Approximately 100 people, including members of the Pueblo, Navajo and Apache tribes, have also expressed an interest in more training and becoming involved with the Alliance.

PORTALS DISASTER RECOVERY GROUP (DIRG)

A model for cooperative disaster management that arose out of a metropolitan Portland, Oregon, consortium is the Disaster Recovery Group, otherwise known as DIRG (PORTALS, disaster recovery group members). DIRG is the disaster response arm of PORTALS, a consortium founded in 1993 to meet the research and educational needs of libraries in the greater Portland region through cooperative and creative access to information resources and services. What makes the consortium somewhat unique is its composition. Private and public universities, community colleges, public libraries and an historical society in the states of Oregon and Washington are members of PORTALS. In the summer of 2000, PORTALS Library Council, the consortium's governing body of library directors, sought out other possible cooperative activities to undertake. The council agreed that disaster planning and management would be mutually beneficial for PORTAL's membership.

At DIRG's first meeting in August 2000, the PORTALS Executive Director convened selected representatives from seven of the institutions. First on the agenda was a discussion of what was meant by disaster planning. It was agreed that disaster prevention and recovery, and initial and follow-up responses to disasters were most important. If there are disaster plans or initiatives from the larger institutions, the library should connect to them. Each member institution would necessarily develop an individual list of emergency contacts.

The notion of a disaster plan template with a general outline that could be customized for each library arose at the meeting. The template would include common background information, local and regional human and facilities resources available for libraries, mutual aid agreements, and a list of emergency response supplies. Model plans and disaster management information would be scanned into the PORTALS website.

In fact much of the background information utilized to begin establishing DIRG was borrowed from SILDRN that in turn had used the IELDRN model to establish itself. A mutual aid agreement, the list of emergency response supplies useful for individual libraries as well as the outfitting of containers for cooperative disaster supplies, were adopted from these vanguard cooperative entities.

Training was an obviously critical need in order to provide knowledge for PORTALS members and to initiate library disaster planning. Arranging for a two-day workshop that would focus on both institutional and inter-institutional planning ensued.

Lastly, establishing a mutual aid agreement, following IELDRN's model, was determined a priority. This would require the commitment of each council member, but would allow for a corps of trained workers to be available on a volunteer basis to assist another library in the event of a disaster. In the end, after drafts of a mutual aid agreement were brought to the Library Council for its review, the Council members agreed that wording be added to the consortium's bylaws rather than having a separate agreement. The bylaws state that each PORTALS member will 'maintain a current disaster preparedness plan and participate in mutual recovery aid when needed' (PORTALS, Bylaws). The council accepted the DIRG charge: 'DIRG will facilitate emergency response preparation, promote emergency response awareness, and coordinate emergency response training for member libraries'.

DIRG sponsored its first major training in late autumn, 2000. Tom Clareson, then of Amigos, presented a two-day workshop held in two different locations that covered the basics of disaster preparedness and recovery. The first day's session held at a community college focused on what constitutes a disaster, disaster prevention, setting priorities, and creating a disaster plan. In an empty industrial building, the second day provided hands-on experience recovering material damaged in a disaster. Labouring to salvage various media drenched in water enlightened participants to the real challenges involved in responding to a library emergency.

A follow-up training for disaster management took place in the spring of 2001. Julie A. Page, Preservation Librarian at the University of California, San Diego, organized and facilitated a session entitled, 'Exercising Your Disaster Plans'. Developed with Sheryl Davis, Preservation Librarian at the UCR, the exercise centred on a scenario describing a plausible disaster befalling a library.

Before the groups convened, members of DIRG, coached ahead of time, acted out a short, 15-minute demonstration of the tabletop exercise. Roles corresponding to personnel designated to respond in case of a disaster were assigned to workshop attendees. These roles included a budget/finance officer, facilities director, art librarian, cataloguer/recorder, and library director, each role placed in a different group. Each role's designees were briefed on what their particular perspective towards the disaster response would be.

After separating into groups, the teams were given a copy of the library's abbreviated disaster plan with an accompanying map of the library's floor plan. The discussion of the group as it grappled with how to respond to the disaster was subtly guided by a DIRG member facilitator to ensure that teaching points outlined in the instructor's script were covered. Most importantly, the need for planning emerged, as it became evident that even with a plan, there were many other issues to face under difficult circumstances. Other critical points raised during deliberations were the need for creating a command centre, dealing with staff, assessing damage, and following or reordering salvage priorities depending on the extent of damage incurred by the disaster. After approximately 45 minutes, the groups ceased their individual discussions to share as a whole the lessons of the exercise.

Later in the spring, DIRG members presented an abbreviated version of the 'Exercising your disaster plan' training to the PORTALS Library Council members. A short demonstration of the tabletop exercise preceded the library directors' enacting the roles in response to the scenario.

During the academic year, DIRG documentation was made accessible at the PORTALS website. Minutes from DIRG meetings (PORTALS, disaster recovery group documents), the template disaster plan (PORTALS, disaster prevention and recovery template plan) and disaster recovery information links (PORTALS, disaster recovery information links) are found at PORTALS committees under governance. One of the aims of DIRG's emergency preparedness effort was to develop a list of local resources that can be called upon for assistance in the event of an emergency. In the autumn of 2001, as a step towards this goal, DIRG members were able to visit a cold storage facility located in the town of one of the private university members of PORTALS, thanks to the local DIRG member. A letter of understanding between PORTALS and the cold storage company that does not stipulate any obligation, but recognizes the possible use of the facility by DIRG libraries will be considered by the Library Council.

Another intention of DIRG was to situate and furnish a cooperative emergency response cache in the greater metropolitan area. The supply centre would be accessible to all PORTALS members on an as needed basis to assist in the salvage of library materials. This project required funding to succeed. A proposal to fund the supplies and emergency preparedness training was being developed and funding sources identified as this chapter was being written.

DIRG members continued to undergo disaster planning training by participating in a group tabletop exercise and sharing in the process of completing institutional disaster plans.

REGIONAL ALLIANCE FOR PRESERVATION (RAP)

Another model of organizational cooperation that includes disaster management can be found in the Regional Alliance for Preservation (RAP) (Regional Alliance for Preservation, 2002a). RAP began in 1997 as a pilot project of the Commission on Preservation and Access in Washington, DC to foster cooperation among the Preservation Field Service programmes funded by a major supporter of preservation activities in the USA, the National Endowment for the Humanities (NEH). The participants in the pilot programme chose to continue RAP as a cooperative programme when the funding concluded a year later, and expanded the alliance to include members of the Association of Regional Conservation Centers (ARCC). The alliance publishes an occasional newsletter and maintains a website.

The mission of the 14 member organizations is 'to provide comprehensive preservation information to cultural institutions and the public throughout the United States' (Regional Alliance for Preservation, 2001). This purpose is effected through serving as a national network of preservation/conservation organizations committed to reaching the broadest audience with coordinated outreach endeavours. Also RAP disseminates information on preservation through education, publications, references and its website. Finally, RAP strives to foster awareness about the importance of preserving the nation's cultural heritage.

RAP has not established its own headquarters or staffing. Clients interested in its activities are requested to contact individual members' websites for further information. The RAP website is well arranged to meet the needs of potential users. The education and outreach page headlines disaster assistance below which is a list of the RAP members who may provide on-site or telephone emergency consultation, emergency hotline listings, and emergency preparedness training (Regional Alliance for Preservation Outreach, 2002b). For example, RAP member The Southeastern Library Network (SOLINET) lists several training activities related to disaster management under its workshops such as Disaster Preparedness, Disaster Recovery and Hurricane Preparedness: Surviving the Big One (SOLINET(a)). SOLINET also provides disaster mitigation and recovery resources including emergency response products, publications and videos at its website (SOLINET(b)). NEH-funded preservation field officers are available for consultation in the event of an emergency.

LEARNING THE LESSONS
Sheryl Davis and Kristen Kern

WHY NETWORKS FAIL

We are aware of a number of networks that were discussed but never got off the ground and others that ceased activities after a short period of activity. While one person with institutional support might succeed in starting a network and even keep it going for a while (a strong leader from a lead institution is crucial for success), a network is a collaboration of equals. If the leader is too strong and controlling the other members become resentful and may decrease their participation.

Constant membership turnover can cause a network to falter. If membership on the network board is viewed as fulfilling criteria for advancement, some institutions assign a different person every year. The lack of continuity can be a problem. The whole point of a network is shared responsibility, but on every network board a given number of members will be there only because they were assigned the task by their home administration. The work of the network can grind to a halt as the few active members wear out.

To ensure continued productive activity, each network needs a core of members who are committed to the mission and goals of the network (and are supported by their home institution). The core may be only two to three members, but can be quite effective even if the other members' participation is 'half-hearted'. In successful, long-running networks, even the most committed people will have periods of time when they must reduce network activities due to other work demands or burnout. One hopes this only happens to one core member at a time.

CONCLUSION

Reviewing the models presented in this chapter, it is apparent that cooperative efforts to prepare for emergency response can take different forms with the same purpose of ensuring an effective response to unexpected events. Knowing that serious emergencies can occur, groups both informally and conventionally organized have coalesced to share the task of preparing for and responding to emergencies. Sponsoring training sessions, developing and sharing resource lists and contacts, and writing disaster plans are activities that build momentum for, and maintain resolve in, disaster preparedness.

The examples of disaster management initiatives discussed above illustrate that disaster management immediately becomes a priority when a devastating event occurs. For example, the wild fires in New Mexico spurred the preservation community in the state to establish a disaster response group based on the O-DRAT model.

In the case of a consortium such as PORTALS, the motivation for becoming involved in disaster management was to pursue an on-going set of activities that are clearly mutually beneficial for its membership. Participating together in training, education and disaster planning, DIRG is developing into a team.

State libraries also can play an instrumental role in disaster management. In Oklahoma, the Administrative Archivist in the Department of Libraries provides leadership for disaster planning education and response through the efforts of the O-DRAT. Likewise in New Mexico the State Librarian and State Archivist offered a contact point for disseminating emergency response information.

It is also true that experience is a great teacher. Whether it is hurricanes in the southeast, tornadoes in the central part of the country, fires in the southwest or earthquakes along the Pacific coast, emergencies increase awareness of the necessity to be prepared or suffer unwarranted consequences. As described in the models presented, individuals as members of preservation alliances, library consortia, state agencies and other cultural institutions have understood the value of working cooperatively and have actively engaged to manage the challenges of potential disasters.

No matter what the individual diversities of libraries in a region may be, they are all charged with preserving the collections in their care. Uniting together in regional networks makes good sense. The more libraries that do it, the better the chance of protecting our precious resources.

NOTES

1. This section based on: Davis, S. (1989) 'Networking for disaster preparedness', in *Building on the First Century: Proceedings of the Fifth National Conference of the Association of College and Research Libraries*, Chicago: American Library Association, pp. 295–7.
2. This section based on: Davis, S. and Page, J. (2002) 'Reactivate, reanimate, revive: The California Preservation Program Perseveres', *Society of California Archivists Newsletter*, March, 2.

REFERENCES

Amigos (2002) 'Welcome to Amigos', available at: <www.amigos.org/index.html>. See also, Amigos Library Services, 'About Imaging and Preservation Service', <www.amigos.org/preserve.htm> (accessed 9 September 2002).

Butler, R. (1986), 'Los Angeles Central Library fire', *Conservation Administration News*, 27, pp. 1–2; 23–24.

Colorado Preservation Alliance, 'Disaster Recovery Resource List', available at: <www.archives. state.co.us/cpa/disaster/disasterresourcelist.htm> (accessed 6 September 2002).

Davis S. and Page, J. (2001) California Preservation Clearinghouse, Los Angeles: University of California Riverside Library.

Davis, S. and Page, J. (2002) 'Reactivate, reanimate, revive: The California Preservation Program Perseveres', *Society of California Archivists Newsletter*, March, 2.

Federal Emergency Management Agency, available at: <www.fema.gov/> (accessed 5 July 2002).

Harrington, G. (2002), telephone interviews with Gary Harrington, Administrative Archivist and Preservation Officer, Oklahoma Department of Libraries, on 2 and 16 April 2002.

Heritage Emergency National Task Force, available at: <www.heritagepreservation.org/ PROGRAMS/taskfer.htm> (accessed 4 September 2002).

Inland Empire Libraries Disaster Response Network, (2000a) *Mission*, available at: <www.ieldrn.org/ MissHist.htm> (accessed 5 March 2002).

Inland Empire Libraries Disaster Response Network, (2000b) *Disaster Plan*, available at: <www.ieldrn.org/sample.htm> (accessed 1 January 2002).

Library of California (2001) 'Welcome to The Library of California – a Network of California Libraries', available at: <www.library.ca.gov> (accessed 6 September 2002).

Los Angeles Preservation Network (2001) 'List of disaster supplies and suppliers. Designed for use with a Disaster Preparedness and Collection Salvage Plan', available at: <www.isd.usc.edu/~melindah/lapnet/supplist.htm> (accessed 6 September 2002).

Los Angeles Preservation Network (2002) *About us*, available at: <www.lapnet.org/AboutUs.html> (accessed 7 January 2002).

Massman, A., telephone interview with Ann Massman, Southwest Studies Librarian, Center for Southwest Research, the University of New Mexico Library and former Chair, New Mexico Preservation Alliance, on 21 March 2002.

PORTALS, Bylaws at the Portland Area Library system, available at: <www.portals.org/bylaws.html> (accessed 4 September 2002).

PORTALS, disaster prevention and recovery template plan, available at: <www.portals.org/DisasterPlanTemplate.html> (accessed 4 September 2002).

PORTALS, disaster recovery group documents, available at: <www.portals.org/committees.html> (accessed 4 September 2002).

PORTALS, disaster recovery group members, available at: <www.portals.org/DIRG_members.html> (accessed 4 September 2002).

PORTALS, disaster recovery information links, available at: <www.portals.org/DIRG_info.html> (accessed 4 September 2002).

Regional Alliance for Preservation (2001) *About RAP*, available at: <www.rap-arcc.org/welcome/rabout.htm> (accessed 6 September 2002).

Regional Alliance for Preservation (2002a), available at: <www.rap-arcc.org/> (accessed 6 September 2002).

Regional Alliance for Preservation (2002b) 'Education and Outreach', 'Disaster Assistance', available at: <www.rap-arcc.org/welcome/rfield.htm> (accessed 6 September 2002).

San Diego Imperial Library Disaster Response Network (SILDRN) (2002) available at: <www.orpheus.ucsd.edu/sildrn/> (accessed 1 January 2002).

SOLINET(a), workshops, available at: <www.solinet.net.workshops/Inventorylist.cfm#Preservation> (accessed 6 September 2002).

SOLINET(b), disaster mitigation and recovery resources, available at: <wwww.solinet.net/preservation/preservation_templ.cfm?doc_id=71> (accessed 6 September 2002).

University of California Preservation Advisory Group (1999) *Charge University of California Preservation Group*, available at: <www.library.ucsb.edu/ucpag/ucpag.html#charge> (accessed 7 January 2002).

7 Psychological aspects of disaster management

Maj Klasson

BACKGROUND

People have always tried to prepare for bad times. As a very small child during World War II, I remember being carried on a stretcher by my mother and the women in my little village in southern Sweden, pretending to be wounded, as a training exercise in case that war should enter our peaceful country. Later on, especially in the last decade, several big disasters opened our eyes to how innocent citizens, war victims, people exposed to bank robberies, fire victims and others suffer from shock and stress disorders and need treatment of some kind. Methods for treating these victims have developed into programmes for traumatic stress management.

My own interest started when the public library in my hometown was the target for an arson attack that had devastating effects. I had the opportunity to collect information during the first 24 hours after the fire and for several subsequent years, until one year after the rebuilt library had been in use (see Appendix 7A for a chronology of events). The information focused on users, staff, politicians and other people involved in library management or development and their experiences and stories from the night of the fire and the following months. It all resulted in a research project and the production of articles (for instance, Klasson, 1999a; 1999b; 2000b; 2002; Klasson and Persson, 2000; Rydsjö, 2000), a monograph (Klasson, 2000a) and some conference papers. Students have also produced their masters theses using this material at the Swedish National School of Librarianship.

In some cases reactions after disasters can continue for several years. McFarlane (1990) found that people surviving the forest fires in Australia in 1983 (28 people dead and several injured) suffered for several years from stress disorder symptoms – 42 per cent suffered from mental disorders, 50 per cent showed a significant increase in clinical symptoms and in psychological problems. Weisaeth (Holen, Sund and Weisaeth, 1983) describes the reactions among survivors just after a catastrophic fire: anguish, sleeping difficulties and fear of the disaster site was present in about 80 per cent of the people directly exposed to it. Cobb and Lindemann (1940) found that almost 50 per cent of the survivors admitted to hospital after a fire suffered from emotional disturbances eight days after the fire. Holen (Holen, Sund and Weisaeth, 1983; Holen, 1990) performed a longitudinal study (over eight years) on survivors after the Alexander Kielland disaster (an oil platform in the North Sea which tipped over and fell into the water). He compared them with a control group and found that the survivors had a higher degree of sickness, and more and longer periods of sick leave than the control group.

It is not easy to find examples from the library world of psychological debriefing at fire sites, floods or war zones. Linköping is one of a few Swedish public libraries where a big library fire has occurred. Another is the Boxholm public library (Mäntykangas, 2000), one of several case studies in a dissertation by Arja Mäntykangas, a doctoral student at the Swedish National School of Librarianship. Through a database search, (mainly internet websites and LISA (Library and Information Science Abstracts), I have found several articles on large library fires. Articles from this literature search mainly describe the restoration process in relation to materials, acquisition and preservation (see, for example, Kennedy, 1995; MacKinnon and Morgan, 1989). In only a few articles are the psychological effects mentioned. Now and then, there are brief remarks that 'personnel required counselling in order to come to terms with the consequences of the disaster and the effect on their working life' (Simpson, 1994 on the Norwich Central Library fire). In Norwich, the Assistant Director, John Creber, organized immediate crisis treatment for staff (see Chapter 9). He noted that that two years after the fire staff still found it difficult to talk about it.

Thorburn (1993) writes that the effect of an arson attack is on the same scale as bereavement and there is a drastic drop in staff morale. Full briefings and occasional tours of the damaged site play a large part in their acceptance of the disaster and help the staff through the difficult times. Hammond (1996) and Stoker (1994) mention stress counselling at the library. Stoker ends his article by citing the novelist Malcolm Bradbury: 'After people and paintings burning books is the worst thing.' Stoker also points out the importance of the library for citizens and the role of the local newspaper as a means of asking for support from the community. In Linköping *Östgöta Correspondenten* filled the dual role of information source and channel for support. Watson (1989) also notes this in his article on the Los Angeles Public Library fire. Seven major Los Angeles television stations sent film crews to the library and ran reports. 'Ironically this devastating fire turned out to be the best publicity opportunity the library ever had. The fire helped focus public support, that's a terrible way for something like that to happen, but there is no question that it did.' People's awareness of libraries changed, which resulted in donations and other support. This was also the case in Linköping. In a fire in a skyscraper and a multi-storey library at Jacksonville, the catastrophe inspired cooperation between individuals and groups (Hubbard, et al., 1995).

Since no one died in the fire at Linköping, the number of people with high level disorders was less than in more severe disasters. Even less dramatic events, however, cause some problems for individuals.

THE LINKÖPING LIBRARY FIRE

On 20 September 1996, a fire was intentionally started by a pyromaniac at *Stadsbiblioteket i Linköping* (the Central Town Library, Linköping). On that day the building was crowded. Linköping University was celebrating its annual *Humanistdygnet* (Humanist around-the-clock) event of popular presentations and lectures, based on research at the university and disseminated to the citizens as a form of communication between researchers and the surrounding community. Four hundred people strolled around and listened to poets and story tellers, researchers and writers, when someone cried: 'Fire!'. Ten minutes after the fire was discovered the whole building was an inferno.

The fire-fighters directed their actions towards preventing the fire spreading to neighbouring buildings, among others, a home for the elderly. It was Friday night and the staff at the home were mostly inexperienced young women, who had a terrible time trying to call relatives of the elderly people by phone when the service was disrupted by the fire.

Water was not poured on the library because of the risk of water damage to the collections, especially in the cellar where the literature from more than half a millennium of collecting was stored. Small fires gave off smoke for several days. Townspeople gathered outside the library. The shock was great and triggered a lot of feelings. People from all over Sweden sent letters and offers of help: authors, cultural workers, politicians, other libraries and a large number of ordinary people wanted to give their support for rebuilding the library. Newspaper articles, television and radio programmes reported from the site.

THE DAYS AFTER THE FIRE

In the days after the fire, several things happened: the health organizations, *Kommunhälsan* (the Municipal Health Department), and *Previa* (another programme for health support in the local community) started planning and performing psychological debriefing of staff. Different work groups were formed comprising politicians, staff and other relevant municipal officials (security, police, and so on), who took care of the immediate work. Valuable material in the fireproof cellar was evacuated and the material brought to safer places such as cold storage areas; this involved crawling and crouching in intense heat while packing and removing smoke or water damaged material. The stench was pervasive. The ceiling was hanging down and full of cracks. People had to get temporary work places, insurance companies needed information, evaluation of the lost material had to start as soon as possible and the extent of damage to the computer system and local databases had to be established. The police called library staff and some of the *Humanistdygnet* participants for questioning several times. A temporary main library had to be opened soon and a new library had to be planned; for that purpose a competition was arranged for architects to submit plans. A project leader for the first year of work was appointed.

On Saturday, the day after the fire, a large demonstration against violence and racism was organized with help from the local paper, *Östgöta Correspondenten* (*The Östgöta Correspondent*). Several hundred people gathered by the castle and beside the library ruins. Some cried, others were in a state of shock. Library staff, faces white, huddled together in the middle of the square. Well-known individuals from the local community stood on a platform outside the castle. Among them were the Mayor, the Bishop, the County Governor, the Head of the University Library and the Town Library, the university Vice-chancellor, professors of local history, the Town Chancellor, spokespersons for the students, and researchers who had used the centuries-old collections.

A few days after the fire a billboard was put up on the initiative of young students (16–19 years of age) from the high schools in the central area. It was used especially by children and young people, and, in some cases, adults. High school students were allowed to demonstrate outside the library ruins and hundreds of notes filled the billboard. Later, a local support group was created. Every Friday outside the library, and later in the winter, inside the temporary library, authors, researchers, politicians, and so on, gave speeches or presentations on the theme of libraries, freedom of speech and free access to books. These activities were kept alive until the opening ceremony of the new library in spring 2000.

Initial research dealt with the psychological effects of the fire in the first year after it happened. This covered the debriefing of staff, changes in work tasks and their subsequent effects, reactions from users, such as demonstrations for democracy with calls for solidarity and a non-racist society, and reactions to the loss of study-places caused by the fire. The next few years' research concentrated on the architectural competition, rebuilding, user reactions and staff reflections on the various processes. During the last phase of the project I and others carried out a study of the impact of the new library, its introduction and management.

The research data consisted of interviews, questionnaires, written notes on the billboard ('The Billboard for the Freedom of Speech'), newspaper articles and letters-to-the-editor in the daily newspaper, audio tapes, video tapes, pictures, and so on, produced in the restoration and rebuilding processes. As mentioned earlier, this chapter concentrates on disaster management and thus excludes some of the other aspects of the fire. Most empirical examples, usually in the form of quotations, come from the analyses of qualitative interviews revealing individuals' real experiences.

RESEARCH INTO THE HUMAN IMPACT OF THE FIRE

In the period after the fire, I started to conduct interviews with librarians, both managers and front line staff. I also interviewed politicians, municipal officials, health unit personnel, fire-fighters, and library users of all social classes and ages. All in all about 40 tapes (60–80 hours of recordings) were made, collecting stories from the days of the fire and the period that followed. A doctoral student, and former head of a public library, Christina Persson, took part in several of the interviews and analyses (some analyses from the interview study will be incorporated in her forthcoming dissertation). The interviews were taped and analysed by qualitative methods. Usually the analysis started immediately after the recording with our reflections on the interviews. Presented below are some examples from a part of the study concerning experiences during the fire and in the following six months. The anonymous quotations, mainly from interviews with staff are slightly edited. All interviewees have been very generous and allowed us to share their experiences and feelings. When we met them, debriefing had been carried out and finished. Most of them were in a phase where they had had time to elaborate on their thoughts. They could reflect upon the situation and choose what to tell us. We did not want to intrude into their lives in the first few weeks when so many things were in a mess. We have a lot of informal conversations from that period, but nothing we will present as quotations. Although some time had passed since the fire they give a very intense picture of what it was like when the fire started, and afterwards.

Reading the texts, it is possible to see the different stages of the recovery process after a shock. Several interviewees express 'a sense of unreality' and speak of their feelings of 'being locked up'. The shock makes time stand still, but after a while things feel normal again:

> When the information was given by the politicians I felt numbed. I did not care. But then, afterwards, I went with my friends and close colleagues to a café to have a coffee. And suddenly I felt OK. Colleagues were the best medicine. To talk and talk with people who knew …

I was strolling around in the library waiting for friends coming from the last seminars when a young blond girl descended the stairs calling out in a trivial casual tone 'The library is on fire'. I did not get frightened or stressed. I helped immediately to get people out of the building like a busy bee. I could not understand the seriousness of the situation. Then when I saw the large windows fall out with a big bang on the grass, I partly grasped that it was a big fire. The full reaction did not come until I was at home in the middle of the night. The teenage daughter had to comfort her mother.

People *repressed* the strange situation by keeping themselves occupied in lots of detailed routine tasks, and in a state of *not being vulnerable*:

When the alarm went off we were occupied with closing the circulation desk. So we continued to put away the material, we counted the cash and locked it in the safe, closed the curtains, rearranged some papers and did all the routines we were used to doing. There seemed to be no hurry. It was not real. We went out through the main door. When we turned around we saw the flames jump from shelf to shelf and suddenly it was all ablaze.

I found myself going through the same procedure every day the week after the fire. In the early morning in my thoughts I went to the library. I went through the usual corridor, down the stairs. Then I looked at the top of the desk where the bird sculpture Phoenix was placed. Then I looked at the picture on the wall showing a square in Malmö: I went behind the desk and welcomed the users dropping in. This sequence of memories passed clear as glass through my mind every morning in the exact similar steps.

Sometimes it was as if the situation never occurred:

When I cycled towards the library site two days after the fire I suddenly *knew* the library was there like before. When I turn around the corner I will see it. It is there. Then I saw the ruin and the ashes.

Then came feelings of *deep sorrow*. '*Han fattas mig*' ('He's left me bereaved') Astrid Lindgren, the famous recently deceased Swedish author of children's books, makes one of her characters say when he expresses his deep sorrow on a relative's deathbed. The same kind of remarks came from several interviewees talking about what the loss meant to them. Not only the building, the interior, their personal things in the offices, but also traces of years of library work:

Suddenly all traces of my work over twenty-five years as a librarian have vanished.

To *lose the workplace* is like losing the 'home at work'. The pictures on the walls, colours, the welcoming of the 'guests', the comfort, the feeling of having a place where you are safe and secure is a vital part of your self-esteem:

Nothing was left. I felt lost. Yesterday I had a job and a place to go to. Today I have a job but no workplace.

Many interviewees expressed *anger and rage* and quite a bit of *frustration*. They felt a need to put the blame somewhere:

I felt anger and rage. Why did the police not do anything to avert the disaster! We knew of the threats beforehand. Why did they not do anything?

Why did it take so long for the firemen to come? And why did they stop pouring water over the flames?

The fire-fighters actually arrived three minutes after the alarm. Many interviewees gave the same impression: The feeling of *time standing still or being prolonged*:

Afterwards I see myself strolling around in the library, up and down the stairs, talking to friends, my eyes catching every detail of the collections, exhibitions, people and scenes for hours. But according to my watch it all happened in a few minutes!

We tried not to create panic so we moved slowly and talked in calm voices and we felt as if we had all the time in the world. But in reality it was a case of minutes!

The fact that it was an arson attack made some interviewees feel *queasy and frightened*:

Every time I heard sounds like the sound of a fire engine I was frightened. And I did not want to go down in the cellar. I turned around and looked over my shoulder if I heard an unknown noise.

For the first time in my life I felt Evil come close.

and, the feeling of *being an outsider*:

I am trained as a voluntary fireman, but I did not have the authority to do anything! It was terribly frustrating! Why did they do this and not that! My feelings were inside the library and I was standing there as an outsider!

Being tired, burned-out – managers were aware that staff were tired. Someone said, with black humour, 'we are fierce spirits who are burned-out!' Demand for activity at work was very low the first few weeks after the fire. Those who wished could stay at home occasionally, but very soon reality knocked at the door. Lots of work was waiting to be done and problems to be solved. The first heavy work had already been performed: the evacuation of the material from the fireproof cellar. The temperature was 80°C at the hottest spot and the ceiling had to be strengthened so that it did not fall down:

I cannot forgive myself for taking part in the evacuation. I have two children at home! What would have happened to them if the ceiling had come down on me?

Now, staff were charged with several tasks simultaneously. First, they were processing their reactions after the fire, coping with anger, sorrow and sometimes *guilt*: 'could I have done something to prevent the damage?' Second, they had to start evaluations of the collections. Third, they began work on the damaged printed material and restoration of the lost library collections. Fourth, a

149

temporary library was to be opened and, finally, the planning of a new library had to start immediately. Those who were 'homeless' had to get a temporary workplace at branch libraries, something that was not always a success. The dichotomy *generalist–specialist* became obvious. Some main, central library staff expressed the view that the branch libraries worked less efficiently than they themselves did and some branch library staff said that the main library staff were less flexible and less able to do several things at the same time. Chatting with customers, a typical branch library staff occupation, for example, could either be interpreted as inefficient, or a means of making contact with users. Some interviewees pointed out how interesting it had been to learn new things from each other.

Fall in morale: sometimes interviewees felt down and indifferent. So many things had to be performed at the same time and for staff with an average age of 57 years it could only be moderately rewarding to work towards a solution that might just be put into effect by the time of their retirement.

Support group and rhetoric: many people outside of the local support group provided moral support, but also expressed their expectations for the rebuilding of the library: traditional values on the one hand, and Sweden's most excellent, up-to-date IT library on the other. Interviewees showed some ambivalence towards the support group's tendency to stress quick action. It became impossible for the politicians as well as the library managers to ask for a longer period of reflection on how the new library could take advantage of the situation, and create something less traditional. The process of producing concrete plans for a new library had to start almost the day after the fire. It built on the idea that the system had a main, central library and several branch libraries. Among branch library staff ideas about a system with equally important branches in a network were growing. Maybe the main library should not be that big? Maybe the branch libraries should grow instead?

Shift in hierarchies: The new situation required competence of a kind that had not been the case before. It demanded people with ability to handle unexpected situations and great stress. A lot of *expanded learning* took place and staff could either break out of the stress phase and use the new situation as a learning opportunity, or break down, leave the organization, or stand still and refuse to engage in the development work. Some shifts in hierarchies took place at the end of the first year.

One of the innovations managers were interested in trying was a higher degree of *teamwork*. They also wanted to engage staff in planning the new library. Everyone should be a member of at least one team. Two years after the fire there was one team still working: the team for literature acquisition. In time for the opening of the library, a little more than three years after the fire, through the application of quality management and delegated power, management had set up a more team-oriented organization.

PSYCHOLOGICAL DISASTER MANAGEMENT

The day after the fire, planning for disaster management started. All kinds of tasks were waiting for urgent solutions, such as saving and rebuilding the collections, restoring material, setting up a temporary library, insurance questions, conservation of the surviving rare books, and so on. Those processes relating to the material side of the disaster have been described in a book by library staff (Jacobson-Schacht, 2000), but the psychological effects of the disaster on staff also called for attention. When dealing with psychological aspects of behaviour it is important to recognize that what influences people is not the actual situation, but how *they* experience it. Another principle is that human information management has its limits. A person's mind is not able to manage more than five to ten information units simultaneously. Too much information creates stress and bad judgements can follow. Psychologists also talk about the tendency for behaviour to follow a situation, thereby being inconsistent at times. When new experiences occur, knowledge processes like thinking, learning, memory processing and reflection begin. These mental activities are called cognition.

People in a major crisis, therefore, have to replace negative or malfunctioning thinking patterns with constructive and functional ways of thinking. Cognitive therapy is a common form of crisis therapy, which may be useful in psychological problem solving. A milder form is debriefing. Debriefing is not used on sick people, but on normally functioning people who react to an abnormal situation such as, for instance, a fire. It was used after the Linköping library fire of 1996.

WHAT IS DEBRIEFING?

Psychological debriefing is a systematic strategy to help people through periods of extreme psychological stress in relation to catastrophes of different kinds. The mental processes after an incident of arson trigger feelings very much like those experienced during bereavement: sorrow, fear, anger, rage, hate, guilt, shame, tiredness, indifference, denial that it happened, and lack of enthusiasm. Debriefing is not a psychiatric method directed to abnormal behaviour; it is more a method for learning how to cope with extreme stress in crises and handle normal, although very strong, feelings in these situations. The goal of debriefing is to lessen the effect of the critical incident and speed up recovery (Weisaeth, 1996). In a state of shock or deep stress, individuals pass through different stages:

- shock, lasts minutes or days
- reaction, lasts four to six weeks
- reparation, six months to one year
- reorientation.

Atle Dyregrov, a Norwegian psychiatrist, has conducted several studies on debriefing. He has also written manuals and academic books on the subject (Dyregrov and Mitchell, 1988; Dyregrov, 1989; 1992; 1997). Debriefing is used not only on people who have experienced disasters and traumas, but also to help personnel working with victims of disasters, rescue teams, healthcare workers, police and fire-fighters, to cope with their feelings. Dyregrov and other researchers have found that debriefing shortens the period of severe shock and helps people to recover more quickly.

DEBRIEFING AND EMOTIONAL STRESS MANAGEMENT

The morning after the fire in Linköping library, the two organizations responsible for the healthcare of municipal employees started to plan the debriefing of those individuals who had been present on the night of the fire and during the difficult evacuation work of the next two days. The library organization consists of two departments: the public library with its main library and several branch libraries, and the information bureau. The latter deals with municipal information, consumer information, information for refugees and immigrants, and so on. The head of the whole organization is Tanja Levin, who is not a librarian herself, but came from the information bureau. The information bureau was the main target of the arsonist. It had received several threats during the months before the actual fire, some of which had also been delivered to the library. Staff at the healthcare services, *Previa* (responsible for staff at the information bureau) and *Kommunhälsan* (responsible for staff at the library) heard about the fire early on Saturday and came to the site.

In the debriefing process a psychiatrist, Dr Thomas Eriksson, with experience of debriefing soldiers in Bosnia, took responsibility for the more severe cases, including acting as a counsellor for managers and assistant managers. Dr Eriksson had long experience of counselling high-ranking officials and managers, teaching among other things, how to be a competent leader in crises. Before the debriefing took place a tradition was established. It consisted of daily, informal, morning meetings with coffee, information and 'sympathy', open to everyone. Staff from different parts of the library system could meet and talk and exchange information about the fire and subsequent activities. Experts from the police, municipal security service (for example, fire-fighters), politicians from the town council, and others, were invited to answer questions or to give information. For many of our interviewees this was the best therapy for overcoming problems in the period after the fire. The first two days of the treatment mainly involved the presence of health service staff being available to talk at any time. On Monday 3 September, three days after the fire, formal debriefing started.

The debriefing material that was used at Linköping comes partly from the SOSCON conference on organization and leadership in crises (Weisaeth, 1996), and a presentation by the psychiatrist Lars Weisaeth. He describes the debriefing method as a process with several phases: introduction, factual, thinking, reaction, symptoms, learning, and reorientation. Three hours or less is needed for formal debriefing. This was not the case in Linköping where the groups met twice in a few days and then had a follow-up meeting 14 days to a month later. Some individuals had individual consultations as needed in between. Daily meetings also provided an opportunity to analyse and process facts and feelings. At the first meeting most of the time was spent identifying what happened, what people did, thought and felt. The second meeting repeated this but spent a little more time considering the future. At the last meeting very little time was taken going over the past, the participants concentrated on how to deal with the present situation and the immediate future, according to an interview with Bengt Ericsson of *Previa*. Debriefing consists of the following phases (author's translation):

● *Introduction phase*

The leader describes the goals and the rules. The rules are as follows:

- Once you are a member of a ring, a defined group, you have to be present every time. You are not allowed to be absent. If you are, you will be asked to come back. It is important that no one stays behind.
- Within the group you speak freely but you do not tell anyone outside the group what has been said.
- You are expected to share your experiences and feelings with the others, but you are allowed to choose to be silent.
- You speak about your own experiences, not of others. You use rounds, you answer the questions one after another, nothing is too small or dull, and all reactions are all right.
- No documentation is allowed. [Examples of reactions, and so on given in this chapter come from later interviews.]
- No criticism or actions are taken against anybody. No reaction is 'wrong'. No accusations are directed at persons by name.

153

- *Factual phase*

  During this phase you talk about 'What happened' and 'What did you do when it happened?' Everyone describes his/her exact memories.

- *Thinking phase*

  During this phase members talk about what they thought when the disaster happened and afterwards.

- *Reaction phase*

  During this phase members talk about what they thought was their worst experience and what things they would rather have missed. They also add their thoughts on how they can handle the present situation.

- *Symptoms phase*

  In this phase the conversation turns to how they felt physically, mentally and emotionally at the time that it happened, afterwards, and at the moment?

- *Learning phase*

  During this phase the theme is how you define what a normal reaction to an abnormal situation is, from a physical, mental and cognitive point of view.

- *Reorientation phase*

  In order to be prepared for the future you must discuss how you feel right now, if some things went wrong, was there anything that was OK? And what did you learn for the future?

The debriefing opened with the creation of a number of groups, selected in 'rings'. Some rings had full debriefings but some had only a kind of structured conversation. The first ring of about eight persons consisted of people who were present and working the night of the fire. The next group were those who evacuated the material from the cellar in terrible heat.

Then several more rings were formed from people with similar experiences. Those who did not have any formal debriefing were staff from the branch libraries whose workplace was located elsewhere. Some of them did afterwards regret that they did not have any debriefing. Their recovery from shock might have been easier.

THE EVALUATION OF THE DEBRIEFING

Six months after the library fire Dr Thomas Eriksson was asked by the authorities to produce an evaluation of activities connected with the psycho-social treatment. He carried out interviews with library staff and staff at the information bureau. He also was in contact with doctors, health organization personnel, personnel administrators, the police and security (firemen). Library and information bureau staff were able to express their opinions about the support and actions that took place after the fire. They also answered two questionnaires, a General Health Questionnaire (GHQ 28) and the Impact of Event Scale (IES 15), which are used to provide an assessment of psychological health conditions. Eriksson describes the results as follows.

First, he summarizes the difficulties, starting with the threats against the information bureau and ending with the situation six months later. Staff had a lot to say about police inefficiency, their own lack of work, disappointment towards politicians, and so on. But the two health organizations received very positive comments. Staff appreciated that they were there all the time at the beginning and that they offered a meeting place and information. As regards the health conditions measured by the scales above, more than half of the staff experienced headaches, tiredness, anguish and sleeping difficulties – higher than is normal. More than half of the staff showed symptoms indicating medium or strong emotional reaction after the fire. They still showed these symptoms six months later showing that it obviously takes a long time to get over an incident like arson.

Eriksson (1997) suggests that there should be a plan of action for extreme incidents. Every work site should have a plan which is easily accessible and known to everyone, with contact details of relevant persons listed.

COMMENTS ON THE DEBRIEFING

All interviewees were positive towards the debriefing they had received, or thought that it did not do any harm. As already noted, those who did not have a debriefing, such as branch library staff, wished they could have had some. The first year revealed some problems such as the enforced work, the disappointment because, according to staff, 'the wrong architect' won the competition, conflicts between external organizations' experts and local senior library managers. The interviews and the informal conversations reflect a period of dissatisfaction on several topics. You could call it the difference between

- pure system thinking contrasted with more organic thinking
- rationality set against relationships and feelings
- trespassing into territories and questioning the knowledge of authorities against defending local know-how
- the indulgence and demand for quick results against patience and acceptance of the fact that psychological processes take time.

But as time goes by and the work becomes more stable, the remarks become more positive. In interviews with staff several years after the incident very few feel that they have any symptoms. They usually say: 'We do not talk of the fire any longer. Now we concentrate on the work in our new library, which is, we understand, very well liked.' The very skilful and pedagogic architect succeeded in creating a dialogue with staff. This seems to have reduced the dissatisfaction of the first phases of planning the new library. In press articles and the municipal information newsletter, they express more and more satisfaction with the way they feel.

CRITICAL VIEWS OF DEBRIEFING

Not all voices on debriefing are in favour of the method and suggest there are difficulties in interpreting results (Robinson and Mitchell, 1993; British Psychological Society Working Party, 1990). Martin Deahl (2000) has written an article on the controversy and challenge of psychological debriefing. He has reviewed several articles, some of which are very critical of the method's ability to create positive effects, such as minimizing post-traumatic stress. Critics usually complain about the difficulty of finding controlled experiments where effects can be established with an acceptable amount of certainty. And there are a lot of comparative studies where no significant effects can be measured. Deahl argues that many of those psychological debriefing studies have 'methodological shortcomings'. Some of the problems with these studies are:

- *Some debriefing is not of high quality*: 'The last decade has witnessed the emergence of a disaster industry.' It has become more and more of a media circus after catastrophes and 'a lot of diverse professional groups – psychologists, social workers, the clergy and psychiatrists ... appear in the wake of a disaster to offer identical interventions in an uncoordinated and sometimes overlapping manner. More worrying, lay workers and volunteers with little professional background and training descend in hordes on disaster sites to offer assistance.'
- *Lack of baseline data*: You do not always know the state of psychological health of the participants in the study, their earlier experiences, whether they have had any training in catastrophe management before the catastrophe, and so on. That makes it difficult to make comparisons of effects.
- *Variable timing*: Time spent on debriefings has varied, from just a few hours to several sessions with some interval in between. Sometimes it has been offered immediately after the accident/catastrophe and sometimes several weeks or months afterwards. The disaster itself can have been of shorter or longer duration.
- *Varying trauma exposure*: Variation in the magnitude of disaster, and how close the participants came to the centre of it plays a part that is not always considered.
- *Low response rate and sampling bias*: People have to agree to take part in studies. Some choose not to, sometimes because of a lack of confidence in psychologists, sometimes for personal reasons.

- *Results from questionnaires are sometimes compared with results from interviews*: Comparing qualitative studies with quantitative creates difficulties in interpreting similarities and differences.

I would like to add that the majority of the critics of psychological debriefing come from the field of medical science. Most of the research money comes from big pharmaceutical corporations and enterprises that need to know if their medicine is effective or not. Measuring physical outcomes is a way of establishing if that is the case. Critics from the medical and natural sciences, with a research tradition of controlled experiments and strict, quantitative studies often refuse to accept that studies of a more phenomenological nature are of equal value in establishing good scientific knowledge about the effect of psychological debriefing. The concept of evidence-based medicine or evidence-based nursing has a strong hold in the medical and nursing professions. Ranking orders of accepted research methods based on the degree of significant results are in use. Randomized, controlled experiments are most highly valued and case studies and qualitative studies least valued.

There are, however, many researchers within the social sciences, including the present author, who undertake qualitative research and hold a different opinion. We feel that when one deals with emotions, very personal feelings and problems, qualitative interviews under conditions of complete trust between interviewer and interviewee make it possible to achieve more meaningful and deeper knowledge. The interviewee's voice, his/her own words, facial expression and body language together give a better insight into the phenomenon of Post Traumatic Stress Disorder (PTSD). Interviewees may give the best evidence on how different target groups experience and describe the effects of disasters and inform the process of overcoming the problems which PTSD causes. Interviewees may also be the best evaluators of what they have learnt from their experiences.

One of the results that researchers agree upon in the studies on psychological debriefing is that debriefing which lasts longer and is repeated after a month will have a better effect than a single session. Richards (2001) has arrived at the same conclusions in a study comparing critical incident stress debriefing (CISD) with critical incident stress management (CISM). The latter method includes other actions like pre-incident training, counselling and advice, follow-ups of more severe cases by psychotherapy, recurrent meetings, team training and so on. Better results come from integrated programmes where debriefing is but one part of a battery of activities (Mitchell and Everly, 1997). In the Linköping case we have found that several other activities accompanied the psychological debriefing, and so maybe we should talk of CISM instead.

CRITICAL INCIDENT STRESS MANAGEMENT IN LINKÖPING

Besides the debriefing, other activities that might have had an impact on psychological processes in the aftermath of the fire include:

- Informal communication among colleagues – moving staff around the remaining library branches, working together on immediate evacuation, reparation and restoration tasks brought staff closer together. Sharing experiences of the fire and the very strong emotions it evoked made the peer group a resource for healing and reflection.
- Teambuilding – building teams in the workplace helps to strengthen feelings of support and actions among members of the group and to develop organizational goals and culture.
- Pre-training of staff in case of disasters – there had been some evacuation training in case of a fire. Staff had also received regular instructions on how to carry out surveillance of the library premises and act on suspicious situations, as several serious threats had been delivered in the months before the fire.
- Individual treatment of the most vulnerable cases by debriefing experts.
- Informal information meetings every morning where time was set aside for casual conversation. Experts from the police, the fire brigade and municipal security service were invited to give information and answer questions asked.
- Support groups – it is important to draw attention to the cooperation and communication between library staff and support groups. Several arrangements were made this way.
- A channel created by the local media for users to express their love of, and sympathy for, the library and its staff. This channel also made it possible for citizens to express their rage against the arsonist, organize demonstrations for the rebuilding of the library and keep informed citizens' interests alive until the opening of the new library.
- Users' support and sympathy as shown orally, in writing, by flowers, by demonstrations for a new library, in positive comments in questionnaires and interviews, in articles and in the notes on 'The Billboard for the Freedom of Speech'.

USER REACTIONS

As pointed out earlier, users did not take part in any debriefing which was given exclusively to those staff who were present the night of the fire and those who took part in the dangerous rescue of materials from the cellar. So how did users express their feelings and what did they do to alleviate the absence of the main library?

Some brief examples on how the users reacted follow. They are presented more fully in other publications (Klasson, 2000a; 2002). The speeches and extrovert behaviour of the people at the Borggården Demonstration was the first example, together with comments in user interviews about the night of the fire. Most of all they include varying degrees of rhetoric: strong feelings, solemn words, core values. Another form of expression is represented by the notes on 'The Billboard for the Freedom of Speech'.

'THE BILLBOARD FOR THE FREEDOM OF SPEECH'

It was pretty stupid what you did. Why didn't you set fire to a tobacco warehouse?

My dear library
Imagine sitting with
a book in the little corner
of the children's department

Necessary was it? We won't let anyone murder the next library/The people's library

In every age people have tried to destroy knowledge
As long as there's been books
There's been people who've wanted to burn them
But the books have lived on
And they're going to stay living! Jacob Blästa School

The library

I hate you who lit the fire and put out the light.

Where books are burned the soul of history is burned. Mette & Sara PO

So bloody unnecessary. Even if I wasn't there that often
We took it for granted, of course there's a library
But not anymore.

Il y a un petit pas entre brûler les livres et brûler les gens; c'est le pas du fascisme!

How will we manage our schoolwork when there isn't any library?

As soon as I saw in the paper that our dearest library had burned down I saw the word *why* in my mind ... Why would someone want to burn down a simple but so special building? The library represents free freedom of speech and print ... And we really mustn't forget the immigrant office. All the wonderful immigrants who have taught us so much need the building and the staff. We hope you all know that we're thinking of you and grieving with you.

Where will we surf on the net now? At Tomas's!

A town's not a town if it hasn't got a library!

As mentioned earlier, outside the library ruins a graffiti board, or, scribble screen called 'The Billboard for the Freedom of Speech' was set up on the initiative of high school students. Children and young people, and also some adults, put up their notes with their thoughts on the fire.

We found the same feelings and topics as we found in the early interviews. The billboard writers express strong feelings of confusion, insecurity and shock. They feel sorrow, rage, hate against the arsonist who is disloyal to other users. They express demands for law, justice, confessions, and punishments. A few billboard writers express a wish to understand the offender and the psychology of his mental health and actions. Some writers use irony as a means of coping with the strange situation. The library is looked upon as a mirror of time, a symbol of free speech, the defender of democracy. It also stands firm against racism. The library stands for good books and culture. It is a 'public home', a social milieu and a meeting place. It is a link to history and the homeland for immigrants. It is like a living creature: it lives, burns, suffers, gets murdered, dies and resurrects. It gives and it receives positive feelings. It offers a positive study environment. The library stands for established values and ideologies in society. It mirrors a societal discourse. The library becomes a discursively loaded artefact whose mission is to disseminate societal thinking patterns.

Some gender differences were identified. Girls wrote most of the poems and boys used irony and witty remarks. Boys also use a lot of swearing. The girls speak of the library as a loved person; they have a relationship with the library. The boys call for justice and punishment. In the few verses boys have produced, a tougher tone is present. Adults use a lot of rhetoric and worry about a shift in attitudes against the 'good society' where you take care of culture and your neighbours. Most notes expressed a strong sense of disgust for racists and arsonists.

QUESTIONNAIRE ANALYSIS

One of the research project's methods of data collection was a questionnaire survey undertaken in cooperation with the first year project leader for the rebuilding of the Linköping public library, Mattias von Wachenfelt (Klasson, 1999; 2000a). About 2000 respondents were asked how the fire had affected their regular library habits and what their hopes were for the future of the library and its services. The questionnaire focused on how users viewed the library service before and after the fire rather than their general feelings. Many of the answers are what one would expect from user studies and the way users tend to answer in similar situations. Access to library resources and to the study environment was of vital interest to the majority of the interviewees. (The study will be published separately.) The questionnaires were distributed eight months after the fire and the users' minds could thus be expected to be preoccupied with the new situation, the rebuilding process, and their own needs.

There are some extra factors evident in responses to the open questions about what the interviewees specifically wanted to add in relation to the library in the year 2000. A very strong emphasis on the social-psychological environment and ethical values such as democracy, freedom of speech, equality between races and solidarity with the less fortunate and the need to build the future on knowledge from the past was found. The fire seems to have influenced people to express feelings, sometimes directed towards the library: love, sorrow, sometimes directed at the arsonist: hate, anger, demand for revenge and punishment. Respondents express all the stages in the process of shock and recovery, although more balanced than in the interviews a few months after the fire and on 'The Billboard for the Freedom of Speech'.

Some new knowledge relating to how to provide channels for users to express and process their feelings was thus gained:

- Help people feel they are there and taking part in the case together with library staff, politicians and other groups.
- Encourage people to participate in the rebuilding work by commenting on the architects' plans, helping to find items for the library, lobbying political parties for funding, answering questionnaires on how they want the service to be in the new premises.
- Organize channels in the press and on billboards for expression of feelings and opinions.
- Keep interest alive by events such as a series of lectures by experts, author presentations, demonstrations, and public information meetings on the rebuilding process.
- Arrange a temporary library as soon as possible, even if it is small, so regular, daily visitors do not forget where to go.
- Users are not only interested in their own affairs and the library as a means for delivering books and information! The library has a very strong symbolic value as a free and open space and as the defender of a democratic society. This must be observed and taken into account in the planning of activities during the period of restoration.

SOME RECOMMENDATIONS

Finally, here are a few recommendations for library managers, based on the research:

- Is there a national library or other body with national responsibility to give advice on disaster management issues and to offer courses on dealing with library materials as well as the psychological side of disaster management? If not, create a network with that aim. The International Federation of Library Associations (IFLA) and the International Committee of the Blue Shield have a lot of experiential knowledge to offer.

- Check your disaster control plan regularly. If you do not have one, create one! (See Chapters 2 and 10 for help with this.) Make sure the plan addresses the psychological aspects of disasters; for example, include details of crisis management teams, doctors and psychologists, and consult with them during development of the plan.
- Prepare a training and education plan on strategies and activities for unexpected crises for middle managers.
- Prepare a plan addressing how to take care of staff in extraordinary stressful situations.
- Prepare a plan for involving users' expertise in restoration work and lobbying for extra finances for rebuilding the library, and collection development.
- Devise a strategy for making the users' situation easier. Can they be involved in the restoration process in any way? How can services they require continue to be delivered with as little disruption as possible?
- Welcome support groups, but do not let them take over. In Linköping a support group was set up. It organized regular information programmes with lectures by celebrities and ordinary people who had something to pass on to the participants, architect, authors, firemen, police, head of the library, the governor, and others. In this way interest could be kept alive and the threat of closing down part of the service was made almost impossible.
- Put up a billboard or space in or near the premises or on the web where people can express their feelings or views about the library. This works as a means of stress relief. The 'Billboard for the Freedom of Speech' in the library park in Linköping acted as a kind of crisis therapy for the community. Many feelings were aired and brought into the open.
- Evaluate the process regularly to get good ideas from different groups of stakeholders. In Linköping, users were asked to take part in questionnaire surveys and interviews by researchers and journalists to reveal their reactions and comments on various issues; they took part in the dialogue for the whole three and a half years of the rebuilding process.
- Be prepared to take care of people's feelings as soon as possible after the disaster and undertake some checking and evaluation during the year after. This seems to have a positive effect on staff and saves a lot of money for managers. A manager with knowledge of psychological disaster management will be a winner, minimizing severe illness and absence from work, and will earn trust and support from his/her staff.

SUMMARY

The arson in Linköping public library affected the whole community. Sweden had not experienced arson on this scale. Compared to what happens in the rest of the world it may seem as though the fire was a minor disaster, but in the local community it moved people and stirred feelings that surprised us. A broader public learned about the method of debriefing. The psychological effect of the arson was apparent among staff as well as among users and followed the pattern of bereavement: shock, with reactions such as sorrow, anger, rage, fear, shame, tiredness, indifference, denial that it had happened, lack of enthusiasm and so on, reparation of psychological status and finally reorientation. Mass-media support was and still is very strong. The visibility of the library has increased. The branch libraries developed a strong sense of pride, high loan statistics and very confident librarians. As a consequence of the fire, Linköping got a new library much more fit for IT use, much better adapted to researchers in archives and local history. Safety plans and the need to take care of precious collections have become a national interest. A lot of work remains to be done on the research project, but we can already see how much information we have gained, and feel very confident that we will add more meaningful knowledge to the psychological aspects of disaster management.

(This chapter is a revised and updated version of a paper presented at a conference sponsored by The International Group of the Library Association 4–6 September 1998 at the University of Bristol and subsequently published in P. Sturges and D. Rosenberg (eds.) (1999), *Disaster and After. The Practicalities of Information Service in Times of War and Other Catastrophes*. University of Bristol. London, Los Angeles: Taylor Graham Publishing, pp. 51–70.)

APPENDIX 7A: SHORT CHRONOLOGY

1996

20–21 September: 'Humanist activities around-the-clock'. The library burns down.

21 September: Crisis meeting. Information to staff. At the library, work started on evacuation of the material in the fireproof cellar, and the creation and start of the temporary Working Group (politicians and library managers) for planning activities after the fire. Public demonstration against pyromaniacs and for the library and freedom of speech.

22 September: Debriefing of staff. A politically formed management group for planning the rebuilding of the library is established. The pupils at Linköping schools, especially at the 'Cathedral School' high school, take the initiative to put up a billboard 'for the freedom of speech' on which they can express their feelings about the fire and its consequences.

21–25 September: A temporary base is established at the House of Concerts and Congresses. Staff from the main library are placed at decentralized library units whose opening times are extended. A mobile library is placed in the centre of the town near the fire site. The programme for seeking premises for a temporary library is produced. A Working Group for the incoming donations of books is established.

October: Start of the evaluation of the damaged and destroyed material which had to be finished by March 1997. The creation of a Working Group for this purpose, engaging consultants and a chosen project leader for the restoration and rebuilding.

2 October: Possible new sites are examined.

3 October: A local committee outside the library is created. It starts public Friday meetings with short presentations and speeches and forms a national committee for the benefit of the library.

21–22 October: The management group for planning the rebuilding goes on a study tour to Malmö and Göteborg town libraries.

23 October: The local committee arranges 'opinion' meeting. The Malmö head librarian gives a presentation.

24–27 October: The library participates in the national fair for Books and Libraries in Göteborg.

November–January. The management group for planning the rebuilding meets different public groups to collect viewpoints on the planning of the new library.

12 November: Decision about rent costs.

14 November: Start of the support group, 'Friends of Books for Children'.

18–19 November: The management group for planning the rebuilding goes on study tour to Tönsberg in Norway to visit a newly built library.

29 November: The temporary main library opens at Storgatan where it is possible to read newspapers and return books. Journals are coming in, and some library loans made, but the library is not working to its full potential.

December: Cleaning of the evacuated books starts. Planned to be accomplished by summer.

5 December: Architect helps the management group for planning the rebuilding to create a local programme for the premises and advises how to carry out the architect competition.

18 December: The work starts with the local programme for the premises.

19 December: The information bureau opens next door to the library.

1997

January: The Swedish School for Library and Information Studies starts formal cooperation.

13 February: Politicians decide to invite five architectural firms to participate in a competition.

25 February: Theme board for the architect competition has a meeting in the Town council about library matters.

March: The new fulltime project leader for the internal planning of the new library will be the Head of the main library. Staff are invited to join different

Working Groups with the purpose of examining the overall work at the library and to plan the new library.

5 March: Information presented to the public in the Town Hall.

26 March: The programme for the local planning is presented to the board in the Council for Education in the municipality (handles school and adult education matters).

7 April: Beginning of the Working Groups. During April and May several study visits are undertaken. Ideas and background materials are collected.

8 April: Decisions are taken in the Town Council about the local programme for the library.

11 April: First meeting with invited architects.

June: A project leader for considering different interests in the process is appointed.

25 June: Architects deliver the competing plans and they are presented to the public.

25 June–26 September: A jury examines the plans.

20–21 August: All staff are given a seminar as a start of the following internal development work.

26 September: The winning architect is presented by the jury.

October: After an initial period of mixed feelings because staff had hoped for another scheme for the new library, the process for revision of the architect's plans begins.

2000

Spring: Opening of the new Town Library is planned to take place. The rebuilding is finished.

REFERENCES

British Psychological Society Working Party (1990) *Psychological Aspects of Disaster*, Leicester: The British Psychological Society.

Cobb, S. and Lindemann, E. (1940) 'Neuropsychiatric observations during the Coconut Grove fire', *Annals of Surgery*, 117: 814–24.

Deahl, M. (2000) 'Psychological debriefing: controversy and challenge', *Australian and New Zealand Journal of Psychiatry*, 34: 929–39.

Dyregrov, A. and Mitchell, J. T. (1988), 'Psykologisk debriefing' [Psychological debriefing], *Tidsskrift for Norsk Psykologforening*, 25: 217–24.

Dyregrov, A. (1989) 'Caring for helpers in disaster situations: psychological debriefing', *Disaster Management*, 2: 25–30.

Dyregrov, A. (1992) 'Manual för genomförande av debriefing', in A. Dyregrov, *Katastrofpsykologi*, Lund: Studentlitteratur.

Dyregrov, A. (1997) 'The process in critical incident stress debriefings', *Journal of Traumatic Stress*, 10: 589–605.

Eriksson, T. (1997) *Evaluering av Branden vid Linköpings Stadsbibliotek* (Draft), Linköping: Kommunhälsan.

Hammond, H. (1996) 'Norfolk and Norwich Library, the emerging Phoenix', *New Library World*, 97, (1130): 24–31.

Holen, A. (1990) *A Long Term Outcome Study of Survivors From a Disaster*, Oslo: University of Oslo.

Holen, A., Sund, A. and Weisaeth, L. (1983) 'Survivors of the North Sea oil rig disaster', a paper presented at symposium at Utstein Kloster, Utstein.

Hubbard, W.J., Saska, R.P. and Lord, G.F. (1995), 'Towering inferno II – recovering from an electrical fire in a multi-storey library', *Library and Archival Security*, 13 (1): 61–75.

Jacobson-Schacht, A.L. (ed.) (2000), *Linköpings Stadsbiblioteks Återuppbyggnad*, Linköping: Linköpings stadsbibliotek.

Kennedy, J. (1995) 'Norfolk Record Office Fire: an initial report', *Journal of the Society of Archivists*, 16 (1): 3–6.

Klasson, M. (1999a) 'Psychological effects of the Linköping fire (and some strategies for overcoming the problems in the first few months)', in P. Sturges and D. Rosenberg (eds.), *Disasters and After. The Practicalities of Information Service in Times of War and Other Catastrophes, proceedings of an International Conference Sponsored by IGLA (The International Group of the Library Association), 4–6 September 1998*, University of Bristol, London, Los Angeles: Taylor Graham, pp. 51–79.

Klasson, M. (1999b), *Linköpingsbor om sina Biblioteksvanor före och efter Branden 1996. En Enkätstudie* [Linköping Citizens on their Library Habits before and after the Fire. A Questionnaire Study], Borås: University College of Borås, Library and Information Science.

Klasson, M. (ed.) (2000a) *Röster. Branden vid Linköpings Stadsbibliotek* [Voices. The Linköping Library Fire], Borås: Valfrid.

Klasson, M. (2000b) 'Röster från klotterplanket' (Voices from the billboard), in *Röster. Branden vid Linköpings Stadsbibliotek* [Voices. The Linköping Library Fire], Borås: Valfrid, Ss. 45–73.

Klasson, M. (2002) 'Rhetoric and realism: young user reactions on the Linköping fire and its consequences for education and democracy', in L. Ashcroft (ed.) *Community, Culture, Competition – the Future of Library and Information Education? Proceedings of the 4th British Nordic Conference on Library and Information Studies, 21–23 March 2001, Dublin*, Ireland, Bradford: Emerald, pp. 142–51.

Klasson, M. and Persson, C. (2000) Röster från branddygnet [Voices from the day of the fire], in *Röster. Branden vid Linköpings Stadsbibliotek* [Voices. The Linköping Library Fire], Borås: Valfrid, Ss.13–44.

MacKinnon, A. and Morgan, V.E. (1989) 'Fire and flood, disaster contingency planning and management for libraries', *HKLA Journal*, 13: 93–8.

Mantykangas, A. (2000), 'Biblioteksbrandeni Boxholm' [The Library Fire in Boxholm], in M. Klasson (ed.) (2000a).

McFarlane, A.C. (1990) 'An Australian disaster: The 1983 bushfires', *International Journal of Mental Health*, 19: 36–47.

Mitchell, J.T. and Everly, G.S. (1997) 'Scientific evidence for CISM', *Journal of Emergency Medical Services*, 2997 (22): 87–93.

Richards, D. (2001) 'A field study of critical incident stress debriefing versus critical incident stress management', *Journal of Mental Health*, 10 (3), 351–62.

Robinson, R.C. and Mitchell, J.T. (1993) 'Evaluation of psychological debriefings', *Journal of Traumatic Stress*, 6: 367–82.

Rydsjö, K. (2000), 'Jag saknarden där tanken ...' [I miss not going to the library ...], in M. Klasson (ed.) (2000a).

Simpson, E. (1994) 'The Norwich Central Library fire', *Paper Conservation News*, 72, 10.

Stoker, D. (1994) 'Only burning people is worse than burning books', *Journal of Librarianship and Information Studies*, 26 (4), 177–9.

Thorburn, G. (1993) 'Library fire and flood – successful salvage, but beware of the cowboy', *Aslib Information*, 21 (2): 76–8.

Watson, T. (1989) 'Out of the ashes: the Los Angeles Public Library', *Wilson Library Bulletin*, 64 (4): 34–8, 41.

Weisaeth, L. (1996) 'Organisation och ledning i kris. Emotionellt ledarskap', *SOSCON, Arlandastad 28–29 Mars*, 1996.

8 The Croatian experience 1991–1995

Kornelija Petr

For both individuals and peoples, memory is an integral part of existence. The memory of the peoples of the world is of vital importance in preserving cultural identities, in linking past and present and in shaping the future. The documentary heritage in libraries and archives constitutes a major part of that memory and reflects the diversity of peoples, languages and cultures. But that memory is fragile. (Abid, A.: Memory of the World. Preserving our Documentary Heritage)

Cultural heritage (library collections) should not become a subject of war trophies or war reparation. It is against the international law of our century. (Klaus Dieter Lehmann, Katya Genieva: 1998 IFLA Conference – quoted in Law, 1999: 7)

INTRODUCTION

A great proportion of the world's cultural heritage gradually disappears because of the effects of 'natural' causes: acidified paper, leather, film, and so on, deteriorate or disappear because of light, heat, humidity or dust. Unfortunately, disasters also threaten the more rapid deterioration of the material preserved in libraries. According to Derek Law (1999: 6) disasters are always unexpected, but can be divided into predictable and unpredictable ones. The predictable are mostly natural, and, occasionally, man-made, such as fire, flood and earthquake. The unpredictable disasters, much more difficult to deal with, come in the shape of violence: armed conflicts and wars seemed to be an unavoidable element of the twentieth century, and have already marked the beginning of the new millennium. And, however numerous or diverse reasons and causes for the destruction of cultural heritage may be, armed conflicts and wars seem to be the reason for the most massive destruction, ever since the Library of Alexandria, which was destroyed on several occasions: first in 47 BC, during the civil war between Julius Caesar and the followers of Pompey the Great, when Caesar was besieged in Alexandria, and then in three subsequent big fires. But we do not have to go so far into the past to find examples of war-affected or ruined libraries. It is enough to think of the two World Wars from the past century, or the one waged on the territory of former Yugoslavia in its last decade.

There are two ways in which national cultural heritage preserved in libraries can be destroyed during war: direct damage through bombing (and often subsequent fires or water from pipes) or through looting. One of the most valued war trophies brought back to the home country by the conqueror is the book, or other documentary evidence of the defeated nation's cultural heritage. Destroying cultural heritage or taking it away has significance for the conquerors for a number of reasons: the conquered nation is prevented from scientific and cultural progress, it is impoverished both spiritually and financially (because books and manuscripts may have a great value), and, most importantly, the national cultural memory is destroyed and the conquered nation loses its connections to its history and identity. Sometimes the conquered nation becomes assimilated and disappears from history. But not every army leader or looter is interested in books and other library materials. In order to understand the value of library holdings and their meaning on a grander scale, one has to be at a certain level of development and must appreciate the value of a book; in other words, one must be aware of the importance the written word has for the spiritual and material life of a nation. For the defeated nation it is always better to be conquered by civilized army leaders because, in that case, there is still a hope that the library holdings will not be completely destroyed, only moved to another location or country. This might not be the case if the conquerors are illiterate and uncivilized, because they might see an enemy in every book or document written in, for them, unfamiliar language or characters (Stipčević, 1999: 327).

The war which Serbia fought against Croatia between 1991 and 1995 was one of those wars in which the aggressor's intention is not merely to occupy a foreign territory, or to break the resistance of the native population, but to destroy the whole nation, its culture, history and all its memories (Stipčević, 1993: 5). The nation's memories are kept and preserved in its museums, libraries and archives. These institutions, together with numerous other cultural sites – churches, schools, cemeteries, historic buildings – became the targets of Serbian aggression with the aim of annihilating Croatian nationhood and everything connected with it.

It was a conflict of two ideas: Serbian, which sought ethno-territorial expansion, and Croatian, which sought its full independence and sovereignty. Serbia wanted to change borders and expand its territory, while Croatia defended its present-day borders and territorial integrity. Therefore, it was neither an ethnic nor a civil war, but an aggression against Croatia conducted by Serbia using the federal army (previously a joint army composed of all the Yugoslav nations) (Klemenčić, 1993).

THE 1991–1995 WAR IN CROATIA: IMPACT ON THE CROATIAN LIBRARY AND INFORMATION SYSTEM

The war in Croatia severely affected the Croatian library and information system in a number of ways: normal information flow was interrupted, subscription to foreign periodicals abolished and work on some projects stopped. Slovenia was the only ex-Yugoslav republic with which Croatia had relatively normal transport, economic, information and communications relations. Communication and economic relations with the other republics of the former Yugoslavia were interrupted. The normal information flow between the republics of the former Yugoslavia was interrupted as a direct result of this war; there was no exchange of information, journals or books, no inter-library loans, no professional meetings and no cooperation (Kunštek, 1992: 156).

When war broke out it was, for a certain period of time, impossible to subscribe to foreign periodicals or to buy foreign books. The reason lay in the fact that the old system of large book and journal distributors supported by the government, characteristic of all former communist countries, fell apart because of inflation and difficulties caused by the war, and it took time before Croatia got its own distributors. During the war, the Ministry of Science and Technology tried to coordinate subscriptions to foreign periodicals; obtaining foreign journals through the intervention of the state is still going on. However, the problem of insufficient funds caused by the very low level of the economy in a country at war prevented the acquisition of enough books and periodicals to allow normal education and research work to proceed.

The war also interrupted work on the project to create a 'Scientific and technical information system in Yugoslavia' (SNTIJ). The project, whose headquarters were situated in Maribor, Slovenia, had started several years before the war. It was planned to have two stages. During the first stage a specialized information system for 23 various subjects was to be created. Croatia was in charge of coordination of information in the fields of 'Tourism', 'Resources and products' and 'Economy'. The project had many shortcomings: it paid little attention to the acquisition of new books and periodicals for libraries; it focused on creation of databases and not on library collections, thus neglecting libraries and concentrating on specialized information services and centres. It seemed that a new communication infrastructure was its only goal. It was developed mainly by computer scientists, with very little cooperation with librarians and therefore had very little effect. The only good thing that came out of this project was the fact that it provided libraries with computers (Jelušić, 1992: 83). However, even though some of the libraries became computerized, not all of them did. In fact, many Croatian libraries did not have a computer at the beginning of the war, and those that did used a variety of software. Librarians possessed insufficient IT

171

knowledge to take full advantage of the facilities; communication and co-ordination between libraries was poor, and only a few libraries had access to international databases.

In 1989, work began on a new JUBIB (Yugoslav Bibliography) database in connection with the SNTIJ project. This was created and maintained by the Yugoslav Bibliographic Institute in Belgrade based on the catalogues of various institutions. The work on this database was also interrupted by the war.

In 1980 the National and University Library in Zagreb began an automation programme. The UNIMARC format was chosen as the national format (Willer, 1982: 57). This project was one of few that was not interrupted by the war, and now there are 14 libraries (academic, special and public libraries) that form the CROLIST (Croatian Integrated Library and Information System) network. In 1991 Croatia initiated another project which also survived the war: the Croatian Academic and Research Network (CARNet) was created with the objective of providing academic institutions (and academic libraries) with access to the internet and international databases. All Croatian academic institutions are now part of this network.

LIBRARIANS

Reduced number of staff

When the war broke out many people left the dangerous war-affected parts of Croatia. Local authorities allowed some groups of people to leave, such as mothers with small children, or school children and their teachers. In some areas whole schools moved to safer places, as was the case with Osijek's schoolchildren, who moved to Crikvenica, a little town on the north coast of the Adriatic Sea. In Croatia, as is the case all over the world, library staff consisted mostly of women, so the movement of women from the war zones meant that library staffing was reduced. But every day, danger, fear and a sense of the absurdity of keeping libraries open when people should be saving their lives and possessions, also made a great number of people leave the war zones.

Some people of Serbian[1] origin supported and joined the aggressors, and their families moved to Serbia. A report about the Gospić library during the war shows that the library had three librarians before the war. Two of them left the town even before the war had started on that territory (Subašić, 1992: 91). The fact that they left the town before the first attacks leads us to believe that they were, as other Croatian Serbs, warned and knew in advance what was about to happen in that area and left while there was still time.

Library staffing was also reduced because young male librarians had to join the army. Consequently, library staff were reduced, in most cases, to a few brave women. They had to cope with all the difficulties that libraries experienced during the war such as stock protection, evacuation, cleaning the debris, and so on.

Working conditions

Working conditions were extremely difficult. In the majority of cases, however, libraries responded well and organized their activities in such a way that they were able to provide the best possible service under the circumstances. In many cases, librarians had to give up routine work and clear up the mess after the library had been hit. The Scientific Library in Zadar received several direct hits at the beginning of October 1991. When people got out on the streets the following morning, they noticed books lying in the street; the damage to the nineteenth-century building was so great as to indicate that that building was the specific target of the enemy's attack. Librarians climbed to their offices on the third floor with apprehension, which turned out to be justified when they saw blue sky through the gap in the ceiling, the destroyed offices and books mixed with parts of the office furniture, computer equipment and catalogue cards.

After the initial shock, priorities for damage control had to be determined. The most important thing was to cover the holes in walls and the roof, clear up the debris and save everything that wasn't completely destroyed in the attack. And, the whole time, Zadar was without electricity and running water. The librarians' work was interrupted daily by general alarms or air raids when they would all run to the nearby shelter. They moved all the books, boxes with catalogue cards and reference collection from the reading room, and the rest of the material to their depository. Until the end of 1991, a period of three months, librarians worked on dusting and removing the glass chips from the books, depository and offices, saving the salvaged catalogue cards, checking and rewriting the destroyed ones, and retrieving data about the destroyed books. During that period everybody was treated the same; the head of the library worked next to librarians and cleaners. When the work was finished, librarians joined the efforts to save the libraries (or more precisely, the collections, because the librarians saved only library material that was not destroyed by the retreating Yugoslav National Army) in Zadar's army barracks (Peljušić-Katić, 1992: 93).

In Vukovar, 1991 was a difficult year from the very beginning, even before it became obvious to everybody that Croatia was heading into war. However, the library tried to maintain its normal functions. Problems in Borovo Naselje started in May 1991 after 12 Croatian policemen were ambushed and killed in Borovo Selo. Borove Naselje and Borovo Selo are small villages in the vicinity of Vukovar where the population consisted mainly of Croatian Serbs; Vukovar public library had branch libraries in the villages. Librarians working there had a difficult time getting to and from work. In the initial stage of the war, before the first conflicts

Figure 8.1 Zadar town library
(Source: T. Aparac-Gazivoda and D. Katalenac (eds) *Wounded Libraries in Croatia*, Croatian Library
Association, 1993. Reproduced by permission of Zadar City Library and Croatian Library Association.)

had broken out, Croatian Serbs would block roads which would make it impossible for anyone, regardless of nationality, to go to work or school. After heavy shelling in September 1991, the head of the library was informed that the ground floor windows were shattered, but that the library holdings were intact because the Croatian army had guarded them. Something had to be done, that was obvious, but what?

The head of the library called five librarians and arranged to meet at the library. They had to return several times without reaching their destination because of the loud detonations of an attack in progress. It was also impossible to approach the library without warning the Croatian army that the librarians were coming; otherwise the soldiers might have mistaken them for looters and shot them. Back then, at the beginning of the war, it was still possible to protect the holdings and coordinate library activities. The damage from the first hit on the library, regardless of the shattered glass, piles of bricks and books damaged by shrapnel, was not too bad. Since librarians had no tools for clearing the debris, they postponed going to the library for a few days. However, very soon that part of town became completely cut off and inaccessible (Kukuljica, 1992: 76).

A number of librarians lost their lives in the war. In Vukovar public library, two out of ten librarians died during the war. One joined the enemy and died in combat fighting against his former colleagues and neighbours. The other, Marija Brkić, died under the walls of her home when it was destroyed in one of numerous shelling attacks. She was due to retire on 1 September 1991, but during August, despite being on holiday, and in September, she insisted on helping her fellow librarians to clear the library debris. The head of the library tried to dissuade her, thinking of Marija's age, her impending retirement, and the fact that clearing debris is such hard work, but Marija insisted saying she had spent her whole professional life surrounded by books and that her intention was to help preserve them. Only a month later, in October 1991, she died in a shelling attack (Kunštek, 1992: 75).

The public library in Novska was also significantly damaged in the shelling attacks. Two librarians looked after the library holdings for the whole period of the war; they protected them and evacuated the most valuable volumes to the branch library in Lipovljani, which functioned without interruption the whole time. The secondary school library from Novska also evacuated its complete holdings to Lipovljani (Jednačak, 1992: 84).

The public library and reading room in Sisak was fortunately spared during the war and was open every day for its users, but librarians themselves were often trapped in the library during the general alarms. The children's department of the Sisak public library received a direct hit in September 1991. Four librarians worked for almost the whole of 1992 in rooms whose windows had planks instead of glass and were lit by artificial light. Working conditions were much worse in

Figure 8.2   Destroyed reading room of the Slavonski Brod public library
(Source: T. Aparac-Gazivoda and D. Katalenac (eds) *Wounded Libraries in Croatia*, Croatian Library
Association, 1993. Reproduced by permission of Zadar City Library and Croatian Library Association.)

Zadar where library windows also had planks instead of glass, but where there was not even any electricity and the librarians had to work by candlelight.

Working conditions in Slavonski Brod were difficult as well: the general alarm was in force for almost a year (from spring 1992) during which time air raids and shelling attacks did not stop. The public library had to move six times, often to inadequate quarters with no proper shelter and where librarians worked with difficulty. At one time, the attacks became so heavy that the librarians had to leave the area of Slavonski Brod and move outside the town. They returned in the autumn of 1992 and moved into the basement of the High School, also damaged in the attacks but not as heavily as the public library building. During that winter, librarians worked without heating, with only plastic on the windows, because the glass had been broken in the first attacks on the town. At the beginning of 1993 they had to move the library again into the new quarters on the ground floor of the school, where they shared the reading room with their hosts (Crnković-Nosić, 1992: 78).

In the territories directly affected by the war, where the general alarms and air raids were being signalled on a daily basis, the population, and consequently the number of library users, decreased and the 'safer' territories in Croatia received a huge number of displaced persons and refugees.[2] These people had lost all their possessions and, some of them, their loved ones to the war. The majority were peasants who had been used to manual labour all their lives, and now found themselves with nothing to do. All of a sudden, the libraries in these areas recorded an increase in the user population. The public library and reading room in Sisak (Jednačak, 1992) operated efficiently in spite of the war and the difficulties it brought. At the Children's library department in Sisak and at the Ironworks (the most important factory in Sisak and the area which also provided space for the library), new play areas were created for the children of Sisak and the numerous refugee children. The new volume of work made it necessary to employ new staff, so four pre-school teachers, refugees from Petrinja, were employed who, together with other librarians from the library in Sisak, were exceptionally active in working with the children. The central department of the library focused on work with displaced students and their parents.

Areas with mixed populations (Croats and Serbs) experienced a decrease in user numbers even before the war broke out. In Vukovar, for instance, a significant decrease in children using the library was noticeable, particularly after the massacre in Borovo Selo in May 1991. It is a general belief that a great number of Croatian Serbs had been warned about what was going to happen on the territory of Croatia and, as a result, most of them sent their wives and children to relatives or friends in Serbia. A few even sold their homes and moved with their families to Serbia.

A decrease in user numbers was also noticeable during the intensive attacks on towns on war-affected areas. At these times these places were almost deserted and soldiers made up the majority of the population (Slavonski Brod in 1992, Osijek in 1991, Pakrac in 1991). University towns also lost some of their student population as male students and younger staff became soldiers; some moved to safer areas, and some students continued their education at other universities in Croatia. However, only 10 per cent of students of Osijek University, for example, continued their education elsewhere, while those students remaining in towns under attack continued using the libraries even if they joined the Croatian army.

While war-affected places recorded decreases in user numbers, other places in Croatia coped with a huge number of displaced people and refugees, many of whom were suffering from severe depression due to the loss of their homes or loved ones. For many of them one of the ways out of that situation was reading. Libraries in Zagreb, or on the coast where many of these people found their refuge, recorded a significant increase in users who were not obliged to pay library fees. The increase in reading was not noticed only in territories that were safe, but also in places where the war was still going on. In Dubrovnik, for example, libraries had five times more readers during the war than before it.

Helping libraries in need

Libraries that were not directly affected by the war helped other libraries in many ways: they offered professional help and education to librarians from war-affected or occupied territories, organized collections of books for destroyed libraries and provided shelter for evacuated library holdings. The City and University Library in Osijek, even though damaged in numerous shelling attacks, offered temporary shelter to the librarians and salvaged the library holdings of the Faculty of Agriculture library in Osijek, which was completely destroyed in 1991.

In October 1992 in Vinkovci, there was a Round Table, 'The Public library in war and restoration', where librarians gathered and discussed the possibility of restoration of the public library network. This Round Table also raised the question of re-establishing library activities in the territories where they were interrupted. This was directly connected with the issue of returning to the occupied territories, and the organization of libraries in refugee centres.

The scale of destruction in the war was so great that the Croatian librarians could not deal with it on their own; they needed help from abroad. Help came in many forms. For example, there was an international competition for the design of a new Vinkovci public library, financed by UNESCO from the 'Books for all'

Figure 8.3 Destroyed building of Faculty of Agriculture and Faculty of Food Technology in Osijek
(Photograph: Zdenko Petr. Reproduced by permission of Zdenko Petr.)

fund. Also, the International Young People's Library in Munich donated children's and young people's books on the theme of peace for the Children's Peace Library in Vinkovci.

Many library users and supporters joined the efforts to collect books for destroyed libraries. Croatian libraries initiated a big book collection in autumn 1991. The traditional 'Month of the book' cultural exhibition had as its slogan 'Give a book to a damaged library'. In 1992, another exhibition, 'Month of the Croatian book', was dedicated to the restoration of destroyed libraries. Many donors – national and international, institutions and individuals – donated books or money for the revitalization of destroyed libraries. A group of librarians from Zagreb libraries worked for a year on the selection, cataloguing and classification of these books. In this way, many damaged or destroyed libraries in Croatia were provided with an initial book stock; Vinkovci public library, for example, received about 30 000 books in the period between autumn 1991 and autumn 1992. Also, less than a year after the burning of the old library, Vinkovci library celebrated the deployment of its first mobile library, a gift from the city of Vienna.

Mistakes and wrong decisions

At the beginning of the war in Croatia there were no clear guidelines about what to do and when. Evacuation of the library might seem the best solution, but there were many problems connected with it (for example, transport, new location), not to mention the fact that it might have been interpreted as showing a lack of patriotism. Therefore, librarians were left to their own devices and judgement. Sometimes they made the wrong decision (or failed to make any decision at all) and had to bear the consequences. In the case of Vinkovci public library, which was burned down on 16 September 1991 – the first library to be destroyed during the war in Croatia – priceless manuscripts of famous Slavonian writers such as Josip Kozarac, Vladimir Kovačić and Jozo Ivakić were turned to ashes. As a consequence, the head of the library had to resign from her position. Gospić library had different circumstances. The temporary war manager of the library was himself more or less responsible for the ruin of what was left after the library had been hit. He did not look after the library properly and the library books were carelessly scattered around the boiler-room. In the period between 30 September and 30 November 1991, the users could borrow videotapes only (since the rest of the holdings lay neglected in the boiler-room). The library had to close in December 1991 because nobody in the Gospić cultural centre showed an interest in its problems. It was only after the National and University Library in Zagreb and the Ministries of Education and Culture reacted that the library was reopened in February 1992. Very soon it recorded an increase in users, and expanded its stock through donations of books.

LIBRARY USERS

This war proved that the book is priceless in times of disaster. People read books in shelters during numerous general alarm alerts and air raids; displaced people who lost their homes and were temporarily living in hotels on the coast found their refuge in the world of books; students who remained in towns under attack went to their academic libraries looking for examination literature. All the academic libraries of the Osijek University, except that of the Faculty of Engineering, were open and had users during the war. The university comprised eight faculties: Agriculture, Civil Engineering, Economics, Education, Electrical Engineering, Food Technology and Law at Osijek and Mechanical Engineering at Slavonski Brod. Two academic libraries (Faculty of Agriculture and Faculty of Food Technology) that were completely destroyed and had to leave their premises soon found new homes – one in the halls of City and University Library Osijek, and the other in one of Osijek's kindergartens – and almost immediately started providing services to their users. In 1991 I was one of the refugees who found a temporary refuge in one of the country's coastal towns and who became addicted to the solace the local library offered. I, however, became overnight a librarian who had to return to Slavonia, the war zone, and who was appalled that she was expected to go back and start working in the library. To me it was inconceivable that libraries in war zones were still functioning.

LIBRARY HOLDINGS AND BUILDINGS

Unfavourable position

War and peace have different rules and values. What is considered to be an advantage in peace may very easily turn out to be, if not deadly, then at least a disadvantage in war.

Antonija Kukuljica, head of the Vukovar public library described her last days spent in the glass library building on the bank of the River Danube under constant danger from shells fired on the town: 'The war came to us with the force of a natural disaster and we never even anticipated the scope of the catastrophe' (Javor, 1992: 73). Very soon the librarians started to feel like sitting ducks. What used to be an advantage – the excellent position and a wonderful view of the magnificent forest over the river – became extremely dangerous. Librarians concentrated their work in the part of the library building that was facing the town. The glass panes normally provided a lot of light and created a pleasant atmosphere in the library, but provided no protection during the war. Also, the building had no cellar. One Saturday in August, when gun shots were heard for the first time in the centre of the town, librarians realized that there was no shelter where they, the users, or the books could be protected.

The public library in Slavonski Brod also had problems because of its position. Once a beautiful spot on the bank of the river Sava, during the war it lost all its appeal because it stood directly on the front line. The library suffered its first damage in autumn 1991 when the soldiers of the Yugoslav National Army from the town barracks started shelling the town. The library lost its reading room with valuable reference and periodical collections; the building was quickly repaired, debris cleared, and a new room was allocated as the reading room. This situation lasted until March 1992. Then the enemy attacks started again, but this time they were shelling from Bosnia, just across the river. In the next two weeks the library was again severely damaged and the whole of the book stock had to be removed to the shelter of the library basement.

Evacuation

The war in Croatia surprised everyone and therefore there were no effective plans for the evacuation or preservation of library holdings. (In 1992, the Institute for the Protection of Cultural Monuments requested that a protection and evacuation plan be drawn up. The plan, however, included only 20 historic libraries.) In 1991, the first stage of the war, library managers had to make difficult decisions. Some tried to get help and instruction from other sources, as the head of the Vukovar public library did when she asked for instructions from the local government, but they had none to give. They had neither a plan nor sufficient space for evacuation or preservation of their own archival material and documents, and because these were near the Vukovar police station and the hospital, they were constant targets for the enemy. Vukovar library had no rare material that would demand obligatory evacuation, and the evacuation of the whole library was out of the question. However, it was felt necessary to preserve accession lists, library documentation and staff personnel documents and for that purpose they used an old goods lift (the building used to be a shoe shop) protected by reinforced concrete and situated in the middle of the library building. This, being the safest place in the whole building, was used as a safe for library documentation. Its metal door was disguised and the head of the library assumed the documentation was safe until the Serbians occupied the town (Kukuljica, 1992: 76).

Some libraries evacuated their complete holdings, some only a part, and a great number of libraries did not evacuate anything. In Slavonski Brod many libraries moved to safer areas. In the period between March 1992 and October 1993, the public library had to move six times (the Gymnasium, the original site, the Gymnasium again, the cellar of a private house in the nearby village of Podvinje, the Gymnasium basement, a Gymnasium classroom on the ground floor). Historic libraries in Slavonski Brod (the library of the Franciscan monastery and the Brlić family library) were also evacuated in autumn of 1991 and moved to safer areas, far from Slavonski Brod. The Faculty of Mechanical Engineering library in Slavonski Brod moved twice, but it did not evacuate its complete holdings, so the librarians often had to go back to their original location to retrieve the books necessary for their students. In Osijek, for example, only the museum library evacuated its most valuable books and manuscripts.

The public library in Pakrac had a slightly different situation – 'perfect' protection plans had been made by the local authority prior to attacks on the town. According to the plans, the library holdings were to be evacuated to the wood and timber factory, 'Papuk'. Unfortunately, when the town was attacked, the factory was one of the first places that burned down (Iličić, 1992: 87). The library itself suffered a great deal. The ceiling of the reading room received a direct hit, so the building was uninhabitable. The damaged building was not protected by soldiers (as the library building in Vukovar had been) and consequently equipment (for example, TV, video recorder) and some books from the reference collection were stolen. Besides the stock, only the catalogue cabinet, and part of the circulation records were preserved. In January 1992, the regional library in Bjelovar organized the evacuation of the Pakrac public library. They evacuated the majority of holdings, together with accession lists. Children's books had been mistakenly stored in the library cellar where they were additionally damaged by humidity. The books were returned to the Pakrac library at the end of 1992 when basic repair work on the building had been carried out. The evacuation of the complete Pakrac library (21 000 volumes) to a new location 80km away was a unique example in this war. Until then there had been evacuations of smaller collections, but none of them was on this scale. The evacuation itself was unplanned, initiated by one of the Croatian army commanders who liked books. During one of the numerous ceasefires a group of experts from the National and University Library in Zagreb and the regional library in Bjelovar visited the Pakrac library and agreed that evacuation was the best thing to do. Evacuation, however, is not an easy thing to organize; books can be damaged in transit or through inadequate storage. Sometimes it is better to leave the books where they are, because the new location may not always be the best solution. In Pakrac for example, somebody wanted to protect the children's books and so put them in a damp cellar where they rotted away. The situation in Pakrac revealed all the problems and weaknesses of library disaster management plans (Iličić, 1992: 87). There were also other reasons why it was so difficult to decide to evacuate and why so few libraries did it. First, during the war everybody was constantly harbouring the hope that 'this ceasefire' would last. Second, who should organize the evacuation (new location, workers, transportation) when most of the population, including a great number of librarians, were not around? The situation in war is chaotic and the police and army have other responsibilities and cannot supervise the evacuation of the library. And, last but not least, what to evacuate? Should the evacuation be complete or only partial? Should only the holdings be evacuated or the inventory and equipment as well?

Material damage

During the war numerous cultural sites and monuments became targets of the aggression. According to the *Bulletin of the Croatian Institute for Protection of Monuments* (1992), these included 479 churches, some Romanesque and Baroque, of which over 75 were completely destroyed and 151 seriously damaged; 725 individual immovable monuments registered as cultural monuments which were damaged, such as museums, archives, library buildings; 299 protected historic sites, of which 82 were destroyed; historic city centres of many towns which were systematically shelled, including the city of Dubrovnik, under the protection of UNESCO and the old city of Split which is on the World Heritage List. Many libraries were destroyed by bombs, rockets and shells. Some of these libraries were completely burnt out, others were damaged and incapacitated; the complete library network in certain regions was destroyed. According to data from 1993, 138 school libraries, 23 public libraries, 12 historic libraries (mainly monastery libraries), 3 research libraries, 11 academic and 8 special libraries were either damaged or destroyed (Aparac-Gazivoda and Katalenac, 1993: 11). In Karlovac, for example, five cultural institutions, one of which was the public library, were attacked by rockets and severely damaged in one day (Eleta, 1992: 90). The mobile library parked in front of the library was also hit in the attack. Fortunately the holdings, previously moved to the cellar, were preserved (only 500 volumes were destroyed).

Big military libraries in three academies of the former Yugoslav National Army in Zadar possessed about 500 000 volumes (Pehar, 1994: 120). The army took one part of it when they withdrew, and the other part burnt down. In the 'Đuro Đaković' army barracks in Zadar the books (fiction and encyclopaedias) burned for 23 days. However, Zadar librarians managed to save about 70 000 volumes.

Dubrovnik, a beautiful old town on the Adriatic coast, was under merciless attack day and night. The research library in Dubrovnik, situated in the Skočibuha Palace, one of the oldest and most beautiful palaces in the town, was hit by five missiles at the beginning of June 1992. In its rich history the palace had many occupants, among whom were Polish and Russian emigrants in the eighteenth and nineteenth centuries (Urban, 1992: 96). In 1806, it was destroyed in a gunpowder explosion and remained a ruin for a century and a half. During the 1991–95 war, the beautiful sixteenth-century building was seriously damaged, and its stability, already badly shaken in the 1979 earthquake, was worsened by

Figure 8.4   Destroyed books from Zadar military libraries
(Source: T. Aparac-Gazivoda and D. Katalenac (eds) *Wounded Libraries in Croatia*, Croatian Library Association, 1993. Reproduced by permission of Zadar City Library and Croatian Library Association.)

rockets. Old cracks became wider and some new ones were created in the supporting walls. In 1992, the palace was as badly damaged as in 1806. The biggest gap in the roof was covered the very next morning with canvas. Nevertheless, this could not protect either the building or the book collection from a sudden storm and heavy rain. The majority of the book collection, including 77 incunabula, was initially put on the ground floor and in the cellar, although it was clear that these were unsuitable locations for a longer period of time. Ten per cent of its Croatian deposit copy collection and 10 per cent of the reference collection were destroyed as well as all its catalogues, accession lists, lending data and all computers. Valuable book stock, the Collegium Rhagusinum and Antiqua (around 10 500 volumes), were put in hermetically sealed, metal containers in the vault of the Dubrovnik bank where it remained until 1994. However, the bad microclimate in the vault threatened to damage the valuable and rare books and it was vital that they were removed to a new location. The research library was therefore allocated a smaller palace in the old town centre. Unfortunately, the majority of the book stock (over 200 000 volumes) had to remain in the old, damaged Skočibuha Palace.

The library of the Inter-University Centre in Dubrovnik suffered an even worse fate. It was completely destroyed in a fire caused by several missiles fired at the building in December 1991.

Also among heavily damaged Dubrovnik libraries is the Franciscan Mala braća library dating from around the thirteenth century. The most valuable part of the library is the collection of 2106 manuscripts, 206 incunabula, 3547 rare books (from the sixteenth to the eighteenth century), a musical collection of around 10 000 scores and 130 items of importance for the world cultural heritage (Aparac-Gazivoda and Katalenac, 1993: 50). The premises of the Franciscan monastery were hit by about 50 shells, also damaging the library. Fortunately, the priceless book collection was preserved, mostly due to the brave monks who endangered their own lives to save the collections during attacks.

Book loss due to loans

Next to the material damage to buildings, one of the effects of the war was book loss. A significant part of the book loss was caused by shelling and rocketfire, and subsequent floods from water pipes and leaking roofs or fires. However, another cause of book loss was unreturned loans. The academic libraries of the University J. J. Strossmayer in Osijek had significant loss of this kind: some of their users were trapped in the occupied territory around Osijek, some joined the enemy, some left Osijek or the surrounding war-affected area and found refuge far away, where it was safe. Many of them either took library books with them, or left them at home where they might have been destroyed in shelling together with the rest of their possessions. Many other Croatian libraries had lost part of their stock in a similar way, particularly those in areas inhabited by Croatian Serbs, as was the case at the Grubišno Polje Public Library. The population of that area was forced to move to Serbia and Bosnia by Serbian paramilitary forces and their supporters, taking with them library books or leaving them in their houses, which were later plundered. Looters, as in all wars, were found on both sides.

In Osijek, however, libraries managed to retrieve a small part of that book stock. When, after the reintegration of the occupied territories, former students, mainly Croatian Serbs, of the University took up their education again, some returned books borrowed at the beginning of the war.

Temporary interruption of service

One of the effects of the war was the interruption of library services. However, only on rare occasions were libraries forced to close their doors to users in order to repair damage. They rarely chose to shut down entirely, because they perceived that as a final defeat by the war. The public library in Pakrac had to close its doors to the public after the return of the book stock from Bjelovar at the end of 1992. This was necessary to reorganize and sort out the book stock, but this break in the continuity of their service was perceived as a great loss for the community. In Karlovac, the public library was also closed, but only for 10 days during the fiercest attacks on the town, whilst the repair work on the damaged library was done. The town of Gospić was attacked for the first time on 30 August 1991. The situation in the town was chaotic; the library was closed until 30 September 1991 when the Gospić Crisis Centre instructed that the library should start working. It worked continuously in spite of rocketfire and shelling every day until 25 October 1991, when a tank missile hit the retaining wall, destroying library furniture, equipment, and 2000 children's books.

There were, however, many Croatian libraries, such as the Zadar Town Library or the academic libraries of the Faculties of Agriculture and Food Technology in Osijek, that suffered severe damage and yet made the greatest effort never to close their doors to users.

Figure 8.5 Vinkovci public library
(Source: T. Aparac-Gazivoda and D. Katalenac (eds) *Wounded Libraries in Croatia*, Croatian Library Association, 1993. Reproduced by permission of Zadar City Library and Croatian Library Association.)

INSTEAD OF A CONCLUSION ...

This is an abridged account of the fate of Croatian libraries during the 1991–95 war fought on Croatian territory. As can be seen, neither the libraries nor the country were prepared for this scope of aggression and destruction. Countries frequently affected by natural disasters such as earthquakes, hurricanes, floods or fires are much better prepared for disaster management than were Croatian libraries. According to guidelines on disaster management of the State Records of New South Wales, disaster management 'is the term given to strategies for the prevention, preparedness and response to disasters, and the recovery of operations following disasters' (State Records New South Wales, 2001). Unfortunately, our country did not consider disaster management before the war and was not prepared for the scope of devastation resulting from it. All Croatian libraries, and especially those later destroyed in the war, made a fatal mistake when they did not take the war threat seriously. At the beginning of the war, libraries ignored the first signs of possible disaster; they insisted on normal functioning and planning of their activities. In August 1991, librarians in Borovo Selo near Vukovar worked on preparing the branch library's new premises, because after the holidays the library was to be moved to a new location. In Petrinja, the last meeting of the committee for the public libraries was held in June 1991, where, regardless of the general atmosphere and some incidents that had happened in Croatia, the topics discussed were new acquisitions and the development of librarianship in the area. Why those librarians chose to play ostrich at the meeting and hide behind professional issues when, it is now obvious, they should have discussed evacuation plans in case of a war, is beyond comprehension; they probably genuinely believed the situation would calm down.

Still, professionalism was the one thing Croatian librarians exhibited in this war and this was the only reason that a large number of Serbian books, documents, and important historical scripts from, for example, the Old Bishop's Library in Pakrac, were evacuated and preserved together with books from the public library.

However, in spite of the unpreparedness of the country and its libraries for acts of aggression and the lack of disaster management plans for the preservation of records, libraries proved to be invaluable places of comfort for people. Civilians who were trapped in besieged towns and the soldiers who protected those towns, went to the library and read because it was the last trace of the normal life they had led before the war. Books gave solace to people in shelters during the numerous air raids and general alarms. Refugees and displaced persons, particularly children, found comfort in reading as well. Libraries immediately responded to a new role they assumed in the war – a therapeutic role. It was similar a little later (1992–95) in Sarajevo where, in spite of the harsh reality of a merciless war and the fact that books were being sometimes used as fuel, library services were provided no matter what (see Peić and Telalović, 1999).

How can the experience of Croatian libraries help in the prevention of mass destruction of library holdings elsewhere? The only possible protection is to evacuate promptly to safe places, out of reach of warfare. Valuable and rare materials and manuscripts should be evacuated at the first signs of conflict; nothing valuable should remain in the war-affected area, because cultural institutions are especially vulnerable and often enemy targets, as this war confirmed. Microfilming or digitization of the legal deposit copy, in addition to retrospective microfilming and digitization of rare and valuable material and storage in secondary deposit libraries in the country, is also a good precaution.

This war surprised and frightened everyone in Croatia. But, as Marinko Iličić, the head of the Bjelovar public library, argues, suddenness and unpredictability is the very characteristic of every disaster, including war. During this war, the town of Pakrac, like many other towns in Croatia, experienced a number of problems: the population deserted the town almost completely; the library staff, as well as many other people from cultural institutions were gone as well. While Pakrac was under attack, no one dared enter the town, and even if somebody tried to, it was not allowed. The Pakrac library was fortunately preserved, but it was not the result of a planned set of actions; rather because coincidentally a particular army commander liked books. But what if the army commander were not as keen on the written word? Obviously, it is of the utmost importance to define the duties and obligations of people in case of disasters or armed conflict.

I hope that this chapter will be a warning to everyone who reads it that records kept at libraries, archives and museums must be well protected and plans must be made for their protection well before any disaster strikes. The records they preserve represent a nation's cultural heritage and identity and are too valuable to be left at risk.

NOTES

1. According to the 1991 census, there were a number of minority groups living in Croatia: Czechs, Slovaks, Hungarians, Italians, Muslims, Albanians and Serbians. There were also 15 other nationalities with fewer than 10 000 declared. Among nationalities, Serbs were the largest minority group (12.15 per cent). In its constitution, drawn up before the proclamation of independence, Croatia guaranteed the rights of minorities. Only the Croatian Serbs refused this status and questioned the status of Croats as the only constitutional majority (78 per cent). Other minority groups were satisfied with the status guaranteed by the constitution and fought on the Croatian side when the war broke out. When ethnic cleansing of the occupied territories began, all non-Serbian minorities were expelled together with Croats (Stahuljak, 1999).

2. The Yugoslav army and Serbian paramilitary forces first utilized the technique of 'ethnic cleansing' in Croatia. As a result 333 100 Croatian civilians, including the writer of this chapter,

were displaced or took refuge, 2181 were killed and 6762 injured during the war (*Bulletin of the Office for Refugees and Displaced Persons*, 1993).

REFERENCES

Abid, A. (1996) 'Memory of the world. Preserving our documentary heritage', paper presented at the 62nd IFLA General Conference, August 25–31, available at: <www.ifla.org/IV/ifla62/62-abia.htm>.

Aparac-Gazivoda, T. and Katalenac, D. (eds) (1993) *Wounded Libraries in Croatia*, Zagreb: Croatian Library Association.

Bulletin of the Croation Institute for the Protection of Monuments (1992), September, Zagreb.

Bulletin of the Office of Refugees and Displaced Persons (1993), January, Zagreb.

Crnković-Nosić, V. (1992) 'Kronologija ratnih stradanja Gradske knjižnice u Slavonskom Brodu' [Chronicle of war damage to the Slavonski Brod Town Library], *Vjesnik Bibliotekara Hrvatske [Journal of Croatian Librarians]*, 3/4 (35): 77–8.

Eleta, N. (1992) 'Ratne štete na knjižnicama Karlovačke regije' [War damage to libraries in Karlovac region], *Vjesnik Bibliotekara Hrvatske [Journal of Croatian Librarians]*, 3/4 (35): 88–91.

Iličić, M. (1992) 'Ratna stradanja narodnih knjižnica Bjelovarske regije' [War damage to public libraries in the Bjelovar region], *Vjesnik Bibliotekara Hrvatske [Journal of Croatian Librarians]*, 3/4 (35): 85–8.

Javor, R. (1992) 'Okrugli stol "Narodne knjižnice u ratu i obnovi"' [Public libraries in war and restoration], *Mjesec hrvatske knjige '92*, Vinkovci, 30. listopada 1992 [Month of the Croatian book '92, Vinkovci, 30 October 1992] *Vjesnik Bibliotekara Hrvatske [Journal of Croatian Librarians]*, 3/4 (35): 71–4.

Jednačak, J. (1992) 'Knjižnice u Sisačko-banijskoj regiji 1991–1992' [Libraries in Sisak and Bania county 1991–1992], *Vjesnik Bibliotekara Hrvatske [Journal of Croatian Librarians]* 3/4 (35), 83–5.

Jelušić, S. (1992), *Struktura i Organizacija Knjižničnih Sustava [Structure and Organization of Library Systems]*, Zagreb: Filozofski fakultet, Zavod za informacijske studije Odsjeka za informacijske znanosti.

Klemenčić, M. (1993) 'Causes and dynamic of the war in Croatia', *Acta Geographica Croatica*, 28, 1–245, available at: <www.hr/hrvatska/WAR/causes.html> (accessed 20 January 2001).

Kukuljica, A. (1992) 'Narodna biblioteka Vukovar u ratu' [Vukovar public library in war], *Vjesnik Bibliotekara Hrvatske [Journal of Croatian Librarians]*, 3/4 (35), 74–7.

Kunštek, D. (1992) 'Wirtschaftliche Entwicklung in der Umbruchzeit : Folgen für den Informationsbereich im ehemaligen Jugoslawien', in *21. ABDOS-Tagung, Bratislava und Martin, 25. bis 28. Mai 1992 : Referate und Beiträge*, Berlin: Staatsbibliothek zu Berlin, pp. 150–60.

Law, D. (1999) 'Disaster and after: an introduction', in P. Sturges and D. Rosenberg (eds), *Disaster and After: The Practicalities of Information Service in Times of War and Other Catastrophes*, London: Taylor Graham, pp. 3–8.

Pehar, I. (1994) 'Nestali, uništeni, oštećeni fondovi 1991–1994' [Destroyed, damaged library collections 1991–1994], *Vjesnik Bibliotekara Hrvatske [Journal of Croatian Librarians]* 21.

Peić, S., Telalović, A. (1999) 'Sarajevo: coping with disaster', in P. Sturges and D. Rosenberg (eds), *Disaster and After: The Practicalities of Information Service in Times of War and Other Catastrophes*, London: Taylor Graham, pp. 151–60.

Peljušić-Katić, M. (1992) 'Stete od bombardiranja u znanstvenoj knjižnici u Zadru 1991. godine' [Damage to the Zadar Scientific Library caused by bombardment in 1991] *Vjesnik Bibliotekara Hrvatske [Journal of Croatian Librarians]*, 3/4 (35), 92–4.

Stahuljak, Z. (1999) 'The violence of neutrality – translators in and of the war (Croatia, 1991–1992)', *College Literature*, 1 (26), *Academic Search Elite on-line* EBSCO Publishing, available at: <epnet.com/ehost/login.html> (accessed 20 July 2002).

State Records New South Wales (2001) 'Guidelines on disaster management' available at: <www.records.nsw.gov.au/publicsector/rk/guidelines/disaster/disasterguidelines-02.htm>

(accessed 2 December 2001). (Since this time, and following consultation on this document, the State Records Authority of New South Wales has published (2002) 'Guidelines on counter disaster strategies for records and recordkeeping systems', Guideline No.5, Sydney: State Records New South Wales, available at: <www.records.nsw.gov.au/publicsector/rk/guidelines/counterdisaster /introduction.htm>. It has also published (2002) 'Standard on counter disaster strategies for records and recordkeeping systems', Standard No.6, Sydney: State Records New South Wales, available at: <www.records.nsw. gov.au/publicsector/rk/Counter%20Disaster/toc.htm>.)

Stipčević, A. (1993) 'Instead of an introduction', in Aparac-Gazivoda, Tatjana and Katalenac, Dragutin (eds), *Wounded Libraries in Croatia*, Zagreb: Croatian Library Association, pp. 5–8.

Stipčević, A. (2000), *Sudbina Knjige [Destiny of a Book]*, Lokve: 'Benja'.

Subašić, D. (1992) 'Gradska knjižnica i čitaonica Centra za kulturu Gospić u ratu' [Town library and reading room of the Gospić Cultural Centre during war], *Vjesnik Bibliotekara Hrvatske [Journal of Croatian Librarians]*, 3/4 (35), 91–2.

Urban, M. (1992) 'Znanstvena knjižnica Dubrovnik – dan poslije …' [Dubrovnik Scientific Library – the day after …], *Vjesnik Bibliotekara Hrvatske [Journal of Croatian Librarians]*, 3/4 (35), 94–7.

Willer, M. (1982) 'Format UNIMARC kao medjunarodni standardizirani zapis za strojno čitljivo katalogiziranje i njegova primjena u jugoslavensko bibliotečno-informacijskom sistemu' [The UNIMARC format as an international standard record for machine readable cataloguing and its application in the Yugoslav library and information system], *Vjesnik Bibliotekara Hrvatske [Journal of Croatian Librarians]*, 1/4 (26), 57–64.

9 Aftermath – service continuity and recovery

John Creber

INTRODUCTION

On 1 August 1994, the Central Library of Norwich, England was destroyed by fire. A new, state-of-the-art library was opened on the same site just seven years later. Behind these two simple sentences lies a tragic tale of loss and a long, difficult route to recovery. Before considering the longer-term effects of this

Figure 9.1 Norwich Library fire, 1 August 1994 – exterior view; smoke and water caused as much damage as the flames
(Photograph reproduced by permission of Eastern Counties Newspapers.)

disaster and detailing the road to recovery, it is necessary to put the library into its context and to say a little about the losses sustained.

NORWICH AND ITS LIBRARY – THE CONTEXT

Norwich Public Library was founded in 1857 and, at the time, served the residents of the City of Norwich. In 1974, it became part of the County Library Service for Norfolk and acted as the central library for a population which, by 1994, had reached 760 000. The central library building, which was opened in 1963, also included the County Record Office which contained the County Archive. The total building area was 5388 m² of which 3658 m² was the Central Library. The county system consists of 48 libraries and 17 mobile libraries; it has a total stock of 1.2 million items, approximately 350 000 of which were in Norwich. Norwich Central Library issued around 750 000 books annually and had about 400 000 visitors a year. As well as being the hub of the County Library Service, Norwich was one of the foremost public libraries in East Anglia and its reserve stock of books met interlibrary loan requests from all over the country. Its Local History Collection was recognized as one of the most important collections in England. It was therefore a real tragedy that this flagship library was destroyed in 1994.

THE LOSSES

Even in pure statistical terms the losses resulting from the fire were quite substantial:

- 125 000 lending and reference books destroyed or damaged beyond repair
- 11 500 audio and video items
- 25 000 local history books destroyed or severely damaged
- catalogue of local studies stock
- 75 years of local newspaper cuttings
- all ground floor furniture including shelving
- 30 computers and other IT devices
- the building itself, which was seriously damaged and eventually declared unsafe.

In addition, the contents of the basement, although untouched by the fire itself, were significantly damaged by water from the fire hoses. This included 3 million manuscripts and records which made up the County Archive, the historic Norwich Town Library collection, which dated from 1608 and which contained fourteenth-century items, and the strong-room collection of local studies material, which was exceptionally rare and valuable. The reference and lending reserve stock (500 000 items including photographs and maps) and the newspaper collection were contained in the four floors of the stack tower and many of these were badly smoke-damaged and the newspapers soaked.

However, the losses and damage should not be assessed purely on a statistical basis. The loss in service was immeasurable. A city had lost its library and with it, its access to knowledge and learning. A community had lost its record of heritage. Staff had lost their place of work. The work of hundreds of person-years had been destroyed.

RESCUE AND RECOVERY

It took a day and a half for the fire to be extinguished and for the building to be declared safe enough to enter. After the initial shock and the inevitable panic, the first task was to assess the damage and loss and make arrangements for removing the salvageable items from the building.

Skips were hired for the mountains of paper pulp which had once been books. A local supermarket loaned trolleys to help with the removal from the building of anything that was recoverable. Hard hats, gloves, overalls and face masks were all provided by local companies and staff were organized into teams to assess and

Figure 9.2 Interior of Norwich library: 30 computers were lost in the fire
(Photograph: Don Reader. Reproduced by permission of Norfolk Library and Information Service.)

remove items from the building. The insurers arranged for a Loss Adjuster to be present at the scene and, together with the County Council's Insurance Officer, he made judgements as to what should be written off and what should be salvaged. In this task we were greatly helped by a Director of Riley, Dunn and Wilson (a commercial binding company), who provided advice on what could reasonably be expected to be repairable. This advice produced many surprises. Items which on the face of it were beyond redemption were declared recoverable. For example, many hundreds of items of stock, particularly from the Local Studies Collection were badly charred and soaked with water. The first reaction would have been to add them to the growing pile in the many skips surrounding the building; in many cases, however, the advice was that it was worth saving and repairs might be possible.

The stock of the 2nd Air Division Memorial Library (USAAF) (2nd Air Division Memorial Library, 2002), which had been where the fire started, was little more than a pile of ash and most of it was written off immediately. (The 2nd Air Division of the 8th United States Army Air Forces had been based in Norfolk and Suffolk during World War II.) The main lending and reference stock was badly charred and water-soaked, dust jackets had melted and in some cases whole shelves of books were fused together as one. Although some of the stock could have been salvaged, it was agreed that, with many of the titles available in-print or with similar titles readily available, it would not be worth the cost of recovering and repairing them. So, with a few exceptions they were all consigned to the skip as were the books from the children's library and the remains of the audio-visual collection. Interestingly, the CDs survived intact since they were housed in drawers, but their cases and sleeve-notes, on public display shelves, were totally destroyed so they were all condemned.

One oasis of lending stock remained untouched. A section of the library, which was devoted to biographies and histories, was behind double fire doors which withstood the 1000° temperatures for four hours. These books reeked of smoke and the jackets of some (those nearest the doors) had begun to melt, but otherwise they were unharmed. These, together with the 500 000 items in the four floors of the stack tower, untouched by the fire or water, were destined to be cleaned and returned to service.

Most of the debates about whether to salvage or discard centred on the Local Studies stock. Although the financial value of much of this stock was minimal, the inherent value and loss to the community was immense. After significant discussions with the Loss Adjuster it was agreed to attempt to salvage anything that was other than pulp or ashes. By this stage (days two and three after the fire) the worst enemy of the salvage operation was the damp and the mould that would result, so the rescued items were sent by Riley, Dunn and Wilson to Scotland in a refrigerated truck and then put into a deep freeze until they could be individually examined. About 9000 items were treated in this way. Weeks later, after the initial rescue operation had been completed, staff visited the conservation plant in Falkirk and, with the Loss Adjusters and the experts from Riley, Dunn and Wilson, began to identify the items which could realistically be conserved. Very few items were discarded at this stage and a year later around 8000 items were back in the library in near-perfect condition.

All the stock which was to be rescued, but which could not be sent immediately for conservation, was put into borrowed refrigerated trailers to stabilize and to prevent the growth of mould. It was early August and the middle of a heat-wave, so mould growth would have been fairly rapid. Arrangements were then made, with the help of the Royal Air Force, to use a redundant hangar at a nearby air-base where, inside hastily erected tents, warm air was blown over the books in an attempt to dry them out. These were mainly the contents of the strong room and the historic Norwich Town Library collection, which had been housed in the basement of the building and which were not burnt but severely water-damaged.

Meanwhile a search was underway for a building in which to store those rescued books which only needed cleaning. A vacant industrial unit on an edge-of-town estate was found and work started on converting it for use. The warehouse floor was suited to the storage and cleaning operation and the first floor offices could be adapted for administrative and associated cataloguing work. Every item which was cleaned and rescued had to be recorded in the library catalogue so that at the end of the operation there would be an accurate record of items still in stock. Computers and a lift had to be installed and a team of cleaners recruited and trained. Shelving for 100 000 items was kindly donated or loaned by other library authorities, supplemented by some shelving in storage in Norfolk. The cleaning and cataloguing operation began in May 1995 (10 months after the fire) and the task was completed by the end of that year.

The other major task to be completed in this phase was the rescue of the 3 million records of the County Archive stored in the basement of the building. Although the concrete slab above the store protected these archives from the fire, it could not protect them from the thousands of gallons of water poured into the building by the fire-fighters. Of course, as the lowest part of the building, the basement acted as a giant reservoir for the water and the first challenge was to acquire and deploy pumps to remove this water. However, the removal and preservation of the precious contents of the basement could not wait until it was completely dry and so, with waders and oilskins on, staff began the process of removing this material. The rescued and damp archives were sent, on professional advice, to Harwell (Atomic Energy Authority, Harwell Drying and Restoration Services, 2002), where they were freeze dried before conservation work was undertaken.

It would be wrong to concentrate solely on the impact of the fire on the stock. The staff were, and are, vitally important and they had been devastated by the events of 1 August. Many of them were seriously traumatized. The effect of this disaster on those who had worked in the building for many years cannot be underestimated; some of the staff had worked there ever since the building had first opened its doors in 1963. This was their day-to-day 'home' and, of course, they had put thousands of hours of work into making the collections and services what they were. Tears, depression and an inability to face the reality of the situation were common. A trauma counselling service was made available to them and many took advantage of this facility. For some, keeping active was a form of therapy, and for these there was a huge amount of work to be done. Teams were formed to remove the stock from the building. Other teams were deployed in other branches in the city to help with the dispersed demand for services. Yet others were charged with the task of selecting and ordering the new stock which would be required (see 'Replacement Stock', pp. 201–204). Some, however, found the demands of the rescue and recovery too difficult to handle and, on medical advice, several staff were given an extended leave of absence. Tact and sensitivity was required with all staff and in many cases efficiency had to take second place to TLC (tender love and care).

The users of the library were shocked and angered by the loss. The public blamed the County Council and the Library Service for the loss of their community facility and, in many cases, the staff of other libraries in the city had to bear the brunt of the criticism.

LESSONS LEARNED

- Use value for money *and* value to service criteria on judging what should be salvaged.
- Take expert advice on what is salvageable. You might be pleasantly surprised.
- Work closely with the insurers (or their representatives) from day one to ensure that all costs associated with rescue and recovery are recoverable.
- Know where you can obtain emergency equipment and supplies at very short notice (pumps, lights, boots, hard hats, face masks, food, trolleys, and so on). Don't wait until a disaster to find out. Maintain up-to-date information in your disaster plan.
- Keep written notes of all decisions, as there will be a need to refer back to many of them later.
- Don't underestimate the time it will take to get books conserved or cleaned and back into service.
- Stabilize any salvageable, wet material by chilling or freezing it as soon as possible after the disaster.
- Take expert advice on the most appropriate storage and salvage methods.
- Don't ignore the personal, traumatizing effect on staff and the user community.

POST-DISASTER SERVICE REQUIREMENTS

Alongside the rescue and recovery operation, planning was taking place on the short-term measures required for immediate service continuity. The users of Norwich Central Library still had books they needed to return, requests awaiting collection, on-going reading and listening needs, information enquiries to be satisfied and, above all, the need for information about the disaster and plans for the future.

It was decided that the latter need should be met through regular press statements, a newsletter and an enquiry line set up to the County Council's Press Office. The needs for lending material could be most effectively met through the extension of hours of opening in all other libraries in the city and by the establishment of a temporary, urban mobile library service to those residents in the immediate vicinity of the destroyed central library. A number of displaced Norwich Central Library staff were allocated to each of the branch libraries in the city and the reserve mobile library from the county fleet was deployed in the area surrounding the Central Library. Additional book-stock for both facilities was 'borrowed' from the mobile library reserve stock and by diverting a proportion of stock from other libraries in the county on a temporary basis.

Redundant space in a Norwich County Council building close to the centre of the city was adapted and fitted out to act as a temporary reference library and information point. The space and the location were not ideal, but it was felt that the need for an immediate presence was more important than finding the 'perfect' premises for what was hoped to be a very short-term measure. The material for this information point was made up of quickly acquired basic reference books, a limited number of CD-ROMs, microform materials on local history and online services accessing the County Catalogue.

Normally, internal bureaucratic wheels in local government turn slowly, but the very nature of the emergency and the impact on the community meant that favours were granted, corners were cut and red-tape reduced significantly, to the extent that the temporary information site was opened within two weeks of the blaze. This service was appreciated by the public and the enquiries which could not be answered from the very limited stock and electronic resources were referred to one of the other libraries in the county with significant reference collections, whose staff was augmented by the temporary secondment of specialists from Norwich. In addition, other libraries in the area (university, colleges and special libraries) and neighbouring public library services were very willing to provide support in the form of handling referred enquiries. In adjoining space in the building the County Archivist set up a temporary microform search room where genealogists and others could research family history using hastily purchased microform copies of records.

These short-term temporary arrangements stayed in place until medium-term temporary premises were operational (see 'Service Continuity' below).

LESSONS LEARNED

- It is important for user confidence that some form of immediate service continuity is maintained. The loyalty of the existing customer base might depend on such action, and the non-users in the community will appreciate the efforts being made.
- The deployment of staff to such temporary services helps to rebuild their confidence and morale and keeps them in touch with their users.
- The generosity and support from other members of the library and information community, both locally and nationally can be relied on at times of disaster such as these.

SERVICE CONTINUITY

While these temporary measures filled an immediate gap, they in no way represented a service which would meet the needs of a city the size of Norwich or act as a central resource for a County Library service. From as early as the first week after the fire, work started to find suitable temporary premises which would go at least some way to meeting these needs until a permanent replacement library could be built.

Under normal circumstances, developing a new central library for a city requires a suitable site, the political will to make it happen and the availability of adequate resources; to achieve all that may take several years. The latter two conditions (political will and resources) were in place from the day of the fire. The availability of a suitable site was evidently not. The use of the fire-damaged site was not an option and it became obvious very early in the search that the availability of a building of up to 5500 m^2 would have required one of the major retailers to suddenly vacate their city centre premises to house all the displaced services in a prime location in the city; this was a forlorn hope. Seeking separate premises for some or all of the services became the only real alternative.

A brief was drawn up for the lending library, the reference library, the local history library, the music library and the County Record Office. Apart from the necessary space and the buildings' adaptability for access for disabled people, one of the most significant aspects of the brief was the floor-loading capability. Most town centre premises are built for office or retail occupation where the floor loadings are typically 2 or 3 kN/m^2. The weight of library shelving requires a minimum of 4 kN/m^2 with a point loading of up to 7 kN/m^2. Where compact shelving or stack storage is required the minimum loading increases to $6\,kN/m^2$. After an exhaustive search, only one suitable building was found in a primary city centre location and this, a former furniture retail showroom, was leased for the lending library. The building needed significant adaptation, including the installation of a lift, and the shelving needed load-spreaders on the first floor because the loading capability was barely at the acceptable minimum. The political and legal processes and the adaptations to the building, together with the acquisition of shelving, counters, book-stock and technology, took several months and the building finally became an operational lending library in February 1995, just six months after the fire. Within a further six months the book issues and visitor figures had returned to the levels experienced in the former Central Library. Every opportunity was taken to stress publicly and politically that this was a temporary facility, in case acceptance of the building as a new library might remove any expectation of a longer-term, under-one-roof solution in the centre of the city. For the same reasons, the temptation was resisted to use space in the temporary lending library for any reference or study facility despite a public demand for such services.

The finding of suitable premises for the reference library, the local studies library and the County Record Office took longer. Eventually, a disused office block was chosen which, over its five floors, was sufficient to house all three services. Its location was far from ideal, situated as it was in a secondary shopping centre 2 km from the city centre, but all city centre options had been exhausted and there was a danger that the immediacy of the need would pass and no temporary solution would be accepted. Although access and lifts in this building were acceptable, the fact that it had been used as offices meant a considerable amount of work had to be undertaken to transform it into a useable library and record office. The reference library moved into the new premises in June 1995 and the building became fully operational in the autumn of that year, just over a year after the fire. At first, because of the location and because the public had become used to life without the service, the take-up was slow. Staff took every opportunity to publicize the existence of the temporary facilities and, after a full year of operation, business was back to the former levels.

The political and financial implications of developing two temporary libraries in a relatively short space of time should not be understated. The insurance negotiations were on-going and there was no certainty that all the associated costs of the temporary premises would be met. There was some political feeling that the money would be better spent on a permanent replacement library earlier rather than later, even though the vision of a long-term replacement was beginning to open up many imaginative possibilities. Some of the options for the temporary premises were at a lower order of cost and this appealed to the more cautious politicians. Much hard work was put in by senior library and financial staff to make the case for the preferred solutions. Throughout the whole period, from the immediate recovery period through to the brief for the permanent replacement, the political responsibility was put into the hands of a specifically formed 'Fire Sub Committee' of the Policy and Resources Committee of the County Council. This put the decision-making firmly in the upper echelons of the political hierarchy, but removed direct involvement from the Libraries and Recreation Committee. This inevitably caused some difficulties and, although the library officers made every effort to keep their parent committee informed of decisions and options, there was a significant feeling of disenfranchisement by some of the elected members.

Since, at this stage, it was uncertain how long it would take to establish the permanent replacement library, the leases for the two temporary premises were negotiated to be as open ended as possible with break clauses after three and five years. The actual end date of the leases was seven years and the new building (see 'Conclusion', pp. 210–11) was delivered with just a month to spare.

Other premises were required as well as the two identified above and a search for those was continuing alongside the fitting out of the lending and reference library. Ideally the 100 000 reserve stock (lending and reference), once cleaned, should be co-located with the lending or reference libraries or split between the two sites. However, there was insufficient room at either site to accommodate this quantity of stock and a limited selection only could be stored there. Access to the collections would be required on a daily basis and if storage were to be elsewhere, additional staff and transportation costs would be incurred. The warehouse site identified for the cleaning operation would suffice while the cleaning was in progress, but maintaining a staff presence beyond then would prove too costly. It was eventually decided to rationalize the storage facilities at the County Headquarters and at the Great Yarmouth library and accommodate the stock there, where staff were already on hand to administer the collections. This storage space did not have the right environmental or security conditions for the rare stock of the Norfolk Studies reserve or the City Library collection, so these were stored in spare space in the Suffolk County Archive store in Ipswich, thanks to Suffolk County Council.

The former Central Library had contained a very substantial collection of sets of vocal and orchestral scores for performance hire. Nearly all these had been lost in the fire and, whereas space in one of the city branch libraries would suffice for the staff and limited stock of this collection for a short period after the fire, it became obvious that as the replacement collection was built up more space would be required. Redundant space adjoining another city branch library was leased and adapted to take this growing collection and the service operated from there until the permanent library was opened.

LESSONS LEARNED

- While it is important to set out the ideal requirements for a temporary replacement library, compromises are necessary. If the ideal were insisted upon, the temporary facilities would not be available in time to constitute a genuine continuity of service.
- Compromises over size, location, collocation of service and environmental conditions will be necessary.
- The staff and the public need to be kept informed of progress towards a temporary solution. Six months may not seem long after the fire, but at the time, to the staff and the public managing with the 'makeshift' arrangements, it seemed like an eternity.
- This information, however, must not be allowed to obstruct or compromise the decision-making process. Decisions should not be pre-empted in publicity or staff briefings. On the other hand, staff should not read decisions in the press before they hear about them from senior colleagues. This is not always possible to achieve, but an ideal to strive for.
- The costs and time involved in adapting and equipping a temporary premise are naturally just as great as those required for a permanent library. Staff need to be prepared to cut corners and make quick decisions if temporary timescales are to be achieved.

REPLACEMENT STOCK

What is a library without books? The stock loss sustained in the fire needed to be replaced in some way before temporary facilities could operate effectively. From the very early days after the fire the purchase of replacement stock began. Pre-empting the insurance settlement, £1 million was allocated from the county's insurance reserve to start the process. The first target was the lending stock so that, once a building was found and adapted, the temporary lending library could operate with a full complement of books. Four to six months were allowed for this operation.

In a normal year the acquisition staff, and the processes they manage, handle about 125 000 items with a value of £1.2 million. To meet the replacement target they would be expected to continue with routine work (the rest of the service had to continue as normal) and deal with twice the throughput in a third of the time. This was not possible without a significant increase in resources. New staff were recruited and trained – no easy undertaking itself. The County Training Room was commandeered to act as an extension to the acquisitions unit, and new computer equipment, trolleys, tables and chairs were ordered.

One month after the fire the buying process was underway. Librarians from other parts of the service were asked to help the Norwich librarians with the tasks of selection and ordering. This entailed showroom visits to the leading library suppliers, visits to local bookshops, pouring over lists and catalogues and using the printout of the stock which was on the shelves the day before the fire as a checklist. One third of the stock of the library had been on loan at the time of the fire, but without this printout we would not have known which third. As it was, with a team of up to 12 librarians selecting from more than 10 different sources simultaneously, some duplication was inevitable, but this was kept to a minimum.

One of the principles adopted was to replace like for like but not title for title. This provided us with the opportunity to update the stock and tailor it to the needs of a temporary library. Because of the temporary nature of the planned service and the fact that only about 80 per cent of the shelf capacity of the former lending library was expected to be available, the second principle of purchase was that staff should concentrate on the popular and standard titles, rather than the higher-level academic and senior practitioner stock. As a regional centre, Norwich had always prided itself on its depth of stock to meet these needs, but in the light of the temporary nature of the service for the foreseeable future, Norfolk rapidly became a heavy net borrower from the Inter Library Loan Service rather than the net lender it had been previously. This inevitably put a heavier burden on other authorities and libraries in the region and increased Norfolk's ILL (Inter-Library Loan) costs considerably.

One of the challenges to be addressed was dealing with donations. Inevitably, after a disaster of this magnitude, the local community wanted to help, and one way in which they felt able to do this was to look at the contents of their own bookshelves (or their attics) and offer those books for which they no longer had a use as donations. Some libraries offered sections of their stock; some publishers or booksellers offered a free choice from their stock up to a given value; some publishers simply sent books by post or courier. The quality and relevance of these donations was wide and varied. The generosity of the donors was touching and was genuinely appreciated. However, some of the donations were more suited to a charity bookshop or a jumble sale than a public library. Whereas we needed books to fill the shelves, we did not want to compromise our high standards of stock selection and maintenance and so a tactful letter was drafted in which we thanked the donor for his/her generosity, but stressed that we reserved the right to use the material donated in the best interests of the service, which might include selling it on to raise money to buy further books. This process was formalized in the 'Great Norfolk Book Hunt' which was launched for the Norfolk Studies Library (see below).

Storage of the newly acquired stock until such time as the temporary library building became available could have been a problem if we had not already leased warehouse space for the cleaning and storage of the stack stock. 120 000 items cannot simply be left in boxes. The library suppliers may have undertaken to store the books for us (as they did with the stock purchased for the permanent library), but we were fortunate to have the space available. However, it is an issue which other libraries in a similar situation may have to address.

The replacement of the lost Local Studies stock was a totally different matter. There is no standard supplier of local books by the metre. Most of the stock to be purchased had long been out of print and was, almost by definition, scarce or rare and, in some cases, unique.

The first challenge was to identify the stock which had been lost, estimated at 25 000 volumes. This was not easy since, unlike the general stock, the local history catalogue was on card and not automated and had been destroyed by the fire. A painstaking fingertip search of the ashes and paper pulp that remained was undertaken, looking for any scraps of title pages, chapter headings or page headers which might give clues as to the identity of the damaged material. As a result of this search some 8000 of the missing items were identified. This information, together with the collective memories of staff and regular users and the annotated pages of some local bibliographies, led to the compilation of a shopping list of some 16 000 items. Not surprisingly a search of local antiquarian and second-hand bookshops revealed only a very small proportion of these titles, often at inflated prices.

The task of replacing these items was kick-started by the launch of the Great Norfolk Book Hunt. As indicated earlier, the community was anxious to help the rebuilding process and none more so than those interested in local history. The press and media were particularly keen to harness this enthusiasm and, in partnership with the local newspaper and the local radio station, an appeal was launched for books on the locality. Collection points were set up in all libraries and forms of gift were drawn up to account for the donations. A series of Antiques Roadshow (a popular BBC television show, where members of the public bring various artefacts and antiques to experts for opinion and valuation) sessions were held in main libraries where the finds and donations of the public were examined and commented on by local experts. Books, photographs, maps, pamphlets and ephemera poured into the libraries. The result was an overwhelming response and the donation of a staggering 12 000 items. Not all of them were of local significance, but about a third of the donations were direct matches for items on the 'wants' list and many more were invaluable like for like replacements. Some were loaned by their owners so that microform, digital or paper copies could be taken. Some local antiquarian collectors donated large sections of their own collections, promised them as bequests or passed them over as lifetime deposits.

The overall result, as well as giving a tremendous boost to the replacement programme, forged links with the public which dramatically improved relationships with the user community.

Despite this encouraging start, it was evident that the task of completing the replacement of the lost stock was going to be a long, drawn-out process. Buying from further afield was essential and so perusing antiquarian book catalogues, visits to London and Hay-on-Wye and attending auctions became the daily routine for the local studies librarian. The reconstruction of the Colman Collection (a collection of antiquarian material built up by Jeremiah Colman in the mid-nineteenth century, and donated to the library service by the Colman family) was one of the most challenging aspects of the search. The stock was of high value and many of the items were unique in that they contained contemporary annotations. They were the sort of titles which only rarely appear on the second-hand antiquarian market and were nearly always sold by auction. Telephone bidding and sealed bids to US auction houses became the norm and, at the time of writing, approximately 2500 of the 3700 items lost have been replaced with identical or similar titles.

LESSONS LEARNED

- There is a clear need to prioritize the selection criteria. Decisions need to be taken such as:
  - Are you buying for short-term expediency or long-term need (remembering that the books will date and may be obsolete before a long-term building solution is available)?
  - Are you buying the whole range or just parts of it?
  - Are you aiming to replace title for title or simply like for like?
- The staffing, space and equipment resources for a major replacement programme in a short time are critical.
- Spread the load of selecting between a range of staff with a range of expertise, but build in mechanisms for avoiding duplicate buying.
- Be aware of the impact of the loss and your replacement programme on the inter-lending load.
- Capitalize on the power of public or user appeal for replacements, but be prepared with a clear strategy on donations and communicate this with the potential donors.
- A major loss from an antiquarian collection will inevitably inflate local prices. Be prepared to look further afield for the replacements.
- Keep a record of stock holdings, even if only a title list, off-site either on paper or on computer disk. You will be lost without a catalogue or stock list and it makes insurance negotiations so much easier (see below).

INSURANCE

From the first day after the fire, negotiations started with the insurers on the value of the property and contents destroyed or damaged. Norfolk County Council was self-insured for the first £250 000 of the claim, but discussions started with the loss adjusters appointed by the insurers on the total value of the damage and the cost of the consequential losses. This latter covered the County Council for the cost of providing short-term and medium-term replacement services over and above the costs it would have borne if the fire had not taken place, but it did not cover the costs of making the claim, which were significant. Much senior staff time went into the identification and valuation process and into the negotiations themselves, the additional cost of which had to be borne by the County Council. The first major task was the identification and valuation of the lost stock. For the general lending, reference and audio-visual stock this was based on the printout of all the stock on the shelves the night before the fire. However, it became obvious, and was accepted by the insurers, that a title-by-title valuation of some 125 000 items was not practicable given that many of the titles would have been out of print or superseded by later editions. It would also have been a very lengthy and costly process. Instead, an analysis was undertaken of the non-fiction by class number and current average prices for standard and academic stock by subject were obtained from the Library and Information Statistics Unit (LISU) at Loughborough University (Library and Information Statisics Unit, 2002). These prices were applied to the stock numbers in each classification band according to a formula agreed by the insurers. Average prices were negotiated for the audio-visual and fiction stock and applied to the agreed numbers lost.

The lost and damaged Norfolk Studies stock presented more of a problem, since, as indicated above, no catalogue of the stock survived. The fingertip search mentioned earlier yielded a list of some 16 000 items known to have been lost or damaged beyond repair. This list was sent for two independent valuations (a local antiquarian bookseller and a local auction house). The average of the resultant valuations (which were within 10 per cent of each other) was then applied to the total estimated loss of 25 000 items. After much detailed negotiation a settlement figure was agreed. The damaged but repairable Local Studies stock was subject to a repair and conservation estimate by Riley, Dunn and Wilson. Much discussion took place on the need for conservation, washing and de-acidifying following the effects of the fire and the need for cloth or leather bindings on some of the more valuable items. There were also significant questions from the insurers as to whether microform copies of some of the items (especially the bound newspaper volumes) would not be adequate rather than incurring the high costs of conservation. This discussion turned on whether the loss was simply about the information content or the artefact value as well as the content.

A major loss on which it was very difficult to place a straightforward replacement value was the news-cuttings file: seventy-five years of indexed cuttings of local significance had been turned to pulp by the water. A costing exercise was undertaken on a hypothetical project to photocopy relevant articles from 75 years of the local newspapers and reconstruct the lost file. This was then compared with the cost of creating digital copies of the newspapers from the surviving microfilm and indexing relevant articles from the resultant file. The cost of the latter approach was found to be significantly lower, as well as offering a more flexible approach to the material and a platform for future development.

Although details of the main furniture and major equipment (including computer equipment) in the library were held on an inventory maintained off-site, many smaller items were not recorded. To develop a valuation of these required much taxing of staff memories and the creation of a long list of the items lost or damaged beyond repair. This list was valued by a purchasing agency deemed to be independent. A final settlement sum was agreed in August 1995; the total agreed value was £13.98 million and it was agreed that this would be paid as a cash settlement rather than the more usual payment against incurred reinstatement costs. This form of settlement gave the County Council the flexibility to use the cash in the most appropriate way and gain the benefit of improved cashflow and interest yield. Although the insurance negotiations took over a year, an agreement was reached at the outset, as mentioned earlier, for an 'on-account' release of £1 million for book purchase, and approval to place orders for replacement computer equipment and consequential loss costs were met as they were incurred. This was essential if service continuity was to be guaranteed.

LESSONS LEARNED

- It is important to check the terms and value of insurance cover, particularly to confirm that the cover includes consequential loss, since the cost of managing the recovery process and of establishing and maintaining temporary services can be very high.
- The staff time involved in assessing the value of the loss and processing the claim can be very high, and is not usually covered by the insurance policy.
- It is essential to maintain up-to-date records of stock, furniture and equipment so that any claim can be proved and expedited. Copies of such catalogues and inventories should be kept off-site.
- Be prepared for protracted negotiations and make provision for interim budgets to cover the essential incurred costs during the process.

LONG-TERM REPLACEMENT

From the early days after the fire, alongside the preparation of temporary services, the rescue and recovery of the stock, the purchase of replacement stock and the negotiation of the insurance settlement, work started on the plans for a permanent replacement library. Initially at least, the plan was to rebuild on the site of the previous library on a like-for-like basis, although there was considerable debate over whether some parts of the original building were salvageable. The County Council was keen to see the building replaced as soon as possible and recognized the opportunity for improving and enlarging both the library and the Record Office for relatively little additional outlay should that be the wish of the users. Consequently a survey was commissioned to determine the community's wishes in this regard. With full cooperation from all the local media over 150 000 questionnaires were sent out which elicited a 3.4 per cent response. The questions posed (with substantial supporting information) were:

- Would you support or oppose the possibility of the County Council spending up to an extra £2.75 million to improve the new library?
- Would you prefer the Record Office to be rebuilt on the existing site or rebuilt elsewhere in the Norwich area (separate from the library)?
- Would you support or oppose the possibility of the County Council spending up to an extra £3 million to improve the new Record Office?

Further questions were posed to establish where the respondents lived, their sex, employment and their age-group, and their frequency of use of the previous facilities. The results were a strong vote (73 per cent) in favour of an enhanced library and 55 per cent in favour of an enlarged Record Office. Sixty-seven per cent of respondents indicated that they would prefer the Record Office to be rebuilt or recreated on a site separate from the library. This latter preference was due to a number of factors:

- Long-term researchers preferred an out-of-town site where parking restrictions were fewer and access was easier.
- There was a nervousness about housing the unique records with a public library after the disaster of August 1994.
- The out-of-town site favoured at that time was the University of East Anglia and there was obvious potential synergy between the research activity at the university (in particular the Centre for East Anglian Studies) and the research resources of the County Archive.

However it was also recognized that there was a similar synergy between the Record Office activity and the resources of the Local Studies library. If it was accepted that if the Record Office was to be rebuilt on an out-of-town site then

207

some provision for a secondary search facility should be provided in the Central Library to meet the needs of those researchers who required access to both the archives and the Local Studies stock. To test the validity of this assumption a further study was undertaken which consisted of a telephone survey of users of the Local Studies library or the Record Office (or both), a consultation meeting with representatives of organizations interested in Norfolk life and a meeting with representatives of history departments in schools and colleges. The results of this study confirmed the preference for a Record Office and Local Studies library in separate locations, but with a secondary records search facility in the library.

Extensive desk research was undertaken to establish the expected demographic and societal changes over the next 20 years to contribute to the planning process for the replacement library. In summary this showed:

- a significant (30 per cent) increase in the number of pensioners over the period
- that the number of those pensioners with higher or further education would rise from 1 per cent to 7 per cent
- an increase in life expectancy of up to five years
- a reduction in the number of 16–18-year-olds
- an increase of 25 per cent in the number leaving school to go on to further or higher education
- 70 per cent of all jobs will be 'knowledge based'
- 35 per cent of all jobs will require higher education
- 50 per cent of jobs will be part-time or short term
- 7 per cent increase in Norfolk's population
- 100 per cent increase in leisure time compared with the previous generation
- a significant increase in the availability of home computers
- an increase in computer literacy.

The outcome of this research was that a new central library needed to cater for:

- an older population
- a greater demand for learning
- a greater need for regular re-training of the workforce
- an increase in leisure time
- a greater demand for information
- an increasingly computer-literate user base
- an increasing demand for virtual services.

The options were to develop a library capable of meeting these needs on a standalone basis on the site occupied by the former library or to develop a more ambitious, multi-agency facility using a bigger site. Discussions took place between the County Council, which owned the library site, and the Norwich City Council, which owned the public car-park immediately in front of it, and several other local agencies. The result of extensive discussions was a bid to the UK Millennium Commission for lottery funding for a £80 million building which, as well as the library, would include a business technology centre, a major tourist attraction, a public space, meeting rooms, a café, a digital studio, a multi-media auditorium and a 400-space underground car-park. 'Technopolis', as the project was named, would also be the hub of a countywide computer network incorporating branch libraries and telecottages. After much deliberation this bid was rejected by the Millennium Commission, but a re-scoped, less costly bid was invited.

This revised bid was eventually approved and, as a result, detailed design work began on the Norfolk and Norwich Millennium Project, which later became known as 'The Forum' (see Norfolk County Council Library and Information Service, 'Welcome to the Norfolk and Norwich Millennium Library at the Forum', 2002). This scheme, with a total value of £60 million, incorporated a 4621m² library, a learning centre and a learning shop, a tourist information centre, a visitor attraction, a public open, covered space, cafés and a restaurant and a 200- space underground car-park. The simplicity of this statement disguises the huge amount of work done in a very short time. Only four months elapsed from the rejection of the first bid and the closing date for the submission of the alternative. As well as re-scoping the whole project and redesigning the building, work also had to be continued on the option for a standalone library because there was no certainty that the revised proposal would be completed in time or that it would be accepted. Two years had already passed since the fire and the consequential loss cover would run out in one year's time, so expediting a replacement library was of vital importance to the public and to Norfolk County Council.

However, the bid was successful, building work began on-site in May 1999 and the building was opened in November 2001, seven years after the fire. The library is state-of-the-art and contained on three floors of a spectacular building. It includes the following features and services:

- 120 000 books for loan or reference on the open shelves
- integrated reference and lending stock in subject departments
- 350 000 reserve stock and Local Studies items in a compact storage stack
- an 'Express' popular lending library available on a self-service basis after normal hours
- an eye-catching and fun children's library
- 2nd Air Division Memorial Library for the USAAF
- Norfolk Studies library and secondary search area for Norfolk Records

- a business library and European Information Centre
- self-service terminals
- 220 study desks
- 85 public access terminals and kiosks for internet access, word processing, library catalogue, CD-ROM service
- a digitized collection of photographs and local newspapers
- a programme for further digitization of records from Norfolk Archives.

In parallel with this development, a bid was submitted to the Heritage Lottery Fund for a replacement Record Office. This also was successful and work started late in 2001 on building a new Record Office out of the city centre. This is due for completion in the spring of 2003.

CONCLUSION

The birth of an idea for the replacement of a major central library to the completion of the project can often take many years. Seeking political approval may involve overcoming the obstacles of changing political power during the process, with the inevitable change of political will or thinking about the project.

Figure 9.3 Norfolk and Norwich Millennium Library: Interior view of the first floor
(Photograph: Jacqueline Wyatt. Reproduced by permission of Norfolk Library and Information Service.)

The significant capital and revenue finance necessary for a project of such scope is often not easy to obtain or sustain. The trauma and upheaval experienced following a major disaster is not the most stable of platforms on which to base a planned approach to a new library and the speed necessary for a replacement when a city is deprived of its central library may mean that partnerships are difficult to sustain. The negotiations necessary for a successful partnership are sometimes protracted, and this does not always sit well with the need for urgent decisions. Despite this, the disaster of 1 August 1994 proved, with hindsight, to have been a blessing and Norwich can now boast one of the finest public libraries in the country. As an article in *The Times* (Morrison, 2001) headlined: 'It is not luck but judgement that has produced a superb prototype of the 21st century public library'.

REFERENCES AND SELECT BIBLIOGRAPHY

2nd Air Division Memorial Library (2002) Norwich, UK, available at: <www.2ndair.org.uk/> (accessed 29 August 2002).

Harwell Drying and Restoration Services (2002), available at: <www.harwell-drying.demon.co.uk> (accessed 29 August 2002).

Hammond, H. (1996) 'Norfolk and Norwich Library, the emerging Phoenix', *New Library World*, 97 (1130): 24–31.

Hayman, D. (1995) 'The Norwich Central Library fire', *Survive!*, May, 22–3.

Kennedy, J. (1995) 'Norfolk Record Office: an initial report', *Journal of the Society of Archivists*, 16 (1), 3–6.

Library and Information Statistics Unit (LISU) (2002), see <www.lboro.ac.uk/departments/dils/lisu/lisuhp/html> (accessed 29 August 2002).

Morrison, R. (2001) 'It is not luck but judgement that has produced a superb prototype of the 21st century public library', *The Times*, 2, 8 November: 7.

Norfolk County Council, Library and Information Service, 'Welcome to the Norfolk and Norwich Millennium Library at the Forum' (2002), available at: <www.library.norfolk.gov.uk/millenniumlib.htm> (accessed 29 August 2002).

Pearson, B.P. (1995) *An Inquiry into the Fire at the Norwich Central Library on the 1st August 1994*, Norwich: Norfolk County Council.

10 A guide to sources of information

Graham Matthews

As disaster management is an aspect of preservation management, many sources of information on preservation will contain information on disaster management. It is therefore worth considering general preservation sources (for example, Matthews, G. (2003) 'Preservation management – sources of information', in J. Feather (ed.), *Managing Preservation in Libraries and Archives: Current Policies and Future Developments*, Aldershot: Ashgate) as well as the more subject specific ones below (and others at the end of the chapters in this book).

GENERAL

Guides (books, chapters and short articles) to disaster management for libraries and the broader cultural heritage sector continue to appear, including for example:

Alire, C. (ed.) (2000) *Library Disaster Planning and Recovery Handbook*, New York: Neal–Schuman Publishers. (Based on experience at the Morgan Library, Colorado State University campus, devastated by a massive flood.)

Batchelor, K. (1999) *Records Management: A Guide to Disaster Prevention and Recovery*, DISCPD0013:1999, London: British Standards Institution.

Coult, G. (2001) 'Disaster recovery', *Managing Information*, 8 (8): 36–9.

Doig, J. (1997) *Disaster Recovery for Archives, Libraries and Records Management Systems in Australia and New Zealand*, Topics in Australasian Library and Information Studies Number 12, Riverina Wagga Wagga, New South Wales: Centre for Information Studies, Charles Sturt University.

Dorge, V. and Jones, S. (comps) (1999) *Building an Emergency Plan. A Guide for Museums and Other Cultural Institutions*, Los Angeles, California: Getty Conservation Institute.

East Midlands Museums Service (2001) *The EmmS Emergency Manual for Historic Buildings and Collections*, Nottingham: East Midlands Museums Service. (Available as interactive CD-ROM; for further details see: <www.emms.org.uk>)

Historical Manuscripts Commission (2002) *Protecting Archives and Manuscripts against Disasters*, Advisory memorandum no.6, London: Historical Manuscripts Commission.

International Council on Archives. Committee on Disaster Prevention (1997) *Guidelines on Disaster Prevention and Control in Archives*, Paris: ICA.

Kahn, M. (1998) *Disaster Response and Planning for Libraries*, Chicago: American Library Association.

Matthews, G. and Eden, P. (1996) *Disaster Management in British Libraries. Project Report with Guidelines for Library Managers*, Library and Information Research Report 109, London: The British Library.

Pendry, J. (2000) 'Making a fast recovery', *Managing Information*, 7 (2): 68–70, 72–3.

Society of Archivists, Scottish Region, Disaster Preparedness Working Group (1996) *Disaster Preparedness: Guidelines for Archives and Libraries*, London: Society of Archivists.

Trotta, C.J. and Trotta, M. (2001) *The Librarian's Facility Management Handbook* (Chapter 7, 'Preparing emergency and disaster plans', 139–73.) New York: Neal–Schuman Publishers.

Wellheiser, J. and Scott, J. (2002) *An Ounce of Prevention: Integrated Disaster Planning for Archives, Libraries and Archive Centres*, 2nd edn, Lanham, Maryland: The Scarecrow Press Inc. and Canadian Archives Foundation.

CHAPTERS IN PRESERVATION TEXTBOOKS

Chapters in general texts on preservation often contain chapters or sections on disaster management. These are also useful in seeing disaster management in the broader context of preservation management. See, for example:

Ogden, S. (ed.) (1999) *Preservation of Library and Archival Materials: a Manual*, 3rd edn (Section 3, 'Emergency management') Andover, Massachusetts: Northeast Document Conservation Center, also available at: <www.nedcc.org/plam3/index3.htm>

Swartzburg, S.G. (1995) *Preserving Library Materials: a Library Manual*, 2nd edn, (Chapter 6, Emergency planning and library security, pp. 93–113) Scarecrow Press: Metuchen, New Jersey.

JOURNALS

General library and information science and archive journals contain occasional articles on disaster management. Appropriate abstracting and indexing services will help find these. For specific aspects of disaster management, titles such as *Library and Archival Security* and *Computers and Security*, for example, should be consulted. Preservation titles such as the *Abbey Newsletter, International Preservation News*, and the *NPO Journal* are useful to keep up to date with new publications and conferences and training on disaster management.

BIBLIOGRAPHIES

Day, M. (2000) 'Digital disasters – are you prepared? A Bibliography.' Handout produced for: *Digital disasters: are you prepared? Digital perspectives and Disaster Management*, M25 Consortium of Higher Education Libraries, joint Disaster Management Group seminar, University College London, 23 June 2000, available at: <www.ukoln/metadata/presentations/ucl/bibliography. html>.

Kulzack, D. and Lennertz, L. (1999), 'A decade of disaster: a selected bibliography of disaster literature, 1985–1995', *Library and Archival Security*, 15 (1): 7–66.

WEBSITES

General/international

Conservation onLine (CoOL), Disaster Preparedness and Response, available at: <www.palimpsest.stanford.edu/bytopic/disasters/>.
  Produced by the Preservation Department of Stanford University Libraries, it has an emphasis on North American sources but also includes much of broader worldwide interest either in its content or via links. Provides information/links to resources on disaster management, by organization/author, to disaster plans, case histories, bibliographic resources.

European Commission on Preservation and Access (ECPA), available at: <www.knaw.nl/ecpa/>.
  The European Commission on Preservation and Access (ECPA), established in 1994, acts as a focus for discussion of and cooperation in preservation and access issues for heritage organizations throughout Europe. It is based at the Royal Netherlands Academy of Arts and Sciences. The website aims to be a gateway to information on the preservation of the documentary heritage in Europe and contains routine, but useful, information on news and resources, its own publications, training, links to other sites (worldwide) and a discussion list, EPIC-LST.

United Nations Educational, Scientific and Cultural Organization (UNESCO), Memory of the World Programme

<www.unesco.org/webworld/mdm/index_2.html>.

The UNESCO Memory of the World Programme, Preserving Documentary Heritage offers access through its website directory to wide-ranging information on preservation of worldwide interest. The site (available in English or French) offers information on news and events, links and publications (basic texts, databases, CD-ROMs). See also, its 'Safeguarding the documentary heritage: a guide to standards, recommended practices and reference literature related to the preservation of documents of all kinds'.

UNESCO Archives Portal. Disaster Preparedness and Recovery

<www.unesco.org/webworld/portal_archives/pages/Preservation_and Conservation/Disaster_Preparedness_andRecovery/>.

Provides links to various resources ranging from primers on disaster management, a journal on contingency planning to institutional guides and Emergency Response Action Steps from the US Federal Emergency Management Agency (FEMA – <www.fema.gov/>).

In summer 2002 it made available 'Floods in Europe: damages to libraries and archives, an information service on the damage to libraries and archives in Europe and actions for disaster recovery' (<www.unesco.org/webworld/floods_europe>).

National

Many websites of national or regional associations, organizations and libraries will contain information of interest and use to those in countries elsewhere. The following are examples that contain a variety of information, but it should be noted that many refer to the same resources and to each other.

United Kingdom

National Preservation Office based at the British Library

<www.bl.uk/services/preservation/national.html>

The National Preservation Office, established in 1984, aims 'to provide an independent focus for ensuring the preservation and continued accessibility of library and archival material held in the United Kingdom and Ireland'. It has developed and coordinated a national preservation strategy and offers an information and referral service. Its website provides information about its activities (including strategic plan), committees and publications (free and priced); it produces a range of guidance leaflets on preservation management, security, conference reports, seminar papers, videos and promotional materials and links to other sites, with a 'what's new' feature.

The Society of Archivists
<www.archives.org.uk>
In addition to standard information about the society, its membership, panels, regions, groups, education and training, annual conference, publications, diary of events and contacts, the website includes cover stories and spotlights latest features.

Digital Preservation Coalition
<www.dpconline.org/graphics/index.html>
This is a new initiative (2002) which should include, among its broader coverage, information of relevance to disaster management and digital materials. See, for example, 4.3, 'Storage and preservation' in *Preservation Management of Digital Materials – the Handbook*, first compiled by N. Beagrie and M. Jones (2001), The British Library, now updated by the DPC and available at: <www.dpconline.org/graphics/handbook/index.html>.

United States

American Library Association, 'Disaster preparedness clearinghouse', available at:
<www.ala.org/alcts/publications/disaster.html>
' ... It contains resources, links to the disaster preparedness sites of agencies whose primary role is emergency response or conservation, and information on available training ...'
Amigos Library Services
<www.amigos.org/preserve.html>
' ... a non-profit, grant-funded service which provides preservation information, support and training to librarians and archivists in the Southwestern US ...' It offers assistance with planning and recovery activities, training workshops and a basic disaster plan.
California Preservation Clearinghouse, 'Disasters', available at:
Provides links to a disaster plan exercise, a generic disaster plan (of the Inland Empire Libraries Disaster Response Network, see below and Chapter 6).
California State Archives, 'Disaster Preparedness and Recovery Resources on the Web', available at:
<www.ss.ca.gov/archives/level3_disaster.html>
Provides links to local, federal and other resources.
Heritage Emergency National Task Force
<www.heritagepreservation.org/PROGRAMS/TASFER.HTM>
Previously the National Task Force on Emergency Response, co-sponsored by Heritage Preservation and the Federal Emergency Management Agency. Provides a variety of information, including details of Heritage Emergency

National Task Force (1997), 'Emergency response and salvage wheel', a sliding chart for archives, libraries and museums (see <www.heritage preservation.org/PROGRAMS/Wheel1.htm>).

Inland Empire Libraries Disaster Response Network

'A cooperative network of public and academic libraries in San Bernadino, Riverside, and Eastern Los Angeles Counties which work together to prepare for and recover from disasters' (see Chapter 6).

Library of Congress, Preservation Directorate, 'Emergency preparedness and response', available at:

<www.lcweb.loc.gov/preserv/pubsemer.html>

Northeast Document Conservation Center (NEDCC), disaster assistance, available at:

<www.nedcc.org/welcome/disaster.htm>

Its website asserts that NEDCC, founded in 1973, 'is the largest non-profit, regional conservation center in the United States'. Among other services, it makes available *Preservation 101: An Internet Course on Paper Preservation*, a well thought out and presented programme. Lesson 6 deals with emergency preparedness and offers strategies and tips for writing a disaster plan, with details of printed and on-line resources. NDCC offers a range of Emergency Management Technical Leaflets, for example, Albright, G. (1999) *Emergency Salvage of Wet Photographs*, Technical Leaflet Emergency Management, Section 3, Leaflet 8, Northeast Document Conservation Center, Andover, MA.

Regional Alliance for Preservation

A cooperative programme with 14 member organizations throughout the USA, its mission is 'to provide comprehensive preservation information to cultural institutions and the public throughout the United States'. Initially funded in 1997 as a pilot project of the Commission on Preservation and Access, participants decided to continue RAP and expanded membership to include the Association of Regional Conservation Centers. Available at: <www.rap-arcc.org/leaflets/grfemer.htm> is Reilly, J.A. (1997) *Are you Prepared? A Guide to Emergency Planning*, The Gerald R. Ford Conservation Center, The Nebraska State Historical Society for the Nebraska Museums Association, Omaha, Nebraska.

Solinet Preservation Service, 'Disaster mitigation and recovery resources', available at:

<www.solinet.net/preservation/preservation_templ.cfm?doc_id=71>

'The Southeastern Library Network is a not-for-profit library cooperative providing resource sharing for the educational, cultural, and economic advancement of the southeastern United States.' Founded in 1973, it now has a membership of over 2100 of all kinds of libraries. It provides information about, or links to, products, publications, videos, and leaflets covering a range of topics from protection from wild fires, disaster recovery services and supplies to the contents of a disaster control plan and a disaster prevention and protection checklist.

Australia

National Library of Australia
<www.nla.gov.au/preserve>
The National Library website offers a range of useful information under its Preservation Activities pages, for example, on its collection disaster plan.
National Archives of Australia, *Disaster Preparedness Manual for Commonwealth Agencies*, available at:
<www.naa.gov.au/recordkeeping/preservation/disaster/chapt1.html>
(preservation of digital materials).

DISASTER CONTROL PLANS

Advice on drawing up plans, about specific actions and issues, and reviews of their implementation is widely available. Disaster control plans from various organizations are available via many of the websites above and elsewhere. Some examples are included below.

Council on Library and Information Resources and Cornell University (2002), *Library Preservation and Conservation. Southeast Asia Tutorial*, available at:
Funded by the Henry Luce Foundation, the tutorial is aimed at libraries and archives in Southeast Asia. Within its broad preservation coverage, it includes sections on security and disaster management, offering step-by-step advice, further sources (print and web-based) and cases for discussion.
Graham, R. and Prideaux, A. (2000) *Insurance for Museums. Guidelines for Good Practice*, London: Museums and Galleries Commission.
Henson, S. (2000) 'Writing the disaster response plan: going beyond shouting "Help! Help!"', in *Proceedings of the 9th Annual Federal Depository Library Conference, October 22–25, 2000*. Available at:
<www.access.gpo.gov/su_docs/fdlp/pubs/proceedings/00pro28.html>.
Illinois State University Libraries Plan (2001), available at:
<www.palimpsest.stanford.edu/bytopic/disasters/plans/isudis.html>.
Kaur, J. (1999) 'An investigation into information recovery planning for a large law firm library', *Library and Information Research News*, 23 (73): 24–37.

Lyall, J (1996) 'Disaster planning for libraries and archives: understanding the essential issues', *Provenance*, 1 (2) (<www.netpac.com/provenance/vol1/no2/features/lyall1.htm>).

Maslen, C. (1996) 'Testing the plan is more important than the plan itself', *Information Management and Computer Security*, 4 (3): 26–9.

McColgin, M. (2001) *Soaring to Excellence. Disaster Recovery Plan*, Colorado Preservation Alliance, available at:
<www.archives.state.co.us/cpa/articles/disaster/disasterplan2.html>.

Norris, D.H. (1998) *Disaster Recovery. Salvaging Photograph Collections*, Philadelphia: Conservation Center for Art and Historic Artifacts.

Page, J.A. and Riley, C.A. (2001) 'In an emergency: salvaging library collections', *Serials Librarian*, 40 (1/2): 19–30.

Preiss, L. (1999) 'Learning from disasters: a decade of experience at the National Library of Australia', *International Preservation News* (20): 19–26.

Public Record Office of Northern Ireland (1997) *Disaster Plan*, available at:
<www.proni.nics.gov.uk.structur/preserve/disaster/disaster.htm>.

University of California at Berkeley (1996) *Handbook for Emergency Response*, available at:
<www.lib.berkeley.edu/Staff/Emergency/respindx.html>.

University of Newcastle upon Tyne (1998) *The Robinson Library Disaster Control Plan*, available at:
<www.ncl.ac.uk/bindery/disaster.html>.

See also: 'Websites' above.

DISASTERS – EXPERIENCES

The experiences of others in dealing with disasters can be useful sources of information and advice. A selection of available material is included below; other material is included in publications and websites mentioned elsewhere in this guide to sources.

American Library Association (2002) *Loss and Recovery: Librarians Bearing Witness to September 11, 2001*, produced by *American Libraries*, the magazine of the American Library Association, in cooperation with Library Video Network, Chicago: American Library Association (distributed by Library Video Network, Towson, Maryland). Interviews with some of the librarians who were working in or near the World Trade Center when terrorist attacks occurred. They recall the effects on information and library services and how they have recovered personally and professionally.

Colorado State University, *Lessons of Recovery,* available at: [dead link]. In July 1997, a massive flood hit Colorado State University. The Morgan Library and university bookstore were badly affected. The website compilers laudably aim to share information and to add to this as their recovery process continues. The website offers personal accounts and expert advice, with sections including: lessons, a scholarly review; images from the review, comment from staff and faculty newsletter, news releases, tips from a disaster recovery expert, public relations response to crisis, university emergency operations plan and a specialist in grief talking about coping with it. (See also Alire (2002), p. 350 and Schmidt, p. 21.)

Eng, S. (2002) 'How technology and planning saved my library at Ground Zero', *Computers in Libraries,* 22 (4): 28–32, 34–45.

Fithian, G. (1999) 'The aftermath of the flood at the Boston Public Library: lessons learned', in *Proceedings of the 8th Annual Federal Depository Library Conference, April 12–15, 1999,* available at: <www.access.gpo.gov/su_docs/ fdlp/pubs/proceedings/99pro30.html>.

Grant, A. (2000) 'Benighted!: how the university library survived the power crisis', *Australian Academic and Research Libraries,* 31 (2): 79–90.

Hammond, H. (1996) 'Norfolk and Norwich Central Library: the emerging phoenix', *New Library World,* 97 (1130): 24–31.

Heritage Preservation (2002) *Cataclysm and Challenge. Impact of September 11, 2001, on Our Nation's Cultural Heritage. A report from Heritage Preservation on Behalf of the Heritage Emergency National Task Force,* Project Director Ruth Hargeaves, Heritage Preservation: Washington, DC, available at: <www.heritagepreservation.org/NEWS/Cataclysm.htm>.
Report of a survey of the impact of the events of September 11 on cultural and historic resources at the Pentagon and in Lower Manhattan, with recommendations.

Kenny, B. and Oder, N. (2001) 'Attack on NYC, DC victimizes, strains librarians, libraries', *Library Journal,* 126 (16): 1 October, 16–17.

Loftus, J. (1999) 'Disasters: plans, clean-up, and recovery at Stanford University Libraries', in *Proceedings of the 8th Annual Federal Depository Library Conference, April 12–15, 1999,* available at: <www.access.gpo.gov/su_docs/fdlp/pubs/proceedings/99pro32.html>.

Modigh, B. (2000) 'Looking into the future: new libraries in Linköping and Harnosand', *Scandinavian Public Library Quarterly,* 33 (2): 17–19.

Morrison, R. (2001) 'It is not luck but judgement that has produced a superb prototype of the 21st-century public library', *The Times,* 2, 8 November: 7.

Muir, A. and Shenton, S. (2002) 'If the worst happens: the use and effectiveness of disaster plans in libraries and archives', *Library Management,* 23 (3): 115–23.

Nyuksha, J.P. and Leonov, V.P. (1997) 'Preservation of collections at the Russian

Academy of Sciences Library: a retrospective overview, problems and solutions', *Restaurator*, 18 (4): 201–18.

Special Libraries Association, Virtual SLA, *September 11 Disaster Help and Information Exchange*, available at: <www.sla.org/content/SLA/sept11help/index.cfm>.
Two resources, 'Disaster planning portal', and 'In memoriam' are available. The 'portal is dedicated to the librarians who were killed or injured on September 11th, 2001. SLA offers this Disaster Planning Portal as an ongoing resource to prepare for future natural or unnatural disasters.' The portal provides details of a range of articles, books, videos, and websites.

Tarmann, G. (2000) 'Innsbruck Museum: the most important thing is never to give up', *International Preservation News* (22–23): 22–4.

University of Lyon (1999) *L'incendie du 12 juin 1999* [The fire of 12 June 1999], available at: <www.phebus.univ-lyon2.fr/Bibliotheque/incendie.htm>.

University of Sussex (2000) 'Library salvage operation under way', *University of Sussex Newsletter*, 1 December, available at:
<www.sussex.ac.uk/press_office/bulletin/01dec00/article15.html>.

Webb, C. (2001) 'Disaster recovery in the York flood of 2000', *Journal of the Society of Archivists*, 22 (2): 247–52.

COMPUTERS AND NETWORKS

There is a considerable established and growing literature covering this topic in the areas of computing and business. As the digital library environment and web-based services continue to develop, libraries and archivists are beginning to reconsider this topic, that is, broadening security considerations to cover the growing amount of digital materials (both digitally created and digitized from other formats) available and their preservation and security whether they are threatened, for example, by software or hardware obsolescence, breaches of firewalls protecting networks and systems, power surges, or fire and flood. This is exemplified in the selection of sources that follow. They also provide relevant information and advice and suggestions for further sources of information.

Alire, C. (ed) (2000) 'Technical services in disaster recovery', in *Library Disaster Planning and Recovery Handbook* (Chapter 11, C. Bush, 'It was a dark and stormy night: a technical services overview', 255–82; Chapter 12, D. Cochenour, N. Copeland and J. Farmer, 'Data, data, they want the data', 283–303; Chapter 13, K. Weedman, 'Technology walks', 305–36; Chapter 14, H.R. Lange, 'Technical services: business-as-usual under unusual circumstances', 337–59; Chapter 15, P. Smith, 'Upstairs and downstairs:

implementing a processing center for restoring the collections', 361–82.), New York: Neal-Schuman Publishers.

Barclay, D.A. (2000) *Managing Public Access Computers: A How-To-Do-It Manual for Librarians*, New York: Neal–Schuman Publishers.

Benson, A.C. (1998) 'Building a secure library system', *Computers in Libraries*, 18 (3): 24–9.

Brennan, C. and O'Hara, E. (2002) 'Murphy was a librarian: a case study in how not to handle a systems crash', *Computers in Libraries*, 22 (3): 10–12, 72.

BSI (2000) *BS ISO/IEC17799:2000, (BS 7799-1:2000) Code of Practice for Information Security Management*, London: BSI.

BSI (1999) *BS7788-2:1999, Information Security Management – Part 2: Specification for Information Security Management Systems*, London: BSI.

Cox, A., Currall, J. and Connolly, S. (2001) *The Human and Organizational Issues Associated with Network Security*, JISC Committee for Awareness, Liaison and Training (JCALT) Available at: <www.litc.sbu.ac.uk/jcalt/report.pdf>.

Cravey, Pamela (2001) *Protecting Library Staff, Users, Collections and Facilities* (Chapter 4, Security of electronic files and systems, 79–103), How-to-do-it manuals for librarians number 103, New York: Neal-Schuman Publishers.

De Candido, G. A. (2000) 'Digital disaster planning: when bad things happen to good systems', *Public Libraries*, 39 (5): 258–9. Also available as: G.A. De Candido, *Digital disaster planning: when bad things happen to good systems*, Public Library Association, Tech Notes, at: <www.pla.org/publications/technotes/technotes_disaster.html>.

Hawkins, S.M., Yen, D.C. and Chou, D.C. (2000) 'Disaster recovery planning: a strategy for data security', *Information Management and Computer Security*, 8 (5): 222–30.

Hinde, S. (2001a) 'Lessons learned', *Computers and Security*, 20 (7): 561–7.

Hinde, S. (2001b) 'Incalculable potential for damage by cyber-terrorism', *Computers and Security*, 20 (7): 568–72.

Huleatt, R.S. (2000) 'The fragility of electronic information in the new millennium', *Online Newsletter*, 21 (1): 1–4.

Joyner, C.C. and Lotrionte, C. (2001) 'Information warfare as international coercion: elements of a legal framework', *European Journal of International Law*, 12 (5): 825–65.

Kelly, J.X. (2002) *Cybercrime – high tech crime*. JISC Legal Information Service, available at <www.jisc.ac.uk/legal/cybercrime.html>.

Lazinger, S.S. (2001) *Digital Preservation and Metadata: History, Theory, Practice*, Eaglewood, Colorado: Libraries Unlimited.

Myles, B. (2000) 'The impact of a library flood on computer operations', *Computers in Libraries*, 20 (1), 44–6, 48–9.

Ross, S. and Gow, A. (1999) *Digital Archaeology: Rescuing Neglected and Damaged*

Data Resources: a JISC/NPO Study Within the Electronic Libraries (eLib) Programme on the Preservation of Electronic Materials, London: Library Technology Information Centre, South Bank University.

Royle, C.J. and Schobernd, E.M. (1997) 'Disaster recovery without the disaster', *Technical Services Quarterly*, 14 (4): 13–24.

Shuman, R.A. 'Electronic security issues', in Shuman, B.A. (1999) *Library Security and Safety Handbook. Prevention, Policies and Procedures*, Chicago: American Library Association, pp. 203–50.

Tennant, R. (2001) 'Coping with disasters (Digital Libraries)', *Library Journal*, 126 (19), November: 26, 28.

Wiggins, R. (2001) 'Digital preservation: paradox and promise', *Library Journal, Net Connect Supplement*, Spring: 12–15.

COOPERATIVE ACTIVITY

A local or regional network of mutual support with other archives and libraries can relieve a sense of isolation and provide access to advice and expertise not available within the organization. Central purchase and storage of emergency equipment and supplies and joint training activities may have cost benefits too.

Berthon, H. (2001) 'Preserving together: collaborative library activities in Australia', *International Preservation News* (24): 22–5.

CAVAL Collaborative Solutions
<www.caval.edu.au/welcome.html>
CAVAL – Cooperative Action by Victorian Academic Libraries was established in 1978. 'A leader in risk management training programs for cultural institutions, CAVAL has been running disaster prevention and recovery workshops since 1989. CAVAL has its own purpose-built training facilities at the CARM [CAVAL Archival and Research Materials] Centre.' It has a Risk Management Group and offers risk management services.

Charnes, A.N. and Machovec, G. (2000) 'The role of the Colorado Alliance of Research Libraries in Colorado State University Libraries' disaster recovery', in C. Alire (ed.), *Library Disaster Planning and Recovery Handbook*, New York, Neal–Schuman Publishers, pp. 575–93.

Eden, P. and Gadd, E. (1999) *Co-operative Preservation Activities in Libraries and Archives: Project Report with Guidelines*, British Library Research and Innovation Report 161, London: The British Library.

M25 Consortium of Higher Education Libraries Disaster Management Group, available at:

www.m25lib.ac.uk/M25dcp/home_c.htm.

The site provides a web-mounted disaster plan template and links to other useful sites for use primarily by over 100 academic libraries and archives in the London area.

See also: 'Websites – national', above and Chapter 6.

HUMAN ASPECTS

Effective disaster management relies upon people. To achieve this all staff must be properly trained with regard to their particular roles. Experience of major disasters also shows that appropriate counselling should be available during and after disasters.

Jokilehto, J. (2001) 'Training as an essential part of risk preparedness', *H@R!: Heritage at Risk 2001–2002*, available at: <www.international.icomos.org/risk/2001/training2001.htm>.

Klasson, M. (2002) 'Rhetoric and realism: young user reactions on the Linköping fire and its consequences for education and democracy', *Library Review*, 15 (3/4): 171–80.

Librarians' Consortium, *Library Resources: Concerning the WTC/Pentagon Attacks*, created by Law Librarians as a resource for information in the aftermath of 11 September 2001, available at: <www.1.staff.umkc.edu/lord1/9-11-01-library/>.

Among a range of other information, details of books provided includes a section on coping, which includes dealing with trauma and post traumatic stress disorder.

Matthews, G. and Eden, P. (1996) 'Disaster management training in libraries', *Library Review*, 45 (1): 30–38.

Paton, D. and Flin, R. (1999) 'Disaster stress: an emergency management perspective', *Disaster Prevention and Management*, 8 (4), 261–7.

Pember, M.E. (1995) 'The psycho-social (P-S) factor in counter-disaster planning: the human element', in A. Howell, H. Mansell and M. Roubos-Bennett (comps) *Redefining Disasters: a Decade of Counter-disaster Planning. Papers Submitted by Speakers Wednesday 20–Friday 22 September 1995, State Library of New South Wales, Sydney, Australia*, Sydney: Conservation Access, State Library of New South Wales, pp. 199–206.

RISK ASSESSMENT

Ashley-Smith, J. (1999) *Risk Assessment for Object Conservation*, Oxford: Butterworth Heinemann.

Howe, C. (2002) 'Business risk management: an emerging market?, *Library +Information Update*, 1 (9): 32–4.

Jones, D.J. and Sinclair, J. (2000) *Managing Risks During Renovations*, available at: <www.slnsw.gov.au/plb/publish/papers/managerisks.htm>.

Kenney, A.R. et al (2002) 'Preservation risk management for web resources', *D-Lib Magazine*, 8 (1), available at: <http://www.dlib.org/dlib/january02/kenney/01kenney.html>.

McIntyre, J. (1998) 'A dual approach to risk management', *Liber Quarterly: the Journal of European Research Libraries*, 8 (4): 448–57.

Price, L. and Smith, A. (2000) *Managing Cultural Assets from a Business Perspective*, pub90, Washington, DC: Council on Library and Information Resources in cooperation with the Library of Congress.

Sato, H. (ed.) (1999) *Risk Preparedness for Cultural Properties – Development of Guidelines for Emergency Response. Proceedings of the 1997 Kobe/Tokyo International Symposium*, Tokyo: Chuo-Koron Bijutsu Shuppan.

Standards Australia and Standards New Zealand (1999), *Risk Management* (AS/NZS 4360:1999), Standards Australia: Sydney: Standards Australia and Wellington: Standards New Zealand.

Stovel, H. (1998) *Risk Preparedness: a Management Manual for World Cultural Heritage*, Rome: ICCROM (in collaboration with UNESCO, World Heritage Centre, ICOMOS).

See also: Chapter 3.

SECURITY

Security is an integral part of disaster management which permeates all its aspects, for example, from buildings and facilities, vandalism and theft, to computer networks and systems.

Cravey, P. (2001) *Protecting Library Staff, Users, Collections and Facilities: a How-To-Do-It Manual*, How-To-Do-It Manuals for Librarians, New York, London: Neal-Schuman Publishers.

Hinde, S. (2002) 'Security surveys spring crop', *Computers and Security*, 21 (4): 310–21.

Resource: the Council for Museums, Archives and Libraries (2002) *Information*.

Advice and Guidance: Security, available at: <www.resource.gov.uk/information/advice/00security.asp>.

These web pages provide a range of advice for libraries, archives and museums in the UK, including, for example, security specifications, government indemnity scheme and invigilation guidance.

Robiette, A. (2001) *Developing an Information Security Policy*, JISC Committee on Authentication and Security, available at: <www.jisc.ac.uk/pub01/security_policy.html>.

Shuman, B. A. (1999) *Library Security and Safety Handbook. Prevention, Policies and Procedures*, Chicago: American Library Association. (Chapter 5 'Emergency and disaster management policies and procedures', 149–79.)

Switzer, T. R. (1999) *Safe at Work? Library Security and Safety Issues*, Scarecrow Press, Lanham, Maryland. (Annotated bibliography.)

See also: 'Computers and Networks' above.

WAR, CIVIL UNREST AND TERRORISM

Bosnian Manuscripts Ingathering project, available at:
<www.kakarigi.net/manu/ingather.htm>
A project undertaken by a group of scholars and librarians to recover documents lost in Bosnia, 1992–95, by 'resurrecting the information contained in the burned original manuscripts by using the potential of modern technology and networking'.

Cox, R.J., et al. (2001) 'The day the world changed: implications for archival, library, and information science education', *First Monday*, 6 (12), available at: <firstmonday.org/issues/issues6_12/cox/index.html>.

International Committee of the Blue Shield (ICBS)
<www.ifla.org/VI/4/admin/protect.htm>
'The Blue Shield is the cultural equivalent of the Red Cross. It is the symbol specified in the 1954 Hague Convention for marking cultural sites to give them protection from attack in the event of armed conflict.' The United Kingdom and Ireland Blue Shield Organisation (UKIRB) website, <www.bl.uk/services/preservation/blueshield/content.html>, provides links to these and offers basic disaster advice with links to web and other useful sources.

Kenney, B.J. (2001) 'Central libraries in uncertain times', *Library Journal*, 126 (19): 36–7.

Riedlmayer, A. (1995) 'Erasing the past: the destruction of libraries and archives in Bosnia-Herzegovina', *MESA Bulletin*, (29): 7–11, available at:
<w3fp.Arizona.edu/mesassoc/Bulletin/bosnia.htm>.

Special Libraries Association. Virtual SLA, disaster response information portal, available at:

<www.sla.org/content/Help/webcomms/sept11help/disip/index.cfm>.

' ... a bibliography of resources on disaster responses which may help those who have been impacted by the tragedy of September 11th.'

Sturges, P. and Rosenberg, D. (eds) (1999) *Disaster and After: the Practicalities of Information Service in Times of War and Other Catastrophes. Proceedings of an International Conference Sponsored by IGLA (The International Group of the Library Association), 4–6 September 1998, University of Bristol*, London: Taylor Graham.

United Nations Educational, Scientific and Cultural Organization, emergency programme for the protection of vital records in the event of armed conflict, available at:

<www.unesco.org/webworld/archives/sro_citra/>.

To combat the threat of risks to the archival heritage from recent conflicts, ' ... UNESCO commissioned the International Council on Archives to develop guidelines to help archives to protect their vital or essential holdings.' The programme includes case study reports from Costa Rica, Croatia and the Gambia, a guide to producing an emergency programme and expert reports on specific issues such as fire safety and building hardening.

Valencia, M. (2002) 'Libraries, nationalism, and armed conflict in the twentieth century', *Libri*, 52 (1): 1–15.

van der Hoeven, H. and van Albada, J. (1996) *Lost Memory – Libraries and Archives Destroyed in the Twentieth Century*, prepared for UNESCO and IFLA, CII-96/WS/1, Paris: UNESCO, available at:

<www.unesco.org/webworld/mdm/administ/pdf/LOSTMEMO.PDF>.

See also: 'Disasters – Experiences' above, and Chapter 8.

Index

Page numbers in *italics* refer to figures and tables, *n* indicates notes.